BREAKING THE
GERMAN
DAMS

BREAKING THE
GERMAN
DAMS

A MINUTE-BY-MINUTE ACCOUNT OF
OPERATION 'CHASTISE'
16–17 MAY 1943

Robert Owen

Foreword by
James Holland

Greenhill Books

Breaking the German Dams
First published in 2023 by
Greenhill Books,
c/o Pen & Sword Books Ltd,
George House, Unit 12 & 13,
Beevor Street, Off Pontefract Road,
Barnsley, South Yorkshire S71 1HN

www.greenhillbooks.com
contact@greenhillbooks.com

ISBN: 978–1–78438–962–8

CIP data records for this title are available from the British Library

Edited and designed by Donald Sommerville
Typeset in Garamond Premier Pro
Maps by Peter Wilkinson

Printed and bound by CPI Group (UK) Ltd, Croydon, CR0 4YY

Contents

Plates

All images are from the author's collection unless otherwise noted.

PlateSection 1

Guy Gibson with aircrew of No. 106 Sqn.

Barnes Wallis.

Wellington dropping a 'Golf Mine' over the Fleet.

Arthur Harris; Sidney Bufton (*Air Historical Branch*); 'Charles' Whitworth.

Ralph Cochrane; Harry Satterly.

The Möhne dam and its towers; view from the Möhne parapet.

Part of the briefing model of the Möhne dam; pre-war photo of the Sorpe dam.

Three Dambusters' Lancasters: ED825, ED886 and ED817.

'Upkeep' loaded on W/Cdr Gibson's ED932 AJ-G; Lancaster dropping an 'Upkeep' weapon at Reculver.

Front view close-up of ED825; F/Sgt George 'Chiefy' Powell; F/Lt Harry Humphries.

The Eder lake from above Waldeck castle; the Eder dam looking across the lake towards Waldeck Castle.

The Eder dam from the Michelskopf, showing the two power stations; a bomb aimer's target map of the Eder reservoir.

Drawing by Cuthbert Orde and photo of F/Sgt Bill Townsend; F/Lt David Shannon; F/Lt David Maltby.

Drawing by Cuthbert Orde and photo of P/O Les Knight; F/Lt Robert Hutchison and W/Cdr Guy Gibson.

F/Lt Joe McCarthy; F/Lt 'Mick' Martin; F/Lt Bob Hay.

Plate Section 2

The breached Möhne dam; a ruined house in Neheim.

Unexploded 'Upkeep' examined by the Germans; F/Lt 'Norm' Barlow; F/Lt Bill Astell; pylon at Marbeck, as struck by Barlow's aircraft (*Steve Darlow*).

S/Ldr Henry Maudslay by Cuthbert Orde; damage to the parapet of the Eder dam caused by Maudslay's 'Upkeep'; Maudslay's grave in Reichswald War Cemetery; memorial to Maudslay and his crew at Netterden.

Flooding in Neheim; destruction in Neheim.

A broken bridge and other detritus; the village of Affoldern on 17 May.

Gibson's crew at debriefing.

King George VI talking to F/Sgt Ken Brown; Jack Leggo, Tammy Simpson, Bob Hay, Toby Foxlee and 'Mick' Martin visiting London on 22 June to be decorated for their parts in the raid.

F/Lt John Hopgood; F/Sgt John Fraser; P/O Tony Burcher; the memorial to those lost from Hopgood's crew, near Ostonnen.

Memorial to 54 French prisoners of war drowned at Neheim; the clear-up begins at Neheim.

The flooded steelworks at Hattingen seen at midday on 17 May across the flooded River Ruhr; the village of Himmelpforten and its church; Pastor Berkenkopf; memorial cross on the site of the destroyed church.

The breach in the Eder dam; flooding in Kassel.

Reconnaissance photo of Fröndenberg; the Herdecke railway viaduct.

P/O Geoff Rice; F/Lt Les Munro; F/Sgt Cyril Anderson and his crew (*Dom Howard*).

P/O Warner Ottley; Ottley's grave in Reichswald Forest War Cemetery; memorial to Ottley and his crew at Heesen; Sgt Fred Tees.

S/Ldr Melvin Young; memorial to Young and his crew (*Jan van Dalen*); the broken wreckage of their Lancaster.

Memorial at the Möhne dam; plaque in Harlingen cemetery commemorating P/O Vernon Byers and his crew (*Jan van Dalen*).

Foreword

The Dams Raid on the night of 16/17 May 1943 was and remains one of the most daring, outrageous and brilliantly executed air attacks ever mounted. It's certainly the most famous ever mounted by the RAF, and with some justification too. The Dams Raid is truly an incredible story: an amazing weapon, and 133 men and 19 Lancasters heading out at tree-top height, at night, over enemy territory and dropping their bouncing bombs to smash the German dams. It is a fabulous tale of daring, ingenuity and raw courage. It is also a raid that pushed the technological knowledge of the day to the absolute limit, and it is also an operation rich in the most astonishing human drama.

In May 1943, there was supposed to be only one way to attack a target with a heavy bomber: *en masse*, from 18,000 feet or more, and with the expectation that if the bombs dropped landed within a mile or two of the target, the crew had done pretty well. On the Dams Raid, the thirty-ton Lancasters, carrying a four-ton bouncing (and at the Möhne and Eder dams a *rotating*) four-ton depth-charge, were expected to drop these weapons on a sixpence at a height of just sixty feet. That's the height of a medium size tree. The wings of the Lancaster were 102 feet wide. Sixty feet is ridiculously low. There is almost no margin for error at that height.

Even today, despite a handful of books on the subject, what most people know about the raid comes from the 1955 film starring Richard Todd and Michael Redgrave, which is still regularly repeated on television. It's a terrific film, but if anything, it underplays the achievement, because necessarily in a two-hour movie, so much of the story was left out. Unpick the forgotten details, however, and it quickly becomes clear that a far more extraordinary story emerges – one of politics and personalities as much as science and ingenious engineering, a story of very special but ordinary men rather than the 'Top Gun' of Bomber Command. Wing Commander Guy Gibson, the commander of newly and specially formed 617 Squadron, and Barnes Wallis, the inventor of the bouncing bomb, were real people rather than caricatures – more complex, more contradictory. More interesting. The timing of the raid and its place in the wider war effort, and Second World War as a whole, adds another layer. This was a far more complex, more nuanced episode than most people might think. For the most part, the crews involved were also incredibly young. Gibson was twenty-four; David Shannon, only twenty; John Fraser, bomb-aimer on Hopgood's plane, which was the third to attack the Möhne, was only nineteen. A teenager! He was not the only one.

The effects of the raid were also wider and more far-reaching than most historians have suggested in recent years. After the breast-beating of the film came the denigrators, who claimed the raid was a great PR coup but had little effect on Germany's war effort. This is nonsense. It is true that the dams were repaired by the end of October that same year, five months on, but it is vital to ask why the Germans felt they had to repair them so urgently. This was because they needed to be ready before the winter rains. The dams filled up with water every winter – water that was absolutely vital for industrial purposes but also for the conurbations they supported. They were repaired in time only by a gargantuan diversion of resources, manpower, and expense at a point, in the summer of 1943, when Germany could least afford it. This was the summer the Allies invaded Sicily; Germany's Axis partner, Italy, surrendered; and the German attack at Kursk failed. It was the last time German troops went forward on the Eastern Front. Workers were drawn away from building the Atlantic Wall in France, which then made the Allies' success in Normandy the following summer just that little bit easier.

Rob Owen has produced a timely new account of the raid which fills in so many of the gaps left by the books that have come before. He has been the official historian of the 617 Squadron Association for thirty years, and there is literally no one on the planet who knows more about the raid than him. This is a book that has been gestating a long time, and like the very finest aged whisky is all the better for it. The last survivor of the Dam Busters' crews might, sadly, have recently passed away, but Rob has been following their fortunes for decades. He personally knew many of those brave men, and their families. He gained their trust – and their story was entrusted to him. He has also gathered a greater knowledge of primary sources than any other historian that has come before him and the net result is a book that is the last word on this most iconic of raids. It is destined not only to be read for pleasure but also as a definitive account. Every feature of the raid, from its inception to the science behind 'Upkeep' – the bouncing bomb – to the recruiting of the squadron, to the training and eventual execution of the raid is covered here and in both forensic and very clear detail. He also, rightly, tells the story from the German perspective: this was a human as well as a material catastrophe for Germany and for the many who lost their lives as a result. Rob Owen never loses sight of the human experience, whether it be the boffins, the men of the Air Ministry, the crews, or the Germans and foreign workers whose lives were wrecked as a result.

It is then, a very special, and, I think, rather important book about a truly extraordinary achievement at a key moment in the Second World War. And with the last of the Dam Busters now gone, it is only fitting that Rob's book should appear on the shelves to keep the memory of Operation 'Chastise' alive. It is right that we should remember the effort, bravery, sacrifice and loss of so many, and understand better the far-reaching consequences of this most astonishing air raid in history.

James Holland

Aircrew Participating in Operation 'Chastise'

Aircraft	Pilot	Flight Engineer	Navigator
AJ-G ED932	W/Cdr G. P. Gibson, DSO*, DFC*	Sgt J. Pulford	P/O H. T. Taerum, RCAF
AJ-M ED925	F/Lt J. V. Hopgood, DFC*	Sgt C. Brennan	F/O K. Earnshaw, RCAF
AJ-P ED909	F/Lt H. B. Martin, DFC	P/O I. Whittaker	F/Lt J. F. Leggo, DFC, RAAF
AJ-A ED887	S/Ldr H. M. Young, DFC*	Sgt D. T. Horsfall	F/Sgt C. W. Roberts
AJ-J ED906	F/Lt D. J. H. Maltby, DFC	Sgt W. Hatton	Sgt V. Nicholson
AJ-L ED929	F/Lt D. J. Shannon, DFC, RAAF	Sgt R. J. Henderson	F/O D. R. Walker, DFC, RCAF
AJ-Z ED937	S/Ldr H. E. Maudslay, DFC	Sgt J. Marriott, DFM	F/O R. A. Urquhart, DFC, RCAF
AJ-B ED864	F/Lt W. Astell, DFC	Sgt J. Kinnear	P/O F. A. Wile, RCAF
AJ-N ED912	P/O L. G. Knight, RAAF	Sgt R. E. Grayston	F/O H. S. Hobday
AJ-E ED927	F/Lt R. N. G. Barlow, DFC, RAAF	P/O S. L. Whillis	F/O P. S. Burgess
AJ-W ED921	F/Lt J. L. Munro, RNZAF	Sgt F. E. Appleby	F/O F. G. Rumbles
AJ-K ED934	P/O V. W. Byers, RCAF	Sgt A. J. Taylor	F/O J. H. Warner
AJ-H ED936	P/O G. Rice	Sgt E. C. Smith	F/O R. Macfarlane
AJ-T ED825	F/Lt J. C. McCarthy, DFC, RCAF	Sgt W. G. Radcliffe, RCAF	F/Sgt D. A. MacLean, RCAF
AJ-C ED910	P/O W. Ottley, DFC	Sgt R. Marsden	F/O J. K. Barrett, DFC
AJ-S ED865	P/O L. J. Burpee, DFM, RCAF	Sgt G. Pegler	Sgt T. Jaye
AJ-F ED918	F/Sgt K. W. Brown, RCAF	Sgt H. B. Feneron	Sgt D. P. Heal
AJ-O ED886	F/Sgt W. C. Townsend, DFM	Sgt D. J. D. Powell	P/O C. L. Howard, RAAF
AJ-Y ED924	F/Sgt C. T. Anderson	Sgt R. C. Paterson	Sgt J. P. Nugent

Wireless Operator	Bomb Aimer	Front Gunner	Rear Gunner
F/Lt R. E. G. Hutchison, DFC	P/O F. M. Spafford, DFM, RAAF	F/Sgt G. A. Deering, RCAF	F/Lt R. D. Trevor-Roper, DFM
Sgt J. W. Minchin	F/Sgt J. W. Fraser, RCAF	P/O G. H. F. G. Gregory, DFM	P/O A. F. Burcher, DFM, RAAF
F/O L. Chambers, RNZAF	F/Lt R. C. Hay, DFC, RAAF	P/O B. T. Foxlee, DFM, RAAF	F/Sgt T. D. Simpson, RAAF
Sgt L. W. Nichols	F/Sgt V. S. MacCausland, RCAF	Sgt G. A. Yeo	Sgt W. Ibbotson
Sgt A. J. B. Stone	P/O J. Fort	Sgt V. Hill	Sgt H. T. Simmonds
F/O C. B. Goodale, DFC	F/Sgt L. J. Sumpter	Sgt B. Jagger	F/O J. Buckley
W/O A. P. Cottam, RCAF	P/O M. J. D. Fuller	F/O W. J. Tytherleigh, DFC	Sgt N. R. Burrows
W/O A. A. Garshowitz, RCAF	F/O D. Hopkinson	F/Sgt F. A. Garbas, RCAF	Sgt R. Bolitho
F/Sgt R. G. T. Kellow	F/O E. C. Johnson	Sgt F. E. Sutherland, RCAF	Sgt H. E. O'Brien, RCAF
F/O C. R. Williams, DFC, RAAF	F/O A. Gillespie, DFM	F/O H. S. Glinz, RCAF	Sgt J. R. G. Liddell
W/O P. E. Pigeon, RCAF	Sgt J. H. Clay	Sgt W. Howarth	F/Sgt H. A. Weeks, RCAF
Sgt J. Wilkinson	P/O A. N. Whitaker	Sgt C. McA. Jarvie	F/Sgt J. McDowell, RCAF
W/O C. B. Gowrie, RCAF	W/O J. W. Thrasher, RCAF	Sgt T. W. Maynard	Sgt S. Burns
F/Sgt L. Eaton	Sgt G. L. Johnson	Sgt R. Batson	F/O D. Rodger, RCAF
Sgt J. Guterman, DFM	F/Sgt T. B. Johnston	Sgt H. J. Strange	Sgt F. Tees
P/O L. G. Weller	F/Sgt J. L. Arthur, RCAF	Sgt W. C. A. Long	W/O J. G. Brady, RCAF
Sgt H. J. Hewstone	Sgt S. Oancia, RCAF	Sgt D. Allatson	F/Sgt G. S. McDonald, RCAF
F/Sgt G. A. Chalmers	Sgt C. E. Franklin	Sgt D. E. Webb	Sgt R. Wilkinson
Sgt W. D. Bickle	Sgt G. J. Green	Sgt E. Ewan	Sgt A. W. Buck

Prologue

Operation 'Chastise' – the Dams Raid – of 16/17 May 1943 has gone down in history as one of the greatest feats of arms achieved by the Royal Air Force. It is rightly seen as a triumph of technical innovation by engineers, manufacturers, and groundcrew; of the airmanship, personal courage and determination of the aircrew; and of the unsung diligence of intelligence staff and planners who provided and assessed information to facilitate the execution of the operation.

The operation captured the imagination at the time, and continues to do so, with all the elements of a *Boy's Own* adventure: a seemingly impossible challenge, made possible by scientific endeavour, often in the face of adversity and official frustration, and executed by a hand-picked, highly experienced team, specially trained for the highly secret and daring mission. It was a David and Goliath battle between the attacking aircraft and the combined might of the enemy defences and the seeming invulnerability of the targets they defended.

As one of the epic aerial actions of the Second World War, it has been the subject of a feature film, numerous books, television documentaries and online presentations and doubtless will continue to be so for many more years as new generations of historians uncover new documents and add their own analyses to the works already written. There will always be room for new analysis, fuelled by the discovery of hitherto unconsidered material. It can be argued that in addition to all the narratives already written there are potentially 133 other stories, those of each of the participants in the operation, not to mention the accounts of the experiences of Germans who, like the bomber crews, found themselves involved in a battle not of their making. Some of their narratives have been written; doubtless more will be in future years.

Yet for all the material that has been written and crafted about Operation 'Chastise', much myth endures, which is now gradually being eroded by more detailed study. Many of the seeds of this were sown by Paul Brickhill in his original work *The Dam Busters* – which for its account of the Dams Raid, quarries Wing Commander (W/Cdr) Gibson's own work. Both are master-pieces, yet they were written at a time when wartime secrecy still precluded the revelation of the truth. In 1951 the precise nature and operational use of Wallis's weapon was still classified. It remained so in 1955 when Michael Anderson's film based on these two works was premiered. The design and working of 'Upkeep' were to remain closely guarded secrets until 1962 when they were finally released.

In the words of Sir Barnes Wallis, the weapon's inventor:

> The Germans know about it from the wreckage of aircraft shot down, the Americans know all about it because they were our allies and we gave them a set of plans, the Russians know . . . everybody knows apart from the English [*sic*] who paid for it.

Likewise, the official Air Ministry files relating to the operation remained closed for another decade. It was not until 1982 with the publication of Dr John Sweetman's *Operation 'Chastise' – Epic or Myth*, (later re-issued as *The Dambusters Raid*) that the public were given a comprehensive and detailed study of the development of a weapon to breach the dams and the execution of the operation itself. It was a breakthrough at the time and still today remains a 'must read' for serious students of the subject.

Most works on this subject consider the Dams Raid as a unique operation. This is perfectly valid given the weapon used, the creation of a specialist unit of hand-picked crews, subjected to intensive training, and the results achieved. These traditional narratives of the operation split the events of the attack into three separate elements, based on the allocation of aircraft to targets: those attacking the Möhne and Eder dams, those detailed to the Sorpe, and the final mobile reserve. This simplifies the narrative and enables focus to be placed on each of the waves as a separate entity and their activity to be seen in isolation, without any confusion with the other waves.

There is much to commend this treatment. However, while it makes for easy reading and comprehension, it segregates Operation 'Chastise' from the overall context of the Bomber Offensive and distorts the timeline, thus concealing the synchronicity of events on the night of the 16/17 May 1943. The picture created suggests that the dams were attacked in turn, one after the other and in doing so perhaps contributes to the impression that the Sorpe was of lesser importance than the other two major targets.

However, the planning and execution of the operation was a complex choreography of multi-layered events, taking place across a multiplicity of geographical locations.

The purpose of this work is not to take a revisionist view, nor to undermine the tremendous technical achievement or deny the skill, courage, and airmanship of those who carried out the operation. Rather it is to view the operation from a different perspective and explore whether any new insights can be gained, particularly by viewing the three waves of the operation together in 'real time'. In doing so it will also re-examine some of the elements relating to the preparation and planning of the operation.

In the period before the operation, Wing Commander Gibson owned a dog which he named using a word that is now recognised as racist and highly offensive. The same term was also used as a code-word in the signals procedure on the night of the attacks. The word therefore appears in this book in these contexts as part of the historical record of those different times. There is no intention to endorse racist views or cause offence to readers.

The methodology adopted here is based on over forty years of study of a multitude of sources. Primary amongst these are the briefed routes for the operation and the post-raid report of June 1943. In addition, however, times and positions known from navigation logs, along with German reports relating to aircraft losses, have been used to refine the briefed timings. As may be expected, these are not always co-incident, and sometimes contradictory. In such cases a decision has been taken as to the most likely time and position. In cases where data is not available it has been necessary to extrapolate positions and times from information that is available, based on time distance, speed and heading along with any other evidence. British Double Summer Time, used by the RAF, coincided with German local time at the date of the operation making comparison between German and British reports easier in that respect.

While it cannot be totally error free, the result is intended to provide new insight into this complex and detailed operation. It will doubtless be subjected to further analysis, modification and interpretation as new details come to light.

Chapter 1
Gestation of an Idea

The concept of crippling an enemy's ability to wage war by denying him the means of production vital to his war machine had been in the minds of British strategists at least since 1937 when the Air Staff drew up a series of Air Plans. Amongst these, Western Air Plan 5 emphasised 'the attack on German War industry ... with priority to that in the Ruhr, Rhineland and Saar'. It was further estimated that Bomber Command could achieve this objective by mounting 3,000 sorties over a period of a fortnight against 19 power stations and 26 coking plants identified as critical to German war production. These included the power plant below the Möhne dam, and other facilities, including the Koepchen pumped-storage power plant and the run-of-river power plant on the Hengsteysee near Hagen.

That this could be achieved, given that the RAF's bomber strength at the period comprised some 920 aircraft (with a daily availability of 500 machines), largely Battles, Blenheims, Wellingtons, Whitleys and Hampdens, reflected contemporary innocence and inexperience.

Soon deciding that the task was unrealistic, the Air Ministry came up with an alternative strategy involving only two targets: two dams, the Möhne and the Sorpe, which supplied the Ruhr with 75 per cent of its water requirements. They were easily identifiable, located in countryside to the east of the Ruhr, well away from heavily defended areas and unlikely to have their own defences. Their destruction would result in loss of water for industrial and domestic use and the resulting floods would cause material damage to plant and transport networks. Might it be possible to destroy these dams using existing bombs or torpedoes, or would new weapons be required?

It was clear that the RAF's existing 500-pound General Purpose (GP) bombs would be totally ineffective against such structures and that in wartime such targets would be protected by torpedo netting. Other possibilities, such as dropping semi-armour-piercing bombs at the foot of the air side of the wall, were also dismissed on the grounds that any weapon would need to achieve high velocity and be dropped almost horizontally in order to avoid a glancing blow. The conclusion was that 'dams . . . offer a very difficult target both from the probability of hitting, and the probability of serious damage to the target'. The failure of the Nationalist Army to destroy the Burguillo and Ordunte dams during the Spanish Civil War in 1937 further demonstrated the difficulties of destroying such targets even when charges were placed precisely by hand.

Undaunted, there were those who pursued the idea of aerial attack. In September 1938, a month after the Munich crisis, W/Cdr George Howard, a member of the Directorate of Armament, submitted a secret minute to the Deputy Director of Plans outlining his views on the subject. A successful attack in the early stages of hostilities would cause tremendous psychological as well as material effect. The level of defences for such a target would doubtless increase with time, and certainly after any initial attack: 'no effort should be spared to bring the first attempt to a successful issue'. His preferred weapon for such an attack was the torpedo, but on account of the slow speed of torpedo-carrying aircraft he suggested that immediate high priority should be afforded to the fitting of torpedo carriers to faster aircraft.

He proposed the use of a forward base, either in Belgium (approximately 100 miles from the target) or France (200 miles). The use of aircraft with cruising speeds of at least 200 mph would reduce time over enemy territory, which was certain to be well defended by anti-aircraft guns and fighters. Allowing 30 minutes (60 minutes from France) to reach the target area he considered 15 minutes ample time to execute the attack, building in another 15 for 'combat evasion'. Even if launched from France the entire operation could be completed in as little as 150 minutes (the endurance of a Hawker Demon fighter).

To ensure accurate location of the target (and thereby accepting the failings of night navigation which at this stage was reliant on dead reckoning and/or astro, not that the RAF practised much night flying) the operation would need to take place in daylight, but arrival in the target area could be timed for 15 minutes before dusk, permitting withdrawal under cover of darkness. The threat from enemy fighters could be moderated by a series of diversionary raids against Düsseldorf, Mulheim, Dortmund, Hamm and Münster by bomber formations flying at varying heights and timing their attacks at intervals of 5–10 minutes before the main attacking force arrived at the dam.

That force would comprise one squadron of nine fast torpedo-carrying aircraft escorted by three squadrons of fighters: one preceding to intercept any immediate fighter attack and the other two providing a rearguard. Flying at half-mile intervals, the formations would be stepped up by 500 feet, front to rear, the fighters flying in formations of three to afford tactical flexibility, the bombers in close formation to concentrate their defensive firepower against any attacker.

At a point some eight miles from the target the leading fighters, which would also be carrying smoke bombs, would descend in two lines of sections in line astern, followed by the second fighter squadron's aircraft, each carrying eight fragmentation bombs. After performing a suppression role against the target defences they would climb to 4,000 and 6,000 feet respectively, providing medium-height protection for the bombers. The remaining fighter squadron would provide top cover at 7,000–9,000 feet throughout the entire attack.

As the first squadrons dealt with the defences the torpedo aircraft would descend to 3,000 feet prior to making their attack in line astern at quarter-mile intervals, releasing their torpedoes in quick succession. After the last torpedo had been released the bombing force would climb as rapidly as possible in a northerly direction 'in order to deceive the anti-aircraft gunners'. On reaching 5,000 feet they would turn and head directly back to base, escorted by the fighters, using the same formation tactics as on the outward flight.

Howard had also considered the training and control of the attack. He put himself forward to command the operation, citing his command of No. 111 (Fighter) Squadron, experience of leading fighter formations in attacks for the Air Fighting Development Establishment and leadership of large formations in precision-timed practices for the Hendon displays and the unveiling of the Canadian National Memorial at Vimy Ridge in 1936. Although there was no mention of any specific type of aircraft as the torpedo carrier, he may have been thinking of the Blenheim, Fairey Battle, Hampden or Vickers Wellesley, the last a Barnes Wallis design. (Torpedo-dropping trials were undertaken by a Wellesley, though this aircraft was rather slower than Howard advocated).

Other elements of the plan, such as the carriage of light bombs by the fighters, are also puzzling. The Hawker Demon could carry underwing bombs, but its speed was less than that desired; the Hurricane and Spitfire, coming into service with the optimum performance had yet to be modified to carry bombs. He may have been considering the Blenheim If, shortly to enter service, fitted with a light series carrier. He also stipulated that pilots and gunners for such an operation should be carefully selected. They would need to be well trained and he suggested that 'the raid should be thoroughly rehearsed over an area of water such as Loch Ness in order to ensure that the procedure is carried out as a drill', and suggested that all aircraft should be fitted with radio telephony for intercommunication purposes. He also recommended that further assistance would be obtained were the leader and the deputy leader of the raid to carry out prior reconnaissance of the target from an altitude of 25,000 feet in fast fighters.

Undaunted by the limitations posed by the lack of suitable weapons, the planners, including Howard, persisted and indeed increased their consideration of dams as targets. By July 1939 seven dams in Germany were listed: the Eder and Diemel, Möhne and Sorpe, Lister, Ennepe and Henne. The last five of these, of which the Möhne was the most important, fed the Ruhr area. Six were of the single arch gravity type, which appeared more vulnerable to torpedo attack rather than high- or low-level bombing. The seventh, the Sorpe, of earth construction, was considered more suitable for bombing attack.

Expanding on his original paper Howard then proposed that a series of successive detonations by 440-pound torpedoes at the same point on the target might be attempted. If exploded in contact with the wall the charge would be tamped (and therefore made more effective) by both the water and weight of the torpedo's machinery behind the charge. Assuming each torpedo made a crater 3 feet deep and 20 feet in diameter, then, allowing for failures, 20–25 torpedoes might be needed, each released at a range of 2,000 yards. To achieve such precision Howard suggested that the towers on the dam wall might be used as aiming marks. Reconnaissance could determine whether or not torpedo nets were present; these might have to be destroyed by preliminary bombardment. A glider torpedo to overcome any nets was suggested but discarded since this was still under development.

Looking back at these proposals, they illustrate the over-expectation of the effectiveness of bombing prevalent in the pre-war period and a certain degree of innocence as to the practicalities of operations. It is interesting, however, to note that several elements of this early planning found their way into the final details for 'Chastise'. With a degree of prescience W/Cdr Howard's scheme envisaged a requirement for previous reconnaissance of the targets and that crews should be handpicked and rehearse the attack over a British lake, with the use of the dam's towers as aiming marks. His formation of nine bombers fitted with radio telephony equipment (R/T) for voice communication, presumably to facilitate control of the operation, echoes the nine aircraft in three vics of three that constituted the main force despatched by 617 Squadron against the Möhne and Eder dams. Another of his tactics, the use of fighters for flak suppression, though not used for 'Chastise', was embodied when 617 Squadron undertook their costly low-level attack on the Dortmund–Ems Canal in September 1943.

The planners of 1938 anticipated using larger bombs up to 2,000 pounds, then still under development. Aircraft could carry more bombs than torpedoes, though the latter were likely to be more effective. A compromise might be reached if the dam were attacked simultaneously from each side using both types of weapon. Optimists thought that 18,000 pounds of explosive contained in forty torpedoes and fifteen 500-pound Semi Armour-Piercing (SAP) bombs might produce a breach 40 feet deep and 10 feet across. However, the difficulties of obtaining sufficient hits and timing the detonations of torpedoes and bombs remained insurmountable. Another major consideration was that it was considered impracticable to keep a formation over the target for sufficient time to deliver successive attacks. Each torpedo would have to complete its run and then time be allowed between attacks to let the water calm down between explosions. Once again, these considerations would re-emerge during the planning for 'Chastise'.

By the outbreak of war the matter was no nearer to resolution. Multiple theories were proposed. Evidence from 'a German Jewish émigré, an ex-officer in the Prussian Army who had become a director of companies specialising in the harnessing of water power', suggested that an attack by two or three squadrons of torpedo bombers would be sufficient to cause severe damage to, if not total collapse of the Möhne dam. These figures were disputed by other 'experts'. Some planners now considered that dams were unlikely to prove vulnerable targets to anything other than a large group of mines dropped closely together. Others believed that a new weapon was required and 'that the most advanced technicians should be employed in whatever force is necessary . . . on the development of any weapon which may help us shorten the course of the war. There should be no limits to our efforts in this field.'

Even though no dams had been breached, waters were certainly being muddied. The problem still focussed on the lack of any practical data recording the effect of detonating bombs or torpedoes underwater, against a concrete or masonry structure (a state of affairs that would persist until 1941 when experiments were conducted for Wallis by the Road Research Laboratory).

Despite these difficulties the planners refused to abandon the idea of breaching Germany's dams. In the spring of 1940 the issue refused to go away. Favourable conditions were expected over the coming months. In February 1940 Air Target Intelligence wrote to Wing Commander Baker, Deputy Director of Plans, still maintaining that, as the snow melted and the reservoirs filled, the dams were:

> . . . vulnerable to bombs/torpedoes, and if not these, then mines – or a combination of two or even all three? . . . As a course of action which can be carried out with the minimum force and effort and

result in a major disaster – military and civil – for Germany, there can be nothing to approach it . . . In my humble opinion the small force required for the job coupled with the heavy blow which would be given to the enemy by any success in this direction, make the operation well worth a trial even if there are doubts about it succeeding.

The operation could be undertaken with complete surprise on a moonlit night resulting in negligible losses.

All this was to no avail. The Directorate of Plans did not think the project worth pursuing any further until new or more powerful weapons had been developed.

Five months later, Air Marshal Charles Portal, then Commander-in-Chief, Bomber Command, suggested that 'the time has come to arrange for the destruction of the Möhne dam, which though difficult . . . is by no means impossible provided the correct weapons are available'. Portal supported a torpedo attack on the water side, combined with bombing of the air side. He further suggested that long-delay bombs could be dropped to hinder repair work. Accepting that an attack on 'this most vital target' was not possible because there were no torpedo-carrying aircraft of sufficient range (the fall of France and the Low Countries had denied the RAF the forward bases proposed by Howard) Portal requested that urgent action be taken to extend the range of existing torpedo carriers or modify at least twelve Hampdens to carry torpedoes. Taken from Operational Training Unit (OTU) stocks or the production line so as not to dilute the strength of the operational force, these would become invaluable for long-range torpedo attacks against other dams, lock gates or inland waterways in general (though some were sceptical as to whether torpedoes would run in canals 10 feet deep). Portal's request was rebutted by Air Marshal Sholto Douglas, then Deputy Chief of the Air Staff. He believed that to breach a dam, thousands of pounds of explosive would be required to be detonated in a single explosion: the water pressure on an arch dam supported it and would close cracks. Leaking water would not wear away concrete and experiments firing torpedoes at jetties had shown them to produce only a surface scar. Stalemate again.

Portal became Chief of the Air Staff on 26 October 1940, replaced as AOC-in-C Bomber Command by Air Marshal Sir Richard Peirse. Meanwhile W/Cdr Charles Finch-Noyes of the Ministry of Supply Armament Research Department had calculated that ten charges of 2,000 pounds of explosive detonated in relatively short intervals would be sufficient to destroy the Möhne dam. With the assistance of Squadron Leader (S/Ldr) Noel Pemberton-

Billing two designs were developed to place such a charge against a dam wall with the required precision.

The first design was a self-propelled and directionally stable hydroplane skimmer (toraplane), which could jump buoyed net defences. The second was a torpedo – to travel submerged or semi submerged – and intended to be used for attacking boom defences and harbour breakwaters. These used an ingenious launch mechanism. A cup or weight on a wire would be trailed beneath the attacking aircraft, set up to strike the water at the correct altitude, say 20 feet, about a mile from target. The pull on the wire would release the weapon, ignite the propulsion unit, either steam jet for the surface or a rocket underwater, simultaneously opening the aircraft's throttle to take it clear of any defended area. Impact with the target would destroy buoyancy chambers in the weapon's nose causing the weapon to sink to 40 feet, to be detonated by a hydrostatic pistol.

A Wellington might carry two such weapons, each weighing 3,000 pounds, one under each wing. Ten aircraft would be able to place 20,000 pounds of explosive in 2,000-pound packets at short intervals. Given that it was believed that forty 440-pound torpedoes (amounting to 17,600 pounds) would achieve the desired result, then the Finch-Noyes solution seemed to be the answer sought for over two years.

One of the strengths of the Finch-Noyes scheme was that it could be produced by adapting existing components, so in theory required little development or testing time. Its supposed target may have been harbour moles or breakwaters, rather than dams, which may account for the lack of official support. Although Finch-Noyes was told in August 1940 that his proposal was required urgently, in the end the project came to nothing.

In April 1941, Finch-Noyes wrote to Air Marshal Peirse again proposing his weapon and presenting an outline for a moonlight attack, suggesting that a separate unit be formed and trained for the purpose with specially prepared aircraft. The attackers, now numbering sixteen rather than ten to allow for losses and other failures, would approach at 20,000 feet, then dive down to 5,500 feet, approaching the target at right angles. Released at a range of some 5½ miles from the target the weapon was now designed to glide down, striking the water about half a mile from the dam, detaching its flying surfaces and initiating the propulsion system. Rather than a hydrostatic pistol, a countermining technique might be employed – multiple charges placed at the bottom of the wall, detonated by a final charge.

Finch-Noyes's design was as yet unproven. Accuracy of aim after a freegliding approach was uncertain. The concept of countermining was a difficult and imprecise method of detonation and the critical factor, the exact amount of explosive required to seriously damage or destroy the Möhne dam had yet to be determined. While senior officers were aware of the alleged importance of the Möhne dam they were not sufficiently convinced of Finch-Noyes's proposal to sanction further development.

Meanwhile Barnes Wallis, assistant chief designer at Vickers-Armstrong's aviation section at Weybridge, had been seeking a scientific answer as to the quantity of explosive required to destroy a dam such as the Möhne. His methodology and determination were beginning to bear fruit. In October 1940 he obtained data from tests using models at the Road Research Laboratory at Harmondsworth. By the time Finch-Noyes wrote to Air Marshal Peirse the first meeting had taken place of the Air Attack on Dams Committee, set up to advise the Director of Scientific Research, Ministry of Aircraft Production, on the experimental work necessary to establish the technical possibility of aerial attack on dams. At this stage Wallis was considering a large bomb. Subsequent work with scale models determined that a much smaller weapon could be developed if detonation was in direct contact with the dam wall.

Wallis then set about developing the means of achieving this, with his habitual determination and ingenuity. A spherical bomb, spun backwards prior to release and dropped from low level would cross the surface of a reservoir in a series of decreasing bounces until it struck the parapet of the dam. It would then sink, its spin causing it to remain in contact with the wall until detonated at the optimum depth of 30 feet by a hydrostatic pistol.

By the end of 1942 he produced scaled down prototypes of his weapon which he referred to generically as the 'golf mine'. These were dropped successfully into the Fleet behind Chesil Beach during January–March 1943 He envisaged its development in various sizes to be carried by a range of aircraft: a smaller 950-pound 'Highball' version, two of which could be carried by a de Havilland Mosquito to attack naval targets (other carriers were modified including the Grumman Tarpon/Avenger and Douglas A-26 Invader), and an intermediate size (not produced) for attacking lock gates carried by aircraft such as the Short Stirling and Vickers Warwick. There was also a smaller projectile, 'Baseball', intended to be launched from fast motor torpedo boats. For attacking dams Wallis envisaged a large 9,250-pound version, 'Upkeep', carried by Lancasters. This larger weapon was originally constructed as a cylinder surrounded by a ring of wooden staves held in place by tensioned steel bands, so that the weapon looked very much like a barrel. During development the water pressure on impact shattered the wooden casing and after 18 April trials were conducted using a bare cylinder, which was then adopted as the final form for the operation. Although popularly referred to as 'the bouncing bomb' the weapon was essentially a rotating depth charge. Wallis's preference was to refer to it as a mine.

In February 1943, nearly two and a half years after Portal's original interest in the German dams as targets as head of Bomber Command, he was to play a pivotal role in bringing an attack on them to fruition. As Chief of the Air Staff he brought together the two crucial elements essential to 'Chastise': Air Marshal Sir Arthur Harris and Barnes Wallis. It was an uneasy partnership, in which trust and confidence would gradually emerge, success being made possible by professional dedication and commitment, not to mention the skill, courage and airmanship of a team of 133 young men, soon to become known as 'The Dam Busters'.

Chapter 2

Targets

The Möhne and Eder dams, which had been identified in the pre-war plans, were an essential part of the water-supply network for the Ruhr factories. The immediate source of water for this industrial area came originally from numerous wells which tapped underground sand and gravel beds that held ground water from local rainfall and the River Ruhr. Over-exploitation of this reserve resulting from industrialisation at the end of the nineteenth century caused a severe depletion of the water table, due in large part to considerable variation in the Ruhr's rate of flow between wet and dry seasons. To alleviate this a dozen dams were constructed in the headwaters and tributaries of the Ruhr to capture surplus rainwater during the winter months and release it during the dry season to maintain a constant level in the river. Lakes and filter beds along the river, together with water pumped back from the River Rhine, helped replenish the water-bearing strata. This then supplied reasonably pure water for domestic use and some industrial processes, while other industrial supplies were provided by water pumped from coal mines or drawn from other rivers and canals crossing the region.

The dam construction programme was managed by the Ruhrtalsperren-verein (Ruhr Valley Dams Association) which in 1906 embarked on a major project for a dam in the Möhne Valley, a tributary of the Ruhr, five miles north-east of Neheim. Built during 1908–13, the Möhne dam served to control flooding, regulate River Ruhr water levels and generate hydroelectric power. Capable of containing 134 million cubic metres of water, this was the largest reservoir in the Sauerland, and accounted for some 50 per cent of the storage capacity of the region. The reservoir is fed by two rivers, the Möhne, which enters at the eastern end of the northern arm, and the Heve, entering at the eastern end of the southern arm. The water is carried off by the Möhne valley westwards of the dam and enters the Ruhr at Neheim, five miles to the south-west.

The wall of the dam was constructed of limestone rubble masonry protected against the seepage of water. Built in a curve to provide firm anchorage into the valley sides, the wall was 2,000 feet long, 130 feet high, 25 feet thick at the crest and 112 feet at the base; its foundations were carried at least 6½ feet into the base rock. When the reservoir was full, excess water spilled over through a series of arched openings below the parapet, discharging onto a downstream apron. Normal draw-off of water was by means of four pipes 4½ feet in diameter passing through the foot of the dam and controlled by valves in the round chambers built on either side of the two gabled towers on the crest of the dam. The pipes could be used to discharge water directly into the River Möhne or to the two power stations below the dam. These generated 6,000 kW and 500 kW respectively.

The Sorpe dam at Langscheid, ten miles south-southwest of the Möhne, was the most recent dam in the system. Built in 1922–35, unlike the Möhne, which is a masonry gravity dam, the Sorpe consists of a concrete core, 770 yards long and 33 feet wide at the crest, faced on each side with an apron of earth. The earth facing sloped gently up 208 feet from the valley bottom to the top of the dam making the bank over a thousand feet broad at the base. Upstream of the core the facing was mainly clay and stony clay. The downstream bank contained a high proportion of gravel, rubble and rolled quarry-waste. Water was drawn off by means of a tunnel passing under the dam and discharging into a spillway and then into the equalising basin. A 7,200-kW power station at the foot of the dam would be used as a peak load pump-storage plant; water could flow from the reservoir to the equalising basin through the turbines to generate power at times of peak demand and be pumped back from the equalising basin into the reservoir at times of low load.

The Sorpe was the second largest reservoir in the Sauerland, with a capacity sufficient to provide a year's reserve should there be two consecutive years of low rainfall. The Sorpe was thus available to replenish other reservoirs by a cross-feed system and raise the level of the Ruhr to ensure continuity of supply when dams elsewhere in the system were low, or at times of drought. Between them, the Möhne and Sorpe dams accounted for 75 per cent of the area's storage capacity.

In total the Ruhrtalsperrenverein network comprised twelve dams

	Water volume		
Möhne	134 million cubic metres		
Sorpe	72	„	„
Lister	22	„	„
Ennepe	15	„	„

Henne	11	"	"
Seven smaller dams	12	"	"
Total	266	"	"

In addition to domestic and industrial water supply, these dams also served to protect low-lying areas of the Ruhr valley from flooding and since the construction of the dams many of the former flood plains had been built over. Control of the river level along with part canalisation of its lower reaches meant that the Ruhr was navigable as far as Mulheim for large vessels and to Witten for those of smaller size. The storage of water in the upper reaches and control of flow, together with the damming of the Hengsteysee, Weitersee, and Baldeneysee, permitted the functioning of a number of small hydroelectric power stations. Although generating only a small proportion of the total power needs of the Ruhr area they provided a useful addition to local supplies. Of these the pump-storage station at Herdecke (Koeperhernwerk) was the most important, providing a significant source of peak-time power.

The model experiments conducted during 1941–2 by the Road Research Laboratory at Harmondsworth and its subsidiary at Garston near Watford had focused on a scale replica of the Möhne, since Wallis and the Air Ministry believed that its loss would impair industry and electrical generating capacity. In his second paper on the subject, 'Air Attack on Dams', written during the autumn of 1942 and circulated in January and February 1943, Wallis argued that the effects of water shortage and damage by flooding would be intensified if one or more of the other four principal dams in the Ruhr catchment (the Sorpe, Lister, Ennepe, Henne) could be broken at the same time, but did not single one out. In the same paper Wallis also made the case that the Eder and Diemel dams in the Weser catchment area were also of 'great importance' and that their combined destruction would 'probably' bring about 'an almost immediate cessation of traffic' on the Mittelland Canal and River Weser.

The Eder dam at Hemfurth, some 25 miles south-east of Kassel, was another substantial gravity dam. Constructed between 1908 and 1914 it was built to prevent flooding of the River Weser in the Kassel, Münden, Hameln and Minden areas, generate hydroelectric power and regulate water levels for shipping on the Weser River, and the Mittelland Canal which at that time was under construction. It was 1,310 feet long, 139 feet high, 19 feet thick at the crest and 115 feet at the base. The reservoir contained 202 million cubic metres, making it the largest in Germany. At the foot of the dam there were two power stations, Hemfurth I, generating 13,000 kW and Hemfurth II with a capacity of 17,000 kW. The Diemel dam, constructed during 1912–23 on another tributary of the Weser for flood control and hydroelectric power, was also part of this separate catchment system.

February 1943 However, the Eder and the Diemel do not provide water to the Ruhr district. By advocating these as targets Wallis was in effect establishing two separate target systems, one affecting the Ruhr, the other the Weser, a distinction which was not necessarily fully appreciated by the Air Ministry planners. Wallis reinforced this ambiguity on 15 February 1943 at a meeting chaired by Group Captain (G/C) Sidney Bufton, Director of Bomber Operations at the Air Ministry, 'to discuss the possibility of attacking the Möhne dam with a new weapon'. Focus was purely on the Möhne and Wallis sought to reassure the members that conversion of the aircraft would be easy and release parameters attainable. After a favourable reception he ventured that the Eder, with a capacity twice that of the Möhne constituted 'a most important target'. It was within range and suitable for 'Upkeep'. The gathering agreed that the possibility of a simultaneous attack upon the two gravity dams should be considered.

March 1943 A month later, on 13 March, Bufton informed Air Vice-Marshal (AVM) Norman Bottomley, Assistant Chief of the Air Staff (Operations), that the Möhne and Eder were Germany's most important dams. Reinforcing their importance and suitability Bufton intimated that other potential targets were either out of range or of lesser importance. Planning for 'Upkeep' should be confined to the most important dams, the Möhne and Eder, in that order, ensuring that an adequate effort be devoted to the former before considering the possibility of an attack upon the Eder. By lack of reference of the Sorpe, however, he was diluting the strategic argument of causing the greatest disruption to the Ruhr's industry.

Two days later, the Ministry of Economic Warfare (MEW) issued a memorandum with different conclusions. The economic importance of these two dams differed very widely. The Möhne was of critical importance in the water supply of the Ruhr. Its loss in the late spring or early summer might have serious effects on industrial activity and cause widespread alarm and despondency. The Eder was significant for its flood-prevention functions but 'cannot from the economic perspective, be reckoned a first-class objective'. Since maximum advantage would probably be obtained from an attack during the winter it did not warrant early consideration. MEW re-iterated that the Möhne and the Sorpe jointly provided over 75 per cent of the Ruhr's storage capacity. The simultaneous breaching of these would deprive the River Ruhr of water and hinder bulk traffic for the heavy industries along the river. Of greater significance this would also deprive much of the Ruhr of the main source of its industrial and drinking water at a time when the natural flow of the Ruhr into the Rhine might be very low. The effect would be to produce 'a paralysing effect' on industrial activity.

Countering Wallis's suggestion and focusing on the economic and industrial effects, MEW noted that while destruction of the Eder dam would interfere seriously with water traffic on the River Weser and Mittelland Canal, it would not affect industrial or drinking water supplies. They concluded that far greater and more widespread disruption would result from the destruction of the Möhne or Sorpe dams than of the Eder dam. Balanced against this was the consideration that, although the Möhne and Sorpe were of greater importance than the Eder in terms of industrial effect, the Sorpe was less suited to the effect of 'Upkeep'. Taking everything into account, MEW concluded: 'Therefore it appears that the best objective for these operations is the Möhne dam, and that it would be preferable to concentrate all forces against this one objective to ensure a completely successful operation rather than split the force on a number of objectives.'

This advice now presented a problem. In early March Wallis had noted that 'one properly placed charge is sufficient to breach these dams,' including the Sorpe. By 17 March he had modified his assessment. Immediate catastrophic failure might not occur with the Sorpe. He reassured Bufton: 'If we can shatter the crest and produce a leakage of water, I think natural erosion will do the rest,' though there was no clear indication of how many 'Upkeeps' might be required to achieve this. By mid-March the planners' inclination was to rule out an attack on the Sorpe for tactical and technical reasons.

This was confirmed by a meeting of the Chiefs of Staff Committee on 19 March which considered that the two dams most vulnerable to attack were the Möhne and Eder. Of these, the former was seen to be the more important, tactically more suitable for attack and its destruction 'would have far reaching effects on the enemy's war economy'. The Sorpe, though important, was ruled out as being unsuitable for attack, 'for tactical and technical reasons'. They concluded: 'We consider that initially the planning of operations for "Upkeep" should be confined to attacks on the Möhne and possibly the Eder dam in that order of priority.' On 27 March Portal circulated a memorandum to the Chiefs of Staff Committee outlining the economic consequences expected from an attack on the Möhne and Eder.

Meanwhile, Portal had asked Bottomley to obtain confirmation of MEW's earlier assessment. Bottomley cautioned that

> I do not think that we should confine your paper to the Möhne dam. The preliminary tactical examination made by AOC 5 Group indicates that it may be possible to damage the Sorpe and Eder dams, if not simultaneously at least within a day or two, before defences are adequately strengthened. The cumulative effects of damage to two

or three of the dams would be proportionately great, and we should count on this probability.

April 1943 MEW's revised assessment was forthcoming on 2 April. Titled: 'Economic and Moral [*sic* – i.e. Morale] Consequences of the Destruction of German Dams' it clarified what had been said previously: 'There is every prospect that both the physical and the moral effects of the flood which would be produced [by the breaching of the Möhne dam] are likely to be sufficiently great to justify this operation in themselves, even if there were no other significant effects.' However, it went on to say that 'the destruction of this dam would not necessarily have a large or immediate effect on the supply of industrial and household water in the Ruhr area' on account of the Ruhr industries relying mainly upon water drawn from underground aquifers. The Möhne's main purpose was to ensure these supplies by storing surplus winter rainfall. Thus, the economic effects of breaching this dam would not necessarily be large or immediate. This was counter to Wallis's assessment that breaching the Möhne would have sudden catastrophic impact.

The simultaneous or subsequent destruction of the Sorpe dam would re-inforce the effects of the destruction of the Möhne dam. MEW advised that breaching both the Möhne and the Sorpe 'would be worth much more than twice the destruction of one':

> It is most strongly urged that, if the operational possibilities hold out any reasonable prospect of success, an attack on the Möhne be accompanied, or followed as soon as possible, by an attack on the Sorpe dam.

MEW again pointed out that the functions of the Eder dam, were not related to those of the Möhne and Sorpe and its destruction would in no way supplement the effects of the destruction of these dams. Release of the Eder's reservoir would result in the inundation of mainly agricultural land in the Eder, Fulda and Weser valleys. Four power stations below the dam might be destroyed; these were of limited economic importance but would interfere with the operation of the Preussenelektra power-supply system. No industrial areas would be affected other than possibly low-lying areas of Kassel. It also seemed unlikely that navigability of the lower Weser and Mittelland Canal would be critically affected.

The effects of the destruction of the Möhne and Sorpe dams would be witnessed by thousands. Regardless of the true facts, their morale would inevitably be undermined and could become susceptible to alarmist rumours regarding the supply of drinking water, risk of disease and inability of the fire services to deal with incendiary attacks. As such there were possibilities for exploitation of this situation by political warfare – or 'black propaganda'. Affecting a smaller and more rural population, the impact on morale of breaching the Eder, 'though by no means negligible', would be much less.

Bottomley passed this report to Portal on 5 April. Drawing attention to the conflicting conclusions between Portal's memorandum of 27 March and the latest MEW assessment Bottomley concluded:

> You will note that contrary to our original idea, the destruction of the Sorpe is regarded as the second in order of importance and especially so if combined with that of the Möhne. We should therefore plan for simultaneous attacks on these two to be followed by attacks on the Eder if circumstances allow.

The Sorpe was now a definite candidate and requests were immediately issued to prepare a revised Target Information Sheet, obtain photographic reconnaissance cover and produce a briefing model. However, a final decision on briefing materials for the Eder would not be taken until early May.

Despite concerns about the suitability of 'Upkeep' for use against the Sorpe, Wallis was still fully occupied in perfecting 'Upkeep's' performance and little further attention appears to have been paid to this issue for nearly three weeks. On 24 April, however, at a meeting with W/Cdr Gibson and Vickers test pilots 'Mutt' Summers and S/Ldr 'Shorty' Longbottom, to discuss height and speed of release of 'Upkeep', Wallis noted in his diary: 'Discussed method of attack on Sorpe.'

May 1943   On 5 May a meeting chaired by Bottomley in his office at the Air Ministry and attended by a select number including AVM Robert Saundby (Harris's deputy), AVM Ralph Cochrane of 5 Group, Wallis and Bufton, confirmed the intention to attack the Möhne, Eder and Sorpe dams during the May moon period, or as soon as possible after 14/15 May.

Meanwhile the crews who were to undertake this remarkable operation were being assembled and began training with only the most basic idea of the task in which they had to become proficient. Secrecy meant that knowledge of the target and the nature of their weapon was restricted to a select few senior officers. It was a case of establishing and perfecting basic skills and then honing them to greater precision as 'Upkeep's' development progressed and the criteria for release were refined and became even more demanding.

Chapter 3

Formation of the Force

By February 1943 Harris had become aware of Wallis's 'golf mines', including 'Upkeep', 'which is under consideration for the special purpose of destroying dams, the Möhne dam in particular'. This weapon could be carried only in a specially modified Lancaster. At that stage it was estimated that when dropped at 220 mph from heights of 80–120 feet it would travel 1,200 yards on the surface of the water. Detonated within 10 feet of a dam wall it might breach it to a depth of 30 feet if the lake were full. The Ministry of Aircraft Production estimated that it would take six months to produce the modified aircraft and bombs. Bomber Command was asked to comment on the tactical aspects of the operation in terms of number of aircraft and the length of training required and whether the operation could be conducted in bright moonlight using radio altimeters, or whether the attack would have to be in daylight.

March 1943   On 17 March the War Cabinet Joint Planning Staff reported on their deliberations with respect to the use of 'Upkeep', confirming that, 'The present arrangement for attacks in May on German dams ... should be pressed on with full vigour,' but that a final decision to launch an attack should wait until the results of technical investigations were known.

Meanwhile Bufton had been dealing with Bomber Command on the subject of allocating a squadron to carry out the operation with 'Upkeep'. On 17 March he told AVM Bottomley:

> They propose to form temporarily a special squadron which will be formed on the modified aircraft. They have not yet decided in which group it will be placed as this depends upon the availability of airfield accommodation. They propose to man it with volunteer tour expired crews who will be fully experienced.

AVM Saundby, suggested modifying sufficient aircraft to equip one squadron, which would have to be taken off normal operations in order to train, but that two or three weeks should be sufficient.

Harris, however, was not impressed, issuing his notorious response:

> This is tripe of the wildest description. There are so many ifs and ands that there is not the smallest chance of it working. To begin with the bomb would have to be perfectly balanced around its axis otherwise rotation at 500 rpm would wreck the aircraft or tear the bomb loose. I don't believe a word of its supposed ballistics on the surface. It would be much easier to design a scow bomb to run on the surface, burst its nose on contact, sink and explode. The bomb would of course be heavier than water and exactly fit existing bomb bays. At all costs stop them putting aside Lancasters and reducing our bombing effort on this wild goose chase. Let them prove the practicality of this weapon first. Another toraplane, only madder. The war will be over before it ever works. And it never will!

The Air Ministry's Directorate of Bomber Operations were keen to progress the project and Wallis made light of the dropping requirements, suggesting heights up to 400 feet, and explaining that modifications to the aircraft would take only two days and be easily reversible. It would take only two months to produce the weapon. On this basis it was decided to convert 30 aircraft, with a view to an operation in June. It was also 'desirable to select provisionally the squadrons [sic] for the operation' and to select a crew from each who might undertake dropping trials.

Harris was not supportive, writing to Portal: 'All sorts of enthusiasts and panacea-mongers are careering round MAP suggesting the taking of about 30 Lancasters off the line to rig them up for this weapon, when the weapon itself exists so far only within the imaginations of those who conceived it.' He deprecated any diversion of Lancasters from the bomber offensive, stating that the concept was 'just about the maddest proposition as a weapon that we have yet come across'.

> I am prepared to bet my shirt (a) that the weapon itself cannot be produced as a prototype for trial inside 6 months; (b) that the ballistics will in no way resemble those claimed for it; (c) that it will be impossible to keep such a weapon in adequate balance either when rotating it prior to release or at all in storage; and (d) that it will not work, when we have got it.

Portal assured him that he would 'not allow more than three of your precious Lancasters to be diverted for this purpose' until the weapon was proven in full scale, but also ordered parts for the conversion of 30 aircraft. It was a leap of faith, given that no full-scale weapon had yet been produced, let alone tested. On 17 March Harris rejected the idea of taking a squadron out of the line and ruled that a special squadron should be formed. Accordingly, AVM Oxland, Bomber Command's Senior Air Staff Officer (SASO), wrote to AVM Ralph Cochrane, Air Officer Commanding (AOC) No. 5 Group, at his headquarters at 'St Vincents', a large Victorian mansion on the outskirts of Grantham. In the briefest of terms, he described 'Upkeep', its *modus operandi* and that it was proposed to use it 'against a large dam [*sic*] in Germany'. Harris intended to form a new squadron within No. 5 Group, equipped with Lancasters specially fitted to carry the bomb for this task. To keep their work as secret as possible they should be based 'on their own at some suitable aerodrome in your Group'.

> The operation against this dam will not, it is thought, prove particularly dangerous, but will undoubtedly require skilled crews. Volunteer crews will therefore have to be carefully selected from the Squadrons in your Group.

Some training would be necessary, and there was a degree of urgency since the water level in the dam was likely to be too low after the beginning of June.

Cochrane had only been appointed commander of No. 5 Group the previous month. He was, however, well known to Harris, having previously commanded No. 3 (Bomber) Group and served as a flight commander under him in No. 45 Squadron in Mesopotamia in 1922. Cochrane also knew and had a high respect for Wallis, having first met him at Barrow-in-Furness in 1916 when Cochrane was an RNAS officer and Wallis was designing airships for Vickers. The airship connection later brought them together again at Howden where Wallis was working on the *R-80* and *R-100*.

The selection of W/Cdr Guy Gibson as commander of the new unit was almost certainly made by Harris, who had known Gibson as a junior flying officer operating on Handley Page Hampdens in 1940, when Harris was commanding No. 5 Group. Gibson had then spent fourteen months flying Beaufighter night fighters before returning to Bomber Command, now led by Harris, who had given him command of No. 106 Squadron at Syerston, within No. 5 Group. Gibson was a resourceful and innovative commander, embodying the courage and determination that became known as the 'press-on spirit'. He was highly regarded by Harris, who subsequently described him as 'as great a warrior as these islands breed'. When Gibson was called into

Cochrane's office to be asked whether he would consider doing 'one more operation' it was almost a rhetorical question.

Popular myth records that Gibson personally selected all the crews and that most of them were known to him and had completed at least a tour of operations and were decorated. The reality is less clear cut.

Given that it would be extremely difficult to obtain enough crews who had completed two operational tours, the best option would be to find those who had completed or were coming to the end of their first tour. Equally it was important not to denude existing main-force squadrons of all their experienced crews.

From his time commanding No. 106 Squadron, Gibson already knew Flight Lieutenant (F/Lt) John Hopgood, F/Lt David Shannon and Pilot Officer (P/O) Lewis Burpee, and Gibson also knew F/Lt Mick Martin. The two flight commanders seem to have been selected on Group recommendation: S/Ldr Melvin Young, chosen as 'A' Flight Commander, was already starting his second tour. He became senior flight commander by virtue of age and length of service and the fact that he was already 'C' Flight Commander on No. 57 Squadron at Scampton. Perhaps surprisingly, though, he had no recent operational experience in the European theatre or on Lancasters. (His first tour had been in 1940 flying Whitleys with No. 102 Squadron and he had then transferred to a Wellington unit in the Middle East.) Henry Maudslay had just returned to operations as a flight lieutenant with No. 50 Squadron having completed his first tour. He was promoted to squadron leader and became 'B' Flight Commander.

G/C Whitworth, RAF Scampton's station commander, may have been asked for recommendations. He had instructed Young in the Oxford University Air Squadron and may have sanctioned the transfer of Young's complete flight across to the new squadron. These crews formed a coherent unit (other than Young's own crew who were newly forming). In addition, the flight had only recently been created as part of planned expansion and their transfer would not overly deplete No. 57 Squadron, which would revert to two-flight status. This transfer provided: F/Lt Bill Astell (on his second tour, but like Young his earlier experience had been in the Middle East), P/O Geoff Rice, Flight Sergeant (F/Sgt) George Lancaster and F/Sgt Ray Lovell. (Both Lovell and Lancaster would be posted back to No. 57 Squadron during training and F/Sgt William Divall would be posted to No. 617 Squadron.)

The selection process is unclear, but it appears that 5 Group then sent out a request to its six other parent stations asking for volunteer crews, which produced:

- Waddington: F/Sgt Ken Brown and F/Lt Harold Wilson from
  No. 44 Squadron;
- Skellingthorpe: P/O Les Knight from No. 50 Squadron (which had
  already provided Maudslay);
- Coningsby was closed for runway laying, but No. 97 Squadron at
  its satellite Woodhall Spa provided three crews, F/Lt David Maltby,
  F/Lt Joe McCarthy and F/Lt Les Munro;
- Langar: P/O Warner Ottley from No. 207 Squadron was a relatively
  late arrival on 7 April;
- Syerston: F/Lt Norman Barlow from No. 61 Squadron;
- Bottesford: P/O Vernon Byers from No. 467 Squadron;
- Since Bottesford and Langar had only offered one crew each it may
  have been expedient to turn to Scampton's sub-station, Fiskerton,
  which provided F/Sgt Bill Townsend and F/Sgt Cyril Anderson from
  No. 49 Squadron.

Not all the captains came with their whole crew, necessitating the posting of additional individual members to make up complete crews, a process which was not completed until 7 May. Lancaster and Lovell returned to No. 57 Squadron at a stage too late to train replacements. The final selection left the squadron with 21 crews, a total of 147 aircrew. Of 21 captains, 15 had completed or nearly completed a tour. Of the 147 aircrew, only 29 were decorated (although not all the decorations had been formally gazetted by the time of the Dams Raid).

The airfield within No. 5 Group selected as the base for this new squadron was that at Scampton, four miles north of Lincoln alongside the A15 road, the old Roman Ermine Street. Scampton had been an airfield during the First World War, but the present station dated from 1936 and comprised four large C-Type hangars, together with comfortable brick-built technical and domestic accommodation including a large officers' mess in neo-Georgian style, now all painted in a disruptive camouflage pattern. The airfield itself offered a concrete perimeter track and dispersed hard standings, surrounding the grass flying field. It had been home to Nos. 49 and 57 Squadrons, equipped with Lancasters, but the former had moved out in January 1943 in preparation for the laying of hard concrete runways more suitable for heavily laden aircraft. Their departure left space for the newly forming squadron which was to take up residence in No. 2 Hangar, with its dispersals off the southern and western stretches of the perimeter track. The runway construction would have to wait.

Personnel began to assemble at Scampton from 20 March, but it was not until 8 April 1943 that an Air Ministry Secret Organisation Memorandum recorded 'No. 617 Squadron formed at RAF Scampton in No. 5 Group ... w.e.f. 23 March 1943 ... The aircraft establishment is 16 + 2 Lancaster.' Until 23 March the Squadron was known as X Squadron. Again, folklore suggests that this was unique, that the X implied an aura of mystery and that No. 617 Squadron came into being by re-numbering X Squadron. It was in fact standard practice to label any newly forming unit 'X' ('Y' and 'Z' if more were forming concurrently) until administration had caught up sufficiently to generate a number. The number followed earlier '600–616' series squadrons formed pre-war, which were Auxiliary Air Force Units. No. 617 Squadron was the first of 1943 expansion. No. 618 Squadron, formed at Skitten on 26 March (though many sources state 1 April) within Coastal Command, was to carry out the Mosquito 'Highball' operations, while No. 619 Squadron was a new main-force Lancaster squadron formed at Woodhall Spa within No. 5 Group on 18 April.

By 27 March No. 617 Squadron was ready to commence training. The nature of the task ahead was still a closely guarded secret and Gibson was only told that 'No 617 Squadron will be required to attack a number of lightly defended special targets. These attacks will necessitate low level navigation over enemy territory in moonlight.' The final approach to the target was to be at 100 feet and at a precise speed, which would be about 240 miles per hour, and would likely be carried out over water. Release of the mine was to be made visually plus or minus 40 yards of a point judged either by a landmark on the shore or after a timed run past such a landmark.

April 1943   By the beginning of April, the squadron was equipped with 10 standard Lancasters, one from each of the squadrons which had supplied crews, plus one more from No. 9 Squadron. A training programme had been drawn up. The first week (1–7 April) would practise low-level navigation and map reading while a suitable reservoir was found for training, followed by ten days (8–18 April) practising accurate flying at 150 feet over water. By 16 April crews were required to be sufficiently proficient to practise the full operation. A full moon on 20 April would permit full rehearsals to be conducted under appropriate conditions on either side of this date.

During the first week of April the squadron carried out sixty-two daylight low-level cross-country flights. Ten routes were laid down. The longest ventured to Scotland or Cornwall, others ranged from Yorkshire to East Anglia; 665 practice bombs were dropped from low level with an average error of 50.5 yards. Since there was no moon, bomb aimers used Livingston 'double glazed' goggles, fitted with amber and blue filters to simulate moonlight conditions. Looking at the ground they saw only faint reflections from water features, giving the impression of a starlit night, while sodium cockpit lighting enabled maps to be read normally. Using the same principles four of the squadron's standard Lancasters would soon be equipped with 'two stage amber'. Blue Perspex screens were fitted inside the cockpit and the pilot wore amber goggles to obtain a similar effect. The flight engineer, without goggles and acting as safety pilot, saw a blue-tinted world. To aid observation the pilot would look ahead and to port, while the engineer looked ahead and to starboard. Although every effort was made to keep the Perspex clean it became coated with squashed insects, which could be misconstrued as distant obstructions. If the crewmen moved their heads slightly from side to side it was possible to distinguish the two. Distant objects remained stationary while marks on the screen, being closer, showed relatively greater shift.

Careful planning was the keynote to accurate low-level navigation. Time spent on the ground saved valuable time in the air when wanting to keep out of trouble. Advice on technique was sought from RAF Tempsford, the airfield in Bedfordshire from which operations were flown in support of the Special Operations Executive, dropping agents and supplies into occupied Europe. It was not that they knew where all the defences were (an impossible task), rather that they were well versed in accurate low-level navigation by moonlight.

The main aid to navigation would be visual map-reading by the bomb aimer, using 1/250,000 charts with key pinpoints marked, passing this track information to the navigator who plotted their progress on his chart and maintained his navigation log, calculating the course for the pilot to steer to make allowance for wind and drift. The bomb aimer remained in the prone position for the entire flight making map reading more difficult since the map was near his face. The strain of continually re-adjusting the eyes for near and distant vision added to the fatigue. Moreover, the map restricted the field of view since it was laid over the window. Some bomb aimers preferred to use strip maps which were mounted on wooden rollers on a frame, wound on as the route was followed. The drawback with roller maps was that they only covered a short distance on either side of the planned route, and a slight error in course could very quickly take the aircraft 'off the map'.

Accurate navigation below a thousand feet proved difficult and required different techniques. Landmarks, including contours, or even small, isolated hills, became much more apparent, but small towns disappeared if not passed directly over or close by, and woods lost their shape owing to the smaller field of view. Vertical features such as church spires, power lines, wireless masts and chimneys were useful. Water features such as solitary lakes on track were good, as were railways and rivers which could be checked by the direction they ran and distinctive bends or bridges. Flying along a river or canal it was best to fly to one side so that both pilot and bomb aimer could observe. Suitable landmarks were selected every 5–10 minutes along each leg. To ease strain, specific landmarks were only looked for when they were due. On occasion the navigator would stand up in the cockpit to identify a feature visually and check the bomb aimer's report.

After take-off, navigators synchronised the directional gyro with the compass, then the initial course to the first waypoint was set on the compass. The time was noted and the estimated time of arrival (ETA) at the first point was confirmed, based on speed, wind and distance. After making sure this was reached accurately and on time, the next leg was plotted, and ETA established. Arrival time at each pinpoint was compared to planned ETA and the next ETA adjusted accordingly if necessary. A steady course, speed and constant look-out were essential. If a pinpoint did not appear on time a search was made until it was found. If wind was causing drift to port or starboard the appropriate course change was made, plus the number of degrees to maintain required track to the next waypoint, and the course adjusted to allow for future drift.

Over the sea it was important to establish an accurate course and maintain a constant airspeed, checking compass and direction indicator. Drift would be detected by means of flame floats, the gunners taking a sight on the receding light and reading the angle off the turret ring. While approaching the coast, a good look-out was to be maintained for the next pinpoint. If off-track a course adjustment should be made to reach it and a mental check made of the angle of crossing the coastline.

In addition to visual map reading, an electronic aid, Gee, was also employed over the sea and as a further position checker over the continent. A receiver in the aircraft detected a grid of signals radiated from Britain across Europe and presented them as a display on a cathode ray tube at the navigator's position. Using a Gee chart which had an overprinted signals lattice the navigator could then determine the aircraft's position. In good conditions and with a skilled operator, Gee could provide a position as far as the Ruhr, but being a radio aid, it was susceptible to German jamming and interference. Initially its use was practised in the maintenance section, but by 23 April navigators had their own dedicated training room.

Additional assistance was provided by a new piece of equipment, the air position indicator (API). This was an analogue computer which took inputs from the air mileage unit (AMU) and the distant reading compass (DRC). It continuously computed and displayed the air position in latitude and longitude on odometer style counters. In addition, it indicated the aircraft's true course, provided a supplement to the navigator's manual air plot and made wind-finding easier and quicker. Although accurate, the API required periodic checking against visual pinpoints and re-setting manually if necessary.

The route to and from the target was planned to avoid known flak positions, but there was always the risk of flying over convoys at sea or recently established defences on land. Flying low would deny any defences warning of an attack's approach and help avoid the threat of night fighters. Keeping below 500 feet should conceal the force from radar. A formation of three Lancasters in vic formation with Nos. 2 and 3 only slightly behind the leader and at about 1½ wingspan interval permitted individual evasive action to be taken. With the leader at about 50 feet, Nos. 2 and 3 should be slightly above, giving a small margin should the leader climb suddenly to avoid approaching obstacles.

Various tactics were adopted to reduce the risks.

Light flak required a visual target and was most effective at heights between 250 and 2,500 feet and ranges of about 1,500–2,500 yards. Its shells were generally tracer and appeared as strings of coloured balls, usually red or yellow, curving up towards the aircraft and generally only exploding on impact. Because it was visually aimed, variations of height and course were of very little use for evasion and high speed was the best way to get out of danger. The use of tracer meant it was often possible to avoid defended areas seen firing at other aircraft. If engaged by light flak or searchlights air gunners should fire on the sites in the hope of putting the ground defences off their aim.

Experience had shown that an aircraft was most likely to be shot at when crossing the coast. The best counter was to lose height very rapidly on reaching the coast, crossing it as low and as fast as possible. This added to the map-reader's difficulty in pinpointing his position and not only necessitated a sharp look-out for landmarks when crossing the coast, but also the need to make sure of a pinpoint after the aircraft had crossed the coast and gained height to 500–600 feet. In the case of 'Chastise' this tactic would be adopted on leaving the enemy coast, but on approach to enemy territory the force would stay down and cross the coast as low as possible.

Height was also a critical issue on the final bombing run. Only the three trials aircraft were fitted with a radio altimeter. A pulse from the aircraft, bounced off the water below, was timed and translated into height. The device was ideal over open water for heights up to 150 feet; it was less reliable over the enclosed waters of a reservoir surrounded by hills. It also created a false sense of security, indicating only the ground directly beneath the aircraft, not any sudden rise in terrain ahead. Flying a heavily laden aircraft low at night, the pilot needed to be looking outside the cockpit, not concentrating on his instruments.

Trailing a wire from the aircraft in the manner suggested earlier by Finch-Noyes proved impracticable and an alternative system using two Aldis lamps was instigated.

Though attributed to Ben Lockspeiser of the Ministry of Aircraft Production, its origins lay in the First World War. In 1917 Captain Jenkins fitted his 'Night Height Projector' to a BE 2c, projecting lights onto the ground angled so that their beams met when the aircraft was at a pre-determined height. The idea was resurrected in the inter-war period for assisting flying boats to land at night and later dusted off and trialled for mine-laying operations. Now it was to be used to establish the height of release for 'Upkeep'. On 4 April 1943 S/Ldr Henry Maudslay flew one of No. 617 Squadron's standard aircraft from Scampton to Farnborough for a trial installation.

The front lamp was mounted in the bombing camera position, to port of the centreline and just forward of the bomb doors, directed 30 degrees to starboard of vertical. The rear lamp was some 40 feet to the rear, aft of the bomb bay, in a hole cut into the Lancaster's redundant under-turret blanking panel. The rear beam shone 40 degrees to starboard and 15.1 degrees forwards giving an intersection of the beams at 150 feet – the original release height of 'Upkeep'. With a beam spread of 6 degrees, at a height of 150 feet each spot was 15 feet wide. The spots could be observed by the navigator from the observation blister on the starboard side of the cockpit. As the aircraft descended the front one appeared to be stationary, the rear being either ahead if the aircraft was too high, or behind if too low. At the correct height the spots formed a figure '8' on the water.

On 8 April Maudslay flew the aircraft back to Scampton. Trial runs were flown over The Wash shortly after sunset with conditions equating to those of a full moon. The spots were switched on and the pilot guided verbally by his navigator who could see them from 500 feet. After a few minutes there was no difficulty in achieving runs to within +/-10 feet of the specified height, measured against a specially calibrated sensitive altimeter.

Six sets were available at Scampton by 16 April to permit the squadron to train. A further twenty would be ready for fitment to the modified operational aircraft. Installation took approximately two man-days per aircraft. With the lamps installed, each aircraft was jacked up into flying attitude and the distance between the lamp centres marked on the hangar floor. From these were calculated the positions on the floor through which the beams should shine to intersect at the required height. The lamps were switched on and adjusted until each spot shone on the correct point on the floor. It was precise work, requiring accurate adjustment to ¼ inch. Bolts were then fitted to fix the lamps firmly in position.

Within the next ten days a further three standard aircraft were fitted. Harris again voiced his scepticism:

> I will not have aircraft flying about with spotlights in a defended area. Get some of these lunatics controlled & if possible locked up ... Beams of spotlight will not work on water at glassy calm. Any fool knows that.

Further trials by the squadron proved his fears unfounded since most water had a slight 'chop' and attempts were made to screen the lights from the enemy by fitting a cylindrical shade to the forward light. The crews too had concerns about flying in to attack a defended target at low level 'lit up like a Christmas tree'. Later the rear lamp was repositioned further forward, to the rear of the bomb bay, improving its screening from ground observation and preventing oil and dirt obscuring its glass. The new position also meant that the travel of the spots on the water as the aircraft descended remained as that practised earlier when the lights were further apart.

Accurate estimation of the point of release also proved problematical. The original idea of timing from an established landmark or other known datum soon proved to be impractical. W/Cdr Charles Dann, Assistant Director for Instrument Research and Development at the Ministry of Aircraft Production, was called in to assist with the problem. Dann's first suggestion comprised two marks on the bomb aimer's panel corresponding to the two towers of the reservoir, with a cross piece in the cockpit to fix the position of the bomb aimer's head. Dann went to Scampton on 10 April and assisted in the making of a sight appropriate to the reservoir selected for training.

After this sight had been introduced to the crews, it was then realised that the towers on the Möhne dam were 639 feet apart, whilst those on the Eder were 781 feet. Using the Möhne sighting marks against the Eder would result in 'Upkeep' being dropped over 600 yards from the dam. As a result, the sight was modified so 'as to permit subsequent adjustment'. This may have resulted in the development of the wooden handheld sight, allowing the arms to pivot and adjusting the distance between the sighting pins to allow for target variations.

In practice it proved extremely difficult for the bomb aimer using the wooden sight to support himself, keep the sight steady and operate the release button, whilst being buffeted by turbulence at low level. A third sight, newer and simpler than the original method, developed most probably by the squadron bomb aimers, dispensed with the wooden cross piece positioning the bomb aimer's head and used the sides of the clear vision panel (or marks adjacent to it) as the foresight The framing of the panel served for the Eder, marks on the Perspex for the Möhne. Two pieces of string of the required length were stretched taught to the eye as the rear sight. This proved more accurate and easier to use at night than the smaller rangefinder.

W/Cdr Dann also investigated the possibility of using the existing Low Level Mark III bomb sight for the operation. A complicated device, this involved the bomb aimer watching a graticule resembling a moving 'ladder' of horizontal bars seen against the background of the ground. The speed of the bars' movement was calculated so that, as the target approached the aircraft and appeared to move faster, its movement coincided with the graticule, at which point the bomb was released. A sophisticated sight, it relied greatly on the skill of the bomb aimer. As far as is known the squadron never tested the Mark III for 'Upkeep' (although they would use it in October 1944 for a low-level attack on the Kembs dam using 12,000-pound Tallboy bombs).

It was soon decided that triangulation sights were the simplest and most effective; each bomb aimer used the version he preferred. Already bomb aimers were improvising their own and F/Sgt Clifford, F/Sgt Lancaster's bomb aimer, achieved a remarkable 4-yard error with six bombs. Ironically, the crew's navigator failed to meet Gibson's requirements; rather than have him replaced the crew opted to be posted from the squadron.

By the third week of training the early problems had been solved and flying progressed on a well-organised and extensive scale. On 10 April the moon became available and three night routes were laid down to simulate the actual operation. At the same time the first aircraft with two stage amber was completed. Crews found it easy to fly at 150 feet and providing navigation was from pinpoint to pinpoint there was no difficulty in keeping on track.

Daylight bombing was carried out daily from 100–150 feet on the range at Wainfleet where two white screens, 30 × 20 feet, and 700 feet apart were erected. These blew down in a gale on 26 April. No practice bombs were dropped at the reservoirs selected for training. Only 11½-pound practice bombs were used against targets on the Wainfleet bombing range, conversion charts being used to adjust the plot of these bombs to equate with 'Upkeep's' unique characteristics. These practices perfected crew co-operation and familiarised the bomb aimer with the effect of the towers approaching the markers on his sight.

Speed of release was causing concern. No. 5 Group wanted release at 205–210 mph, but from 15 April, in response to the latest data from trials, crews were instructed to drop at 240 mph.

The mid-upper turrets were removed from the 'Chastise' aircraft to save weight and reduce drag. Generally, the smaller of the two gunners now manned the front turret and stirrups were made to keep his feet out of the bomb aimer's way. Most gunnery training concentrated on air-to-sea firing against smoke floats, to deal with any ground opposition. Owing to the restricted space the bomb-aimer had to remain in a prone position. This put a severe load on the back muscles, twisting the spine and causing undue nervous strain and fatigue. It also restricted the movement of his arms since the main weight of the fore part of the body was taken on the elbows. Consequently, the bomb-aimer had to twist his neck and body uncomfortably to observe through the clear vision panel and use the bombsight. For greater comfort and stability for aiming most bomb aimers modified their aircraft by lowering and repositioning the chest rest.

In convincing Portal and Bomber Command of his idea, Wallis had originally envisaged that 'Upkeep' would be carried on an easily demountable cradle that could be fitted into the Lancaster's bomb bay. Using this, it would take only two days to modify the aircraft for the operation, which would entail removal of the bomb doors and addition of plywood fairings through which a portion of the bomb would protrude. After completion of the operation the aircraft could be made fit for normal operation within 24 hours. However, after receiving instructions to proceed on 26 February, Wallis discovered that the task was far more complex and that it would be necessary to build bespoke aircraft rather than convert existing standard machines. Fortunately, he was able to enlist the immediate and full co-operation of Avro and their Chief Designer, Roy Chadwick.

Together with the Air Ministry and Ministry of Aircraft Production, they agreed on a division of labour. Avro would be responsible for the attachment points for the arms to carry the bomb, the bomb bay fairings, the release wiring, and the hydraulic power for spinning the bomb; Vickers would make the attachment arms and driving mechanism and the weapon itself. Simultaneously Wallis set to work with a will, beginning the general drawings for 'Upkeep' at 11.30 a.m. on 27 February. By 6.30 the following evening they were completed. During this period, he also found time to discuss bearings for the spinning discs that were to hold the weapon, methods of fuzing and tactical considerations. Such intensity – 12 hours a day, often 16 or 17 for seven days a week – was to become the norm for the next two months.

Such was the complexity of the task that by 6 March Portal's original provision for 30 aircraft was amended to 23. To carry 'Upkeep' the Lancaster's bomb doors were removed, and fairings fitted fore and aft. The weapon itself, a cylinder, 50 inches in diameter and 60 inches long was suspended across the bomb bay, supported by two substantial V-shaped calliper arms, each with a rotating disc at the apex which fitted into a circular recess on each endplate of the 'Upkeep'. The right-hand disc was driven by a Fenner V-belt drive linked to a smaller pulley which was driven by a Vickers Janny variable speed hydraulic motor, originally designed for steering submarines, mounted inside the front fairing. The motor was started approximately ten minutes before the aircraft made its attack to begin spinning the weapon, which was clamped between the calliper arms. These were held under tension against springs until release, when the arms were forced outwards, allowing the spinning weapon to fall free.

The first modified aircraft was completed by 6 April, but the first three were allocated for trials and the squadron had to wait until 18 April to receive the first example. The aircraft were delivered direct from Avro essentially complete, but many of the operational requisites, including the fitting of the calliper arms and spotlights had to be carried out by working parties at Scampton.

By 23 April the squadron were still practising with standard Lancasters. Four aircraft had been fitted with the 'spotlight altimeter calibrator' and ten crews had experienced its use. Flying hours were reduced due to servicing needs and less experienced crews were being given priority.

Meanwhile, trials at Reculver on the Kent coast determined that height and speed of release had to be reduced. From 26 April these were modified respectively to 60 feet and 210 mph. By 7 May the final criteria would be fixed as release from 60 feet at speeds between 210 and 220 mph. These would give 'Upkeep' a range of 450–500 yards, of which 250 yards would be along the water. Crews carried out training over The Wash and over the airfield, where observers with theodolites checked the aircraft height. With the bombing height now more than half the Lancaster's wingspan, crews were ordered to climb immediately if the aircraft descended below 60 feet before re-commencing the exercise. As an added aid, the new 'Upkeep' aircraft had an additional sensitive altimeter replacing the visual direction indicator on top of the instrument panel, giving the pilot a 'head up' indication. Bombing results using the new rangefinder were improving although on average were still +/-150 yards, three times the desired range of error.

1–15 May The first of the 'Upkeep' aircraft was fitted with the spotlights at Farnborough and returned to Scampton on 2 May. By 7 May eighteen operational aircraft had been fitted and their crews were proficient at 60 feet. Two more aircraft would be fitted, the final one when a new Lancaster was delivered to replace one badly damaged by spray when S/Ldr Maudslay released an inert practice 'Upkeep' from too low a height at Reculver on 12 May. A final machine, delivered to Scampton on the afternoon of 16 May and used as a reserve, arrived too late for the lights to be fitted.

With the various elements of height, speed and release point mastered, it was now necessary to integrate these into a full operational plan. Eyebrook reservoir, four miles south of Uppingham, already used as a convenient stretch of water since 10 April, was selected as the target. Poles standing in barrels of concrete and linked by camouflage scrim were erected on the earthen dam to represent the towers of the Möhne dam. Tactical exercises to practice command and control co-ordination were planned from 5 May, involving up to ten aircraft at a time.

Attacks would be controlled by W/Cdr Gibson using direct speech. Daylight tests suggested that the Lancaster's existing TR 1196 radios would be sufficient, but a test on the night of 4/5 May proved a complete failure due to background interference. The solution was found in the installation of TR 1143 VHF sets, as used by fighters, which were sourced and fitted within three days.

On 6 May Gibson held a conference with all the aircraft captains, together with P/O Cliff Caple, the Squadron Engineering Officer, and P/O Henry Watson the Armament Officer, and began to pull together each of the elements of training into exercises to mimic the proposed operation. He did not reveal the final targets, although he did go as far as to suggest that the operation would be conducted within the next two weeks.

By 7 May all crews were deemed operational. After the briefing of the previous day they were now flying short dusk cross countries to Uppingham and then on to Abberton reservoir near Colchester, which was used as a stretch of water to represent the second target. The aircraft made individual attacks at 60 feet, under the control of Gibson who directed them by radio telephony (direct speech). Nothing was dropped at these two lakes, and they returned via the Wainfleet range, finally making a low run over the airfield on return to confirm the calibration of their spotlights. Six other aircraft made runs over the Howden and Derwent dams to represent an attack on the Sorpe. The remainder of the squadron carried out spotlight runs over The Wash.

It was now confirmed that 'Upkeep' would be deployed as a cylinder. At Scampton twenty live weapons, along with several inert ones (to be used for practice) were stripped of their wooden casings and statically balanced. With the operation scheduled to take place as soon as possible after 14 May, Cochrane was keen that the crews should drop an 'Upkeep' against a representative target. Aiming marks were set up on the sea wall at Reculver for aircraft to attack at 90 degrees from the sea.

These 'Upkeep' releases by squadron pilots were flown between 11 and 14 May. Not everyone got the opportunity to do so. Some pilots flew as observers with others – including Townsend with Munro and Barlow with

Shannon – to get at least a feel of the handling of the aircraft with a spinning 'Upkeep'. Several of the aircraft released too low and were damaged by spray, including Martin's and Maltby's. They were repairable, but Maudslay's aircraft was beyond immediate unit repair, necessitating the hasty transfer of a replacement to Scampton.

The following two days and nights saw further training. A 'dress rehearsal' on 13 May revealed a number of shortcomings. The following night a much more successful exercise was conducted, although not all crews participated and last-minute serviceability problems and modifications meant that not all the aircraft involved were 'Upkeep' specials.

On 13 May a live 'Upkeep' was released over the Channel 5 miles off Broadstairs. Dropped from 75 feet and spinning at 500 rpm it bounced for 800 yards before sinking and detonating, sending a plume of spray nearly a thousand feet into the air. Two days later a further live weapon, without pistols or self-destruct fuze, was dropped to test the stability of the weapon's filling when subjected to sudden shock.

The crews now had their aircraft, their weapon and had trained to perfect pitch. By 15 May they were keyed up and ready to go.

Chapter 4
Planning for Action

That the operation should focus on the Möhne, and Sorpe and Eder had been established by Portal and Bottomley on 5 April. At that time the operation was still very much in abeyance since no Lancaster had yet been modified to carry the weapon and no full-scale trial had been conducted. Dropping trials with the full-size weapon commenced at Reculver on 13 April but it was not until 18 April that a semi-successful drop was made of a wooden-cased 'Upkeep'. On this occasion the casing shattered, as on previous drops, but this time the central cylinder bounced for 700 yards in the approved manner. Wallis then decided to dispense with the wooden covering and run the bare cylinder. It was not until 29 April and after the reduction of the dropping height to 60 feet, that it was confirmed that 'Upkeep' would perform in its intended style.

5 May With the weapon's performance better established, AVM Cochrane was asked to prepare an outline plan for the operation. Assessments by MEW indicated that the Möhne and Sorpe, serving the Ruhr, were the most important and were to be given priority over the Eder which should also be attacked: 'should circumstances allow'.

Portal's original intention for 30 Lancasters to carry 'Upkeep' might have allowed for two squadrons for the operation. The reduction to 23 and Harris's decision to form a new single squadron now meant that at best Cochrane had 21 aircraft and trained crews at his disposal. He outlined his plan for the operation at a meeting with AVM Bottomley, AVM Saundby and Wallis at the Air Ministry on 5 May.

In preparing his outline, Cochrane was faced with a number of issues. Wallis believed that in theory the Möhne and Eder dams could be breached by a single 'Upkeep' after a perfect drop. Under operational conditions such being achieved on the first run was unlikely, so allowance had to be made for a number of 'near misses' at each of these targets. After much consideration

Wallis had amended his original view that one 'Upkeep' might be sufficient to breach the Sorpe to the assessment that this might be achieved by the cumulative effect of a number of 'Upkeeps' causing the crest to crumble. As a result, a different form of attack emerged for the Sorpe dam from that to be used against the Möhne and Eder. Also to be factored into any planning was the possibility that some aircraft might be lost before they reached the target, thus sufficient had to be allocated to allow for what was euphemistically referred to as 'wastage'.

Unless crews were to be trained in both forms of attack it would be necessary to allocate separate forces, one using spun 'Upkeeps' against the Möhne and Eder, the other using 'Upkeep' unspun, in effect simply as a large depth charge, against the Sorpe. Given the more stringent requirements for the former method of attack Cochrane envisaged that crews deemed to have performed best in training should be allocated to the Möhne, which was the primary target. He hoped that success would be achieved early in the attack, a belief confirmed by Wallis during the meeting, saying that this might possibly be after three weapons had been dropped. All of the 'Möhne force' who had not yet bombed would then attack the Eder using the same methods. Cochrane did not specify how many aircraft should be allocated, but it is of interest that he specified that this force would be controlled by the leader using VHF radio. The decision to equip the squadron with this kit had only been taken on the previous day – although the concept of local control had been agreed earlier.

With regard to the Sorpe dam, Cochrane stated that 'the method of attack on this dam was much simpler' and he proposed detailing 'about four of the crews who did not achieve the highest standards of accuracy in practice' to attack this target. Since the Sorpe was not expected to fail immediately, all aircraft allocated to this would be expected to attack it, there was no need to make provision for any diversion of those still carrying 'Upkeep' (and thus obviating any problems regarding proficiency in both types of attack).

At this stage the format for the operation was very basic – a total force of 21 aircraft and crews, of which 'about' four would attack the Sorpe. This number would be increased to six in Gibson's training programme drawn up the following day. There appears to have been no indication of attacks on other minor dams or the allocation of a third force – which would emerge later as the so-called 'mobile reserve'.

10–12 May Cochrane gave responsibility for the development of a draft plan to Air Commodore Harry Satterly, SASO at No. 5 Group. A draft copy was handwritten and sent to Scampton's Station Commander on 10 May with a request that it should be reviewed by Whitworth and Gibson to highlight any obvious errors or omissions. The copy was the only one in existence and Satterly needed to be able to relate their comments to it. He requested that the draft be re-written incorporating their changes, or they pin slips containing their comments to the original and return it no later than 1600 hrs on Wednesday 12 May.

Satterly's plan was a more detailed elaboration of Cochrane's outline. He proposed that the attack would be carried out by 20 special Lancasters (this number may have been decided to provide a reserve aircraft as insurance against technical failure) flying from their base to the target at low level in moonlight and returning by three different routes. They would take off in three sections of three aircraft at ten-minute intervals followed by single aircraft at three-minute intervals – all twenty aircraft being despatched in thirty-nine minutes.

Each section of three aircraft would fly in open formation. On leaving the English coast, they would descend to the lowest height possible and set their altimeters to 60 feet, remaining at that height until nearing the enemy coast. There, a rapid climb could be made to 3,000 feet in order that an initial pinpoint might be found. If this was not done and a pinpoint inland was selected, then the coast was to be crossed at very low altitude. Two minutes from each planned turning point along the route the leader would climb to 500 feet to check landmarks. Having done so, he would return to low level.

Ten minutes from the target area the formation leader would commence a climb to 1,000–1,500 feet. Seeing this, the other two in the formation would listen on their VHF. Spinning of 'Upkeep' should commence approximately five minutes before each attack (in the final operatipn order this was amended to ten minutes). The leader would then attack the target as quickly as possible, firing a red cartridge immediately he dropped his weapon. This would:

1. Enable all aircraft to see when another aircraft had attacked, thus ensuring that no aircraft would be blown up by another's weapon.
2. Fox Flak men.
3. Enable the rear gunners to see what was happening to the dam.

After completing his attack, No. 1 would climb up, and after waiting for 90 seconds (timed on a stopwatch) detail No. 2 to attack. No. 2's attack would be identical, and when the leader had seen No. 2's Very light and been informed of his attack he would detail No. 3 to attack. By this time, the next formation led by No. 4 should have arrived, and the same procedure would take place, No. 1 controlling all the attacks. Should the leader fall out, Nos. 2 and 3 would act as leader and deputy-leader respectively.

Once Target A was destroyed, aircraft would be diverted both by Morse and voice messages (W/T and R/T respectively) to Target B. There the same procedure would take place. No. 1 would again lead and Nos. 4 and 7 would take over the back-up leadership roles from Nos. 2 and 3, who would return to base. When Target B was destroyed, the leader was to divert all remaining aircraft to Target C. This attack would not be controlled by the leader, but Nos. 1, 4 and 7 were to proceed there and make a reconnaissance.

After completing their attacks, all aircraft would return to base by widely diverging routes, at a very low level, and very high airspeed.

The draft did not detail the special form of attack to be used, stating that it 'has been carried out on many practices', but defined each crew member's responsibility during the run in to the target:

The Pilot	is responsible for	line,
the Navigator	" "	height,
the Bomb Aimer	" "	range,
and the F/Engineer	" "	speed.

Airspeed and height must be exact 'and constant practice had shown that this is possible'. The text also reiterated the requirement to fire a Very cartridge as soon as the attack had been made, to give the leader means to calculate the correct time interval between attacks.

With reference to control by the Leader by radio over the target it explained:

> Each aircraft must also call up the leader when over the target, so that the leader will know that he has arrived. For all intents and purposes, the control of the attack will be exactly like flying control giving aircraft permission to pancake. The only difference will be that to pancake means to attack, and that flying control is literally flying.

13–16 May The handwritten draft and amendment slips were returned to Satterly who then incorporated them into a revised version, which would be fine-tuned again by Cochrane and Gibson on the afternoon of 15 May, before the final Operation Order was typed and issued on 16 May.

At some point during the revision process a proposal was added, seemingly by Gibson: 'It is strongly urged that a dusk raid by Mosquitos on Soest be carried out just before we go in at Z−60 or so. The leader can then report on the visibility. If this is bad we can turn back.' This proposal was subsequently deleted and not incorporated into the final Operation Order.

Further detail was contained in attached appendices, which demonstrates that significant changes were made between the draft plan by Satterly and its final iteration as briefed on 16 May. The most significant concern the timing and composition of the waves and the targets allocated. No. 617 Squadron comprised 21 crews. Satterly's draft plan contained 20 names – the crew of F/Sgt Ken Brown is missing. This many have been due to the illness of Brown's gunner Sgt Don Buntain. Satterly originally divided the crews into each of the three waves of three, a group of six, each flying individually and finally a group of five who were detailed to attack Target C – the Sorpe dam, again despatched individually.

1.	W/Cdr Gibson	} Take-off 21.55	
2.	F/Lt Hopgood		
3.	F/Lt Martin		
4.	S/Ldr Young	} 22.05	
5.	F/Lt Maltby		
6.	F/Lt Shannon		
7.	S/Ldr Maudslay	} 22.15	
8.	F/Lt Munro		
9.	F/Lt McCarthy		
10.	P/O Knight	22.18	
11.	F/Lt Astell	22.21	
12.	P/O Ottley	22.24	
13.	F/Lt Barlow	22.27	
14.	F/Lt Wilson	22.30	
15.	F/Sgt Divall	22.33	
16.	P/O Rice	22.05	} Target C only
17.	P/O Byers	22.10	
18.	F/Sgt Townsend	22.15	
19.	F/Sgt Anderson	22.20	
20.	P/O Burpee	22.25	

The first three groups of three (Nos 1–9) would be led by W/Cdr Gibson and the two flight commanders, Young and Maudslay respectively. These nine aircraft, with the crews who had performed best in training, would initially attack the Möhne dam and then continue to the Eder. The larger number would allow for possible attrition and poor runs and reflected the priority given to the Möhne.

By inference, the second group of 6 (Nos. 10–15) became the so-called 'mobile reserve'.

The final group of five (Nos. 16–20) were allocated to the Sorpe. That the Sorpe was originally listed as Target C (later to be changed to Z) and thus apparently in third place to the Möhne and Eder's A and B, perhaps again reflected the confusion regarding the target priorities and possibly a continuing failure to recognise that the Möhne and Sorpe comprised a target set with the Eder as a separate outlier. This would be reinforced by the fact that the attacks on the Möhne and Eder would be co-ordinated by the Leader using VHF, while those on the Sorpe would be made by crews flying individually. Perception of the Sorpe as a subsidiary target was further emphasised by the belief that attacking it at the same time as the Möhne might confuse the defences – thus suggesting its role was as a diversion.

Of interest too, are the allocated take-off times. The various waves overlap – Rice, heading for the Sorpe takes off at the same time as Young, Maltby, and Shannon, while Townsend clashes with Maudslay, Munro and McCarthy. Likewise, the first of the mobile reserve intermingle with others of the Sorpe wave, suggesting that at this stage the entire operation was scheduled to be contained in a much shorter time span. Subsequent reflection would restructure the timing – delaying the reserve wave by two hours, expanding the overall duration of the operation. Thus the reserve might be used to attack the secondary targets, such as the Lister, Ennepe and Diemel, but would also be at a suitable stage of its flight, when results of the attacks on the Möhne, Eder and Sorpe could be assessed, to permit the reserve aircraft to be re-allocated to the primary targets if necessary.

The reserve and Sorpe waves would be extensively re-cast for the Battle Order on 16 May. Knight and Astell would fly as part of Maudslay's formation while Munro and McCarthy would be transferred to the Sorpe wave.

The re-shuffling of the reserve wave may also reflect Gibson's perceptions of non-commissioned captains: Townsend, Anderson and Burpee (only recently commissioned), originally detailed for the Sorpe, would be transferred to the reserve and eventually joined by Brown, who, with only seven operations, was relatively inexperienced. The reasons for these transfers are not known. Gibson's final choice may have been influenced following releases made by squadron crews at Reculver during 12–14 May. But Maudslay's, Martin's and Maltby's aircraft were damaged by spray during these drops, and Shannon's 'Upkeep' was released too early and sank short, yet none of these crews was re-allocated.

There may have been concern that the original line-up did not have sufficient weight of experienced crews allocated to the Sorpe, suggesting that it was seen to be of lesser importance and reflecting doubt that it was a suitable target for 'Upkeep'. A reconsideration, re-establishing its joint importance to the Ruhr, along with the Möhne, may have prompted the transfer of more experienced crews (Munro and McCarthy) to add weight to this target in the final Operation Order.

The draft operation plan now allocated five aircraft to attack the Sorpe, one more than Cochrane's original suggestion – this may reflect further consideration by Wallis, or insurance against possible losses. To increase 'Upkeep's' chances of success, on 11 May, Wallis wrote to Bufton stating that, after examination of aerial photographs of the Sorpe, he considered that the airside bank was made of heavier material than previously thought. This might not erode easily. Echoing earlier proposals for attacks on dams, he recommended cratering the air side of the Sorpe with conventional General Purpose bombs, ideally 8,000-pounders, to assist in the disintegration of this buttress should the concrete core be cracked by 'Upkeep'. Wallis then sent Bufton a diagram underlining this on 14 May.

By now the 23 modified Lancasters had been produced and 20 delivered to the squadron (though one was now unserviceable having been badly damaged during a training drop on 13 May). On that date the Air Ministry confirmed: 'Authority given to increase forthwith aircraft establishment of No. 617, repeat 617, Squadron from sixteen plus two to sixteen plus four Lancaster aircraft – additional aircraft are already held by 617 Squadron.'

This permitted the allocation of another modified aircraft, currently held by a maintenance unit, to replace the damaged machine and would also allow one of the three being used for performance trials by the Aeroplane and Armament Experimental Establishment (AAEE) at Boscombe Down, to be transferred to Scampton where 56 live 'Upkeeps' were now stored in the bomb dump.

That day, 13 May, the Vice-Chiefs of Staff met to consider the progress of 'Highball'. Development of that weapon had been problematical, jeopardising any proposal to mount an attack against *Tirpitz* simultaneously with that against the dams. Photographs obtained to date of the Möhne dam did not indicate whether the lake level was rising or falling, and further reconnaissance had been ordered of all three targets to decide whether the operation should take place during the May or June moon period. There was a serious danger that the operation might be prejudiced if the Germans began to draw off substantial amounts of water from the Möhne lake before the commencement of the June moon period. In addition, 'Upkeep' was seen as a 'one-shot weapon' owing to the virtual certainty that immediate counter-measures would prevent further attacks against similar targets. Thus, once the operation had been mounted, the modified Lancasters could be reconfigured to contribute to main-force operations.

Concerns that the initial use of 'Upkeep' might jeopardise Mosquito operations against naval units using the smaller 'Highball' weapon were dismissed. 'Upkeep' was now a cylindrical weapon, rather than a padded sphere, and bore little resemblance to 'Highball'. This fact, along with the relatively short range of 'Upkeep', which might suggest conventional 'skip bombing' to the Germans, gave little reason to believe they would be likely to associate it with the principle of a surface bomb employed against capital ships.

Accordingly, the Vice-Chief of the Air Staff, Air Marshal Sir Douglas Evill, sent a message to the Chiefs of Staff, including Portal, who were assembled in Washington to attend the Trident Conference (12–25 May) to discuss plans for the Allied invasion of Sicily, the date for invading Normandy, and progress of the Pacific War. Evill's message summarised the meeting. Explaining that the early use of 'Upkeep' would not compromise 'Highball', he emphasised that with the squadron fully trained and water levels and moon conditions coincident it was now essential that a decision be taken to launch the operation against the dams. He recommended that this be authorised from 14 May. With growing urgency, Evill sent a similar request in a 'most immediate and personal' to Portal at 1040 the following day. Four hours later Washington's reply was received 'Chiefs of Staff agree to immediate use of "Upkeep" without waiting for "Highball".'

There is a popular belief that approval for the Dams Raid was given personally by Churchill, and Wallis himself later believed this to be so. However, there is no evidence to support this. On 25 May 1955, the eve of his re-election, Churchill wrote to his adviser, Sir Norman Brook, Head of the Home Civil Service:

> I saw a very good film called 'The Dam Busters' the other night, and in this it was said that I had expressed strong personal support for the operation and had given directions on the subject. I certainly remember it quite well. I should be much obliged if you would very kindly let me have any material or record of the decision which I made that the attempt should be made in May, and any other material on the subject.

The request triggered an extensive search of official archives lasting five months, including consultations with Portal and Bottomley. Brickhill, who had written, without having access to official Air Ministry records, that the Chiefs of Staff approved the operation, and that Churchill was 'enthusiastic about it', admitted that his comment was based on hearsay and that he had not seen any firm evidence to support it. Brook finally reported to Churchill that, after the most diligent search, 'I have failed entirely to find any trace of a minute or directive about this by you before the message of congratulation which you sent after the operation.' Perhaps to placate Churchill, he concluded that it seemed likely that plans for the development of the weapon, and the projected operation must have been discussed in conversation between the Chief of the Air Staff and the Prime Minister, who had expressed his approval for them.

For the crews at Scampton, 14 May was a quiet day as the ground crews serviced their charges, but there was a definite sense that their waiting was coming to an end. F/Lt Bill Astell spent most of the morning lying on the grass beside his aircraft observing a pair of nearby partridges. 'They don't seem to mind the motors a bit.' With no apparent sense of prescience, he wrote to his father: 'The Air Force does certainly take some funny ideas. Now they have told us all to make wills, so here is mine. Fairly straightforward, I think.'

That evening most, though not all, crews flew a tactical exercise, the so-called 'dress rehearsal'. An attempt the previous night had been only partially successful. Using their familiar training targets of Eyebrook and Abberton reservoirs to replicate the Möhne and Eder, they practised the various elements of command and control and attack technique embodied in the operation order. Crews detailed to attack the Sorpe were tasked to practise over Derwent Valley, while crews of the reserve wave carried out 'tactical runs' over The Wash and North Sea coast.

Chapter 5

Saturday, 15 May

0900 Headquarters Bomber Command received a MOST SECRET cypher message from the Assistant Chief of the Air Staff (Operations) at the Air Ministry.

> Operation 'Chastise' immediate attack of targets X, Y, Z approved.
> Execute at first suitable opportunity.

High Wycombe then contacted Air Commodore Satterly at No. 5 Group Headquarters who spent the remainder of the morning reviewing his draft operation order and Gibson's comments. At mid-day he passed it to W/Cdr Wally Dunn, No. 5 Group's Signals Officer, with instructions to prepare a Signals Instruction covering the control procedure. Provision was to be made for command to transfer to the deputy leader or even third in line should anything happen to the leader. In addition, a simple alphanumeric code was required for individual aircraft to report to base:

a) That 'Upkeep' had been released correctly;
b) The position of the mine's explosion in relation to the target;
c) The state of the target after each attack.

While this was being done, Barnes Wallis, in Weybridge, received a call instructing him to proceed immediately to Scampton. Cochrane then drove from Grantham to Scampton to tell Whitworth and Gibson that the operation would be mounted the following evening, 16 May, and the squadron's flight commanders should be briefed accordingly.

At about 1500 hrs a Vickers Wellington, fresh from the production line, resplendent in Coastal Command's white camouflage scheme and flown by 'Mutt' Summers, touched down on Scampton's grass, carrying Wallis and Major Hugh Kilner, general manager of Vickers aircraft section. There was time for a brief meeting with Gibson, before he set off with Cochrane to Grantham to discuss the final operation order.

At Grantham, Cochrane, Gibson, Satterly and probably Dunn went to work. At this point a number of important details were finalised. These included the deletion of one of the secondary targets, the Henne dam. There were now only six targets for Operation 'Chastise'.

There were subtle changes to the wording. Rather than continuing attacks on the Möhne 'until half the dam has collapsed' they were to continue until 'it has been clearly breached.' 'It is expected that this might require three effective attacks.' The attack on the Sorpe was now to be made by 'specially trained crews' rather than 'the less experienced crews'. These were 'to be controlled on the alternative VHF Channel'. This suggests that McCarthy may have been seen as leading and co-ordinating this wave, presumably in a manner like that used by Gibson. There is no explanation in the final operation order to this effect. In the event, McCarthy's switch to the reserve aircraft, which was not fitted with VHF, precluded such local control. The revised form of attack, parallel to the dam wall and with 'Upkeep' unspun was clearly specified. The codeword 'Zebra' for the breaching of the Sorpe dam which had been added to the draft of 10 May was also deleted, reflecting that any breach was expected to occur over a period and not as an immediate result.

The training plan instigated from 6 May had allotted six aircraft to practise for this target. Now, possibly due to illness, this number was reduced to five. Since this was minimum number recommended by Wallis to be necessary to cause sufficient damage it left no margin for losses en route to the target. Only days previously Wallis had written to the Director of Bomber Operations proposing a modified form of attack. For whatever reason, the idea was not progressed. The fate of the Sorpe would remain in the hands of the minimum number of crews.

It was also possible that there would be some aircraft from Gibson's formation still with their 'Upkeeps' remaining after the Möhne and Eder had been breached. Although Wallis hoped that one bomb alone, placed and performing correctly, would be sufficient to breach the Möhne and the Eder, it was accepted that three might be required for each dam. If so, and discounting casualties, this might leave three out of Gibson's nine to re-direct to the Sorpe after the Möhne and Eder had been breached.

Back at Scampton, there were a few local flights and an air test while the live 'Upkeeps' were prepared. During the afternoon Wallis and Summers moved among the ground staff examining weapons and aircraft as the armourers began loading. The task would not be completed until late the following afternoon.

Delivered from the Royal Ordnance filling factory at Chorley, the 'Upkeeps' had been stored, concealed by tarpaulins, in the bomb dump on the north side of the airfield. The first six explosive-filled weapons arrived on 16 April and by 13 May the remaining 50 had been delivered (two additional live 'Upkeeps' were delivered to Manston for trials). As they arrived at Scampton each bomb was statically balanced. This was done in a similar manner to balancing a car wheel with weights: pieces of ¼-inch steel plate measuring some 8 × 6 inches, obtained earlier from the Ruston Hornby works in Lincoln, ready to be bolted to the circumference. Balancing was done using a special rig that allowed the 'Upkeep' to be rotated freely to determine any heavy spots. A piece of steel plate was then bolted to the lighter side and the process repeated, with the balance plate gradually being machined down until a uniform balance was obtained.

P/O Henry Watson, the Squadron Armament Officer, worked in the bomb dump fitting the 'Upkeeps' with their hydrostatic pistols and then the weapons were loaded onto a Type E bomb trolley modified with a wooden cradle, to transport them out to the aircraft.

To load 'Upkeep' the belt drive on the starboard side was removed and the Lancaster's forward bomb bay fairing hinged open, split along the centreline in the manner of the bomb doors of a standard aircraft. Before the fairing was opened an eyebolt was fitted at former 38 (on top of the fuselage, in line with the tailplane). To this the hook of a Coles 10-ton crane was attached and the tail of the aircraft lifted to a horizontal position. The trolley could then be positioned beneath the aircraft. A loading sling was then placed underneath the 'Upkeep', connected by cables passing through the bomb bay roof to winches positioned inside the aircraft. The bomb was then winched up between the calliper arms and the discs at the apex of the arms fitted into the endplate running tracks (the aircraft's horizontal position permitting a vertical lift). With these in position, the bolts attached to the ends of cables linked to the aircraft's 4,000-pound-bomb release slip were tightened, thus tensioning them to clamp the bomb, but leaving it free to rotate on the disc bearings.

After the bomb was loaded, the aircraft tail was lowered, eyebolt removed and the screw point covered with a rubber cap. The front fairing was then closed and bolted, and the drive belt re-fitted to the hydraulic motor pulley. Once in position the weapon was spun up slowly to check the drive and rotation and confirm balance.

Inert 'Upkeeps' used for training at Reculver and those for operational use were distinguished by their colour. Practice weapons were painted grey, whereas those filled with explosive were meant to be painted dark green, the

RAF's standard colour for live weapons. It seems this was not always the case, however, indicative of the haste with which the mines had been completed and despatched to Scampton.

In *Enemy Coast Ahead* Gibson also recounts that at one stage Wallis appeared 'and said in a strange voice 'We have got the wrong oil . . . We shall have to find some . . . otherwise they may not work.' In the film the incident is transposed to an exchange at the pre-operation meal following the briefing, but in the recollection of P/O Watson:

> The inside of the rims of the centre disc of the bomb was treated with a stiff grease, similarly the outside of the rim of the 'clappers'. Initially we could not get the grease specified and I used one of equal specification advised by Weybridge engineers, but when Wallis heard of this he insisted we sent to Weybridge for the actual specification. I think that on May 15 we had to replace all grease in nearly panic stages.

Another repeated story, originally recorded by Paul Brickhill, possibly relating to that afternoon, was that of an incident concerning the loading of 'Upkeep' on F/Lt Mick Martin's Lancaster AJ-P, P for Popsie. After half an hour the weapon had been hoisted into position, the release arms clamped on either side and the winch cables and strop removed. Accounts then vary. According to Brickhill, 'a fault developed in the bomb release circuit, the release snapped back and there was a crunch as the giant black thing fell and crashed through the concrete hardstanding, embedding itself 4 inches into the earth below'. Other accounts, including one by Martin's Tasmanian gunner Tammy Simpson, record that it 'put a dent in the dispersal tarmac a good inch and a half deep', and attribute the incident to a popular WAAF who sometimes flew with the crews on training flights. She was inside the aircraft and had supposedly accidentally activated the pilot's emergency release lever. Realisation that the mine had fallen off triggered a mass evacuation of the aircraft with personnel sprinting to clear the area before throwing themselves flat on the ground, while others leapt into vehicles and headed away at breakneck speed. While there was no danger of the hydrostatic pistols being triggered, and the shock of impact after a drop of six feet or so from the aircraft was unlikely to cause detonation, there was a danger that the separate self-destruct pistol might have accidentally become armed. Fortunately, the fuzing procedure that allowed the weapon to be armed while in flight ensured that the pistol was still 'safe'. After about four or five minutes Watson approached the deserted aircraft, examined the weapon and declared the emergency over.

While the incident at Scampton was accidental, on this day a formal trial was arranged to confirm that 'Upkeep' would not detonate on severe impact. Off Broadstairs, a live 'Upkeep' but without hydrostatic pistols or self-destruct fuze was jettisoned without spin, officially from 500 feet though according to Bob Handasyde, the Vickers test pilot who undertook the trial, his height was 4,000 feet – for safety reasons. There was no detonation. 'Upkeep' had passed its final test.

1800 Gibson had returned to Scampton in the late afternoon. To maintain security Cochrane had originally issued strict instructions that only the flight commanders (Young and Maudslay) should be briefed the day before the operation, but this appears to have been extended during the afternoon to include Hopgood, who was to act as deputy leader at the Möhne, and Hay, the Squadron Bombing Leader, and possibly also Jack Leggo, the Navigation Leader. They gathered with Wallis at Whitworth's house to run through the outline plan. During the meeting Hopgood pointed out that the proposed route north of the Ruhr from Rees, via Ahsen to Ahlen passed close to a defended area near the Chemische Werk synthetic rubber factory, at Huls/Marl, resulting in a modification taking their track further north via lakes near Dülmen.

The meeting may have been in two parts – Wallis's diary is open to a number of interpretations. It recorded two entries for 15 May: '6 pm – Briefed crews – captains only' and '10 pm – CO's office to finalise method of attack'. Wallis may have confused 'flight commanders' with 'captains' and the second meeting may have been to discuss with Gibson the final method of attack at the Sorpe. Equally it is possible that Wallis wrote his diary after the event and conflated the events of 15 and 16 May.

Discussions concluded towards midnight, at which point (or possibly between the two meetings) Whitworth broke the news to Gibson that his black Labrador, 'Nigger', had been killed by a car on the A15, just outside the main gate. Contrary to popular belief the vehicle did stop. Its owner and a passenger, who was injured in the accident, helped take the dog's remains to the guardroom where they were placed in a detention cell. F/Sgt George Powell, the squadron's disciplinary NCO, was the first to identify the animal. He in turn told Humphries, who then notified Whitworth. The dog had been Gibson's companion for some two years, acquired as a pup while he was serving at West Malling as a flight lieutenant and flight commander with No. 29 Squadron. *In Enemy Coast Ahead*, Gibson wrote: 'Then I was alone in my room, looking at the scratch marks on the door Nigger used to make when he wanted to go out, and feeling very depressed.'

Wallis, not normally sentimental with regards to animals, noted the event in his diary, sensing it might be an ill omen: '1230: Bed. Nigger killed.'

Chapter 6

'Der Tag for 617 Squadron'

0530 Gibson rose before sunrise. After breakfast in the Officers' Mess, his first port of call was the Station Sick Quarters. As dawn was breaking at 0600 he presented himself to the doctor, F/Lt Alan Upton. When Upton had previously advised him regarding a painful carbuncle which had developed on his right lower cheek, Gibson had been nonplussed to be informed that he was working too hard and needed to take time off and relax. Now Gibson was suffering from a flare-up of an intermittent gout-like complaint in his feet but was insistent that he should not be declared unfit to fly. Asked by Upton if this meant that he would be operating, Gibson replied, 'Yes, but if you tell anyone that, you'll be shot.' Upton could offer no instant remedy. At best he could prescribe painkillers. Realising that such medication might impair his judgement, Gibson declined.

Years later, and perhaps with the benefit of hindsight, Upton recalled:

> I should really have grounded him; he was quite unfit to fly. But I knew the whole project depended on his leadership and knowing his qualities I let him go. It was pretty bad losing half the aircraft, but I should have felt particularly concerned had Gibson not returned.

0800 Working parades – ground crew assembled and went out to tend to their charges at dispersal: 'A' Flight dispersal was near the hangars, 'B' Flight further around the perimeter track.

In the hangar urgent work continued on Lancaster ED933 AJ-X – damaged during training on 12 May – in a futile effort to restore serviceability. With no immediate flying programme despite the promising weather, the ground crews conducted their daily inspections.

Leading Aircraftman (LAC) Harold Roddis, an engine fitter for 'A' Flight, recalled:

As far as I was concerned, Sunday 16th May 1943 was going to be the same as every other day since the Squadron was formed. These were my thoughts on leaving the cookhouse after breakfast that Sunday morning to join the rest of the ground crew at 'A' Flight dispersal hut. How wrong they proved to be was revealed by the dramatic events which unfolded during the rest of the day and night.

Flight Sergeant (Chiefy) Smith in charge of 'A' Flight ground crews had no news of the flying programme for the day which was rather odd as the air crews had been practising most days, so he told us to get along to our various dispersals, remove the engine, cockpit and turret covers and carry out our DIs (daily inspections). These, providing there were no snags, generally took between 1½ to 2 hours including re-fuelling. After these had been completed and the Form 700 signed, we just sat around the dispersal and waited. We really were quite puzzled, it was a beautiful day, perfect flying weather.

Meanwhile over in the Station Headquarters and squadron offices alongside the hangars routine administration was being conducted. By about 0900 RAF Scampton had submitted its daily return of bomb stocks to HQ Bomber Command. At High Wycombe, Harris was holding his daily 'morning prayers' meeting and No. 5 Group Headquarters now stood by to receive a signal from High Wycombe decreeing the forthcoming night's activities. To the uninitiated, it was just going to be another day and at this stage only a select few had any knowledge that the long period of intensive training had come to an end and No. 617 Squadron would be operating that night.

0900 Gibson arrived at Number 2 hangar and found Humphries:

> The Wing Commander crashed in just after 9.00 am.
> 'Flying programme Adj.,' he said.
> 'Training programme, sir?' I asked.
> 'O, um, that is yes to the rest of the Station,' he answered. Seeing the look of bewilderment on my face at this statement he said, 'We are going to war at last, but I don't want the world to know about it so do not mention the words "Battle Order", just make out a night flying programme. All who should know will receive their orders verbally.'

With that Gibson retired to his office. At some point during the morning he walked across to the station workshops, a low building behind the hangar, where he asked a flight sergeant to make a coffin for Nigger's remains. The NCO refused to do so and a tense conversation followed. As an observer recorded: 'With that the Wing Commander lost his temper, there were high words with very little wisdom, and the Wing Commander went on his way without getting a coffin made for his dog.'

Gibson also spoke with 'Chiefy' Powell. An immensely practical man, Powell, like Humphries and Sgt Heveron of the Orderly Room, was one of those who ensured the smooth day-to-day running of basic activities. He and Gibson shared a strong mutual respect.

Of the squadron's 21 crews, one pilot, F/Sgt Bill Divall had a knee injury, effectively ruling his crew out; F/Lt Harold Wilson's crew was also omitted, possibly owing to crew sickness. Nineteen crews would be operating. One of F/Sgt Ken Brown's gunners, Don Buntain had reported sick, so was replaced by Daniel Allatson from Divall's crew. Their names were given to Humphries by the flight commanders. The list was duly compiled and titled 'Night Flying Programme', typed up and duplicated ready for distribution to the various sections that were to provide support for the crews – meals, flying rations, flying and safety equipment, transport to aircraft – but as far as they were concerned it would just be as it had been during the previous weeks. No. 617 Squadron was off on another cross-country training exercise.

1000   Confirmation was received that the operation would take place that night. During the morning Cochrane approved Satterly's operation plan, finalised with Gibson the previous day, and it was sent for typing. As 'No. 5 Group Operation Order No. B.976' there was the main outline plus three appendices: A 'Routes and Timings'; B 'Signals Procedure for Target diversions etc.'; C 'Light and Moon Tables'. Twelve individually numbered copies were made, designated 'Most Secret'. Two went to Whitworth at Scampton, three to HQ Bomber Command for personal delivery to the Deputy AOC-in-C or, in his absence, G/C Marwood-Elton (Group Captain, Operations). The remaining seven copies – destined for addresses or files within HQ 5 Group were embargoed until after despatch of the executive signal for the operation, which would not be until late that afternoon.

At Grantham W/Cdr Dunn was informed that the operation would take place that evening and set off for Scampton in order to brief the squadron's wireless operators on the signals procedures.

For the remainder of No. 5 Group stations it was a different picture. At 1015 the message to them from Group Headquarters was that there would be no operations and that all squadrons were to spend the day training and that evening as many crews as possible should take part in a Command 'Bullseye' – a dummy training attack against a UK target. Once again, there was no reference at all to suggest that Scampton would be doing anything otherwise.

Over at 'A' Flight's dispersal P/O Warner Ottley and crew climbed aboard their Lancaster C-Charlie and departed for a half-hour air test to confirm the rectification of a last-minute problem.

1030 onwards With servicing well under way, the aircraft were fuelled, each with 1,750 gallons of 100-octane petrol and 150 gallons of oil. With 'Upkeep' weighing in at 9,250 pounds the aircraft would tip the maximum all-up take-off weight of 63,000 pounds.

Daily inspections completed, bombing-up continued. Armourers fitted and adjusted the .303 Browning machine guns in the turrets and loaded their ammunition. Instead of the usual Bomber Command ammunition mix (ball, tracer and explosive or armour-piercing), the guns were loaded with 100 per cent Tracer G Mark VI which burned for about 500–600 yards. This long-burning tracer would produce a continuous stream of brilliant fire, intended to put the dams' defenders off their aim. The tracer was in short supply and according to one gunner, 'was made up for us by the Ordnance Corps, and only delivered on the morning of May 16'.

Every front turret's two .303 Brownings had a supply of 1,000 rounds per gun, the four in the rear turret each having 2,500 rounds. Each Browning fired approximately 1,150 rounds per minute, thus the front turret had about 52 seconds' duration of fire. It is believed that some crews took additional ammunition and that several captains suggested transferring ammunition from the rear turret to the front in order to ensure the latter could return fire on the homeward journey.

Also included in the bomb load were four 4-pound incendiaries that could be used for navigation and target marking. A special stock of signal cartridges was also required, notably the red to signify release of 'Upkeep' over the target, and those of the designated 'colours of the day'.

1100 W/Cdr Dunn arrived at Scampton. As he did so, Wallis, who had stayed the night in Whitworth's house and was not normally known for sleeping late, had a delayed breakfast and arrived out on the airfield where there was a developing bustle of activity. There he began to inspect the aircraft and discuss any issues with Watson, Caple and the groundcrews. It was a bright, warm and sunny day for those working outside, but that was of relatively little consequence for the aircrew, who henceforth would be preoccupied indoors digesting detail and preparing for the forthcoming operation.

1130   Notification came through of the night's effort planned for other groups: No. 1 Group would not be operating; No. 2 Group was to send 8 Mosquitos to Berlin, Cologne, Düsseldorf and Munster; 8 Stirlings and 2 Lancasters of No. 3 Group would be laying mines in the 'NECTARINES' area (Frisians) along with 20 Wellingtons of the Canadian No. 6 Group; while Yorkshire-based No. 4 Group was to send 6 Wellingtons to lay mines in each of 'JELLYFISH' (Brest), 'BEECH' (St Nazaire) and 'ARTICHOKE' (Lorient).

The squadron wireless operators assembled to receive their signals briefing from Wally Dunn.

The aircraft were to attack in three waves, nine in the first wave, five in the second wave, and five in the third wave. First and second waves were to leave at approximately the same time, the second wave taking a different course from the first; the third wave was to be regarded as a strategic reserve, and was to leave considerably later, the plan being for No. 5 Group Headquarters to direct these aircraft to their particular target by W/T in accordance with the success or failure of the first two waves.

The primary method of control was to be by R/T – direct speech – communication between the leader and the following aircraft. This was to be conducted using a TR 1143 VHF radio operated by the pilot and switched on ten minutes before arriving at the target. This would enable the leader to have tactical control of the aircraft actually over the target, and secondly to take over complete control of all aircraft in the event of failure of W/T communications with Group.

The VHF set used three channels selected using push buttons set for different frequencies. Button A was to be employed by the first wave and Button C, which would also serve as a reserve frequency, by the second wave. If required, the codeword CODFISH sent by W/T would indicate the need to switch channel. Button D was to be used by all aircraft until 2248 hrs and then again from an hour after the attack.

All VHF control was to be in simple language, the collective call-sign being 'COOLER' and each aircraft being given a number, Gibson being 'COOLER 1', Hopgood 'COOLER 2', etc. This system had been practised already on the ground over the past week using a simulated network with twenty sockets, wired in a common circuit running through both flight commanders' offices and round the crew room. Each captain plugged into a socket, and the R/T procedure was practised until all were word perfect and knew exactly what had to be done on each order.

In the event of failure of the leader's VHF set he would inform either No. 2 or No. 4 by W/T and then hand over control, using the appropriate codeword, 'TULIP' or 'CRACKLING' (*see below*). Should the VHF set in any other aircraft become unserviceable the aircraft was to notify the leader by W/T by broadcasting the codeword 'DEAFNESS' twice, using the aircraft's standard T 1154 transmitter.

In the event of a complete failure of VHF control due to equipment failure or its interruption owing to the low height at which the aircraft would be flying and their possible separation in hilly country, the leader of the first wave was to transmit by W/T 'MERMAID' meaning 'Jamming on all R/T control, control by W/T for first wave only.'

The leader would then control the first wave of nine aircraft by W/T using the following codewords:

PRANGER	Attack Target X [Möhne dam].
NIGGER	Target X breached. Attack Target Y [Eder dam].
DINGHY	Target Y breached. Attack Target Z [Sorpe dam].
DANGER	Attack Target D [Lister dam].
EDWARD	Attack Target E [Ennepe dam].
FRASER	Attack Target F [Diemel dam].
GILBERT	Attack last resort target as detailed.
MASON	Return to base.
APPLE	First group listen out on Button A [VHF/TR 1143].
CODFISH	Jamming on Button A. Change to Button C.
MERMAID	Jamming on all R/T. Control by W/T [TR 1154/5].
TULIP	No. 2 take over control at Target X.
CRACKLING	No. 4 take over control at Target Y.

The leader would transmit the appropriate codeword to Group Headquarters who would then repeat the whole message twice, using full-power transmission, so it would be received by the other aircraft in the wave. In the event of having to implement W/T control before reaching the target, each aircraft was to call the leader of the wave by W/T as soon as it arrived. Instructions would then be given by the leader to attack the appropriate target. In the event of failure of both R/T and W/T communication the leader and sub-leader of each wave would resort to visual signals, firing a constant series of green stars over or near the target area to indicate, 'Wait your turn to attack as best you can, when the target is breached proceed to next target.'

Wireless operators were to maintain a continuous listening watch for instructions from Group Headquarters on 4090 kc/s throughout the operation except when transmitting a message notifying completion of their attack for which they would use 3680 k/cs. No other aircraft would be using 4090 kc/s.

As soon as each aircraft had made its attack and released its 'Upkeep' it was to broadcast to Group on the Group operational frequency (3680 kc/s) the code word 'GONER' and a number signifying the result:

GONER 1	Special weapon released. Failed to explode.
GONER 2	Special weapon released. Overshot dam.
GONER 3	Special weapon released. Exploded more than 100 yards from dam.
GONER 4	Special weapon released. Exploded 100 yards from dam.
GONER 5	Special weapon released. Exploded 50 yards from dam.
GONER 6	Special weapon released. Exploded 5 yards from dam.
GONER 7	Special weapon released. Exploded in contact with dam.

To this would be added a further number signifying the state of the target:

8	No apparent breach.
9	Small breach in dam.
10	Large breach in dam.

The code would be completed by a letter identifying the target: A for the Möhne Dam, B for the Eder, C the Sorpe, D the Lister, E the Ennepe or F the Diemel.

Thus GONER 78A, for example, would indicate an attack on the Möhne dam, the weapon exploding in contact with the dam, but with no apparent breach.

On acknowledgement of receipt of this message by Group, aircraft were to revert to the special 4090 kc/s frequency.

From take-off all aircraft were to maintain a listening watch on the TR 1196 R/T set (normally used for short-range communication with base) using Button D. On reaching 03° 00′E on the outbound flight the TR 1196 set was to be switched off. It was to be switched on again one hour after the completion of the attack as the aircraft returned to base.

During the early afternoon all wireless operators practised transmitting specimen messages on a buzzer circuit and each aircraft wave was given its particular signals role.

While the wireless operators were briefed, pilots and navigators were also receiving a preliminary briefing from Gibson. Forty-three years later, questioned on how he felt on learning the nature of the target, Australian Lance Howard, F/Sgt Bill Townsend's navigator replied:

A feeling of relief. Mainly because it was a special and experimental type of raid and not in any way connected with the submarine pens which we had bombed many times from 20,000 feet in 49 Squadron.

Administration and logistics staff were equally engaged as the aircrew began their briefings. The intense secrecy was providing additional problems for Harry Humphries:

> The WAAF Sergeant in the Officers' Mess kitchen, when I told her I wanted full operational flying meals for normal night flying pro-grammes, was adamant that it could not be done. I told her that it was a special occasion, and it was a very arduous flight and also that it had the blessing of the Station Commander. Still, no, she had her orders, and she was sticking to them. I stormed and I cajoled, and I wheedled but to no avail. Finally, I practically had to intimate that it was not really a normal training flight, and let it go at that. She beamed. 'Why didn't you say so in the first place sir, I knew all the time really?' I looked to heaven, cursed all WAAF cooks under my breath, and hastily left the kitchen. Still, the meals had been arranged.

From noon onwards many of the aircrew were grouped in various conference rooms. In F/Sgt Powell's words, the hangars and offices were 'very quiet, like a morgue'. Martin's rear gunner, Simpson, wrote: 'It was the longest briefing I ever attended.'*

Gibson recorded that there was no formal break for lunch that day, refreshment being taken when opportunity permitted. Before doing so, LAC Victor Gill worked on the engines of AJ-A and AJ-B of 'A' Flight. On returning to the dispersal he found that the aircraft had been loaded with 'Upkeep'. The weapons were a red oxide colour, rather than the officially approved dark green, and so was that on Martin's P-Popsie, which was hastily given a coat of black paint, as were some of the others.

1240 Details were passed of the Command Bullseye which involved a long, round-Britain cross-country with a loose (as opposed to concentrated) mock

---

* Paul Brickhill's account suggests that an initial main briefing took place on the afternoon of 15 May. However, Gibson was at Grantham at this time finalising the Operation Order. Michael Anderson's film places it on the afternoon of 16 May, but in doing so also transposes Nigger's death. However, *Enemy Coast Ahead* and John Sweetman's *Dambusters Raid* record a select briefing on 15 May followed by Main Briefings the next day. Additionally, AVM Cochrane's official report on 'Chastise' states: 'Because of the considerable detail which had to be given to aircrews, briefing was started early on the day of the operation' and the Signals Appendix records that Dunn proceeded to Scampton that morning to instruct the wireless operators. The final executive message confirming that the operation was to take place was only issued at 1615 on 16 May.

attack on Birmingham involving searchlight co-operation and interceptions by both day and night fighters.

Participants were advised that No. 5 Group had requested that no aircraft proceed east of 3°E between latitudes 51°N and 54°N after 0200 hrs on 17 May and none were to fly below 2,000 feet during the night of 16/17 May in the area bounded by 54°N 03°E, 52°N 09°E, 51°N 09°E, and 51°N 03°E. Although no reason was given, this was to avoid any potential conflict with 'Chastise' aircraft.

1315 HQ Bomber Command requested Fighter Command to provide intruder operations in an area bounded by 54° 00′N 03° 00′E, 52° 00′N 09° 00′ E, 51° 00′N 09° 00′E, and 51° 00′N 03° 00′E between 2330 and 0030 and again between 0145 and 0300 hrs. No intruder aircraft were to fly below 2,000 feet in this area. Three-quarters of an hour later a similar message was sent to the USAAF, Fighter Command, Coastal Command, Army Co-operation and all bomber groups, warning them of 'special operations tonight 16/17th May' and requesting that no aircraft fly below 2,000 feet in the specified area.

Twenty modified Lancasters had been delivered to the squadron at Scampton. Since ED933 was confirmed as unserviceable this meant that with 19 crews there was no reserve aircraft should there be a last-minute problem. Of the remaining three 'Upkeep' aircraft, ED765 and ED817 were allocated for dropping trials at Manston, while ED825 was at Boscombe Down, as already noted.

1330 The Air Transport Auxiliary (ATA) Central Ferry Control at Andover rang No. 9 Ferry Pool, Aston Down, to ask them to deliver ED825 from Boscombe Down to Scampton. The aircraft was categorised P1/G (Priority 1, Secret equipment) and had to be delivered in a direct flight. The task was taken on by the Ferry Pool's commanding officer, Hugh Bergel.

At Boscombe Down, Bergel handed over his collection chit, signed the log books and was driven out to the Lancaster. He was intrigued by the modifications but knew better than to ask: 'There was a hydraulic motor, connected to an endless belt. It wasn't difficult to see what the whole contraption was supposed to do but why anyone should want to do it baffled me.'

By the pilot's seat was a notice drawing attention to a special lever controlling the hydraulic system, saying that this MUST be kept in the OFF position except when hydraulics were actually in operation. This related to the system for spinning 'Upkeep', but Bergel was still none the wiser. On running up the engines Bergel found that No. 3 (starboard inner) would not run above zero boost unless the fuel booster pump was permanently switched on, but this was not serious enough to ground a P1 aircraft.

1400 AVM Cochrane left No. 5 Group Headquarters to travel by road to Scampton.

At various times during the afternoon, while Cochrane was on his way to Scampton, bomb-aimers and gunners reconvened with pilots and navigators to study models of the Möhne and Sorpe, and photographs and maps of the other targets, and to discuss the routes with which they would be involved as map-readers. This suggests that this briefing may have been held in Scampton's main briefing room with a large map of Europe on the end wall, sufficient tables to spread out charts, and space to allow for model and target study.

Despite the formation of the squadron and commitment to the operation in March, only two target models were available in time to be used for briefing. These had been made by the Central Interpretation Unit, Medmenham, whose model makers – V Section – were housed in Phyllis Court, a Regency country house five miles away in Henley on Thames. Production began with a rigid wood and hardboard-covered base onto which were attached boards of suitable thickness cut to the shape of selected contours. A basic landform was then modelled using plaster over the resulting terraced assembly, carefully representing the valleys, lake levels and river courses. Over this was carefully laid a skin created from maps or photo mosaic, which, when soaked, would mould itself to the landform and provided reference for man-made features, including the dams. The skin was then given a basic colouring to show the position of woods and fields. Since the modellers were working from black and white photographs these were approximated from tone. Trees, hedges and woodlands were applied; roads and tracks were painted in conventional colours. Finally, required annotations such as a compass direction and model number were added and defences such as torpedo booms and known flak positions indicated by red symbols.

Bomber Command had requested a model of the Möhne dam as early as 12 February 1943. At that time the only available aerial photographs were from 1941, and these did not show the dam itself, so the dam and its surroundings were modelled to 1:6,000 scale using ground photographs and a German 1:25,000 map. The resultant model, No. M 328 and known as 'Manchester' to conceal its identity, measured 54 × 42 inches. It was completed on 17 February and sent to Bomber Command. Two days later updated reconnaissance cover was obtained, and the model was modified, being returned to Bomber Command on 3 March.

The model for the Sorpe dam, 'Warrington', M 347, had been requested on 4 April 1943. Again, to begin with there were no vertical photographs, only three ground shots, allowing a 26½ × 21-inch model to be completed by

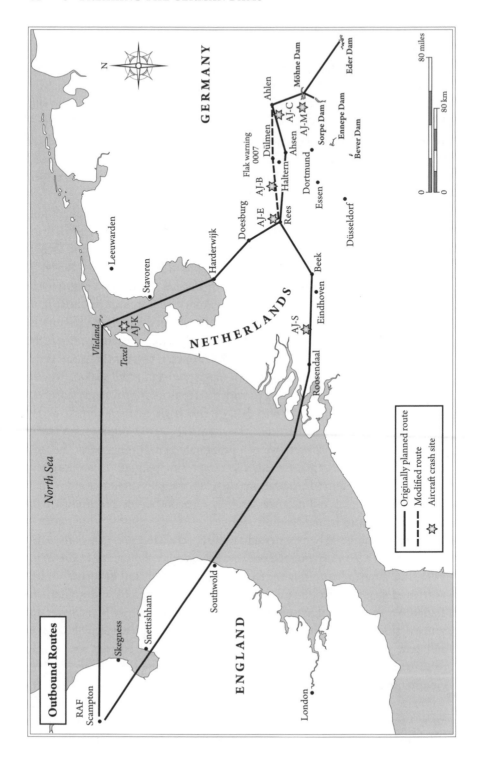

19 April. (Hence Gibson would have seen only a model of the Möhne when he was first informed of the squadron's targets by Cochrane on 5 April).

A request for a model of the Eder was only submitted on 11 May and once again there was no suitable photographic cover, only ground views. Medmenham had been instructed that this was a most urgent requirement and asked to complete it by 18 May. The Eder model, 'Stockport', M 371, the same size as that of the Möhne, was in fact completed by 17 May, but still too late to be used to brief the crews.

Target folders for each of the dams, each containing a printed data sheet, provided details of the dam's location, construction, dimensions and function together with a set of ground photographs taken from pre-war postcards. A stylised target map covered an area six miles around the target with one-mile concentric rings, printed in black and magenta to show up in the dim cockpit lighting. Stippling and hatching identified key features such as built-up areas, woods, and terrain, while features such as rivers and lakes stood out as white.

The aircrews were instructed to examine and study these maps: 'Look at these till your eyes stick out and you've got every detail photographed on your minds, then go away and draw them from memory, come back and check your drawings, correct them then go away and draw them again till you're perfect.'

Although the model of the Möhne indicated with certainty the double-boom torpedo nets, the three gun positions on the dam and the three-gun battery in the fields beyond the compensating basin, there was still concern about a number of strange objects seen on the roadway running along the parapet of the dam. These had first been recorded in April and were approximately 50–100 feet long and 6–9 feet wide, carrying scaffolding or similar and casting shadows across the road. In *The Dam Busters*, Paul Brickhill states: 'There seemed to be only one answer – new gun positions. There must have been a security leak somewhere.' In their reports the interpreters could make no suggestion as to their function, and there had been no security leak. The blocks were in fact clusters of artificial fir trees added to the crown of the dam in an attempt to blend it in with the surrounding lakeside. That this attempt at camouflage would only be effective, if at all, against a low-level attack appears to have been pure coincidence.

As described above, the navigators had been amongst the first to be briefed, given the outline route, timings and forecast meteorological conditions so they could prepare their individual flight plans. The first wave's three sections of three aircraft each would depart at ten-minute intervals and the first section was to reach position 51° 51′N 03° 00′E (in the southern North Sea) at Zero hour (30 minutes after civil twilight). Set course times would be calculated from this point.

They would be routed to the Möhne dam as follows:

Base to Southwold

51°52′N	0300′E	Over North Sea, 30 miles from Scheldt Estuary
51°38′N	0340′E	Scheldt estuary, off western tip of Schouen
51°32′N	04°28′E	8 miles south-west of Breda
51°32′N	05°39′E	Canal junction at Beek en Donk
51°45′N	06°24′E	Rees, on the River Rhine
51°44½′N	07°55½′E	1 mile south-east of Ahlen
51°29′N	08°04′E	Target X, Möhne Dam

Tempsford had recommended obtaining a Gee fix off the coast, then flying between Schouwen and Noord Beveland; straight across Tholen to Roosendaal and onwards to the Wilhelmina Canal 6 miles south-east of Tilburg, following the canal to Beek. Then straight to the bend in the Rhine 9¼ miles south-east of Emmerich, pinpointing on the River Maas and the railway junction at the town of Goch. Pinpointing would be extremely difficult since many turning points were minor topographical features. However, across the Netherlands and the lower reaches of the Meuse and the Rhine there were numerous water features which would reflect the light from a nearly full moon at an altitude of about 30°. Between the Rhine and Hamm the route crossed several railway lines, assisting the map-reader to check his position.

The second wave of five aircraft detailed to attack the Sorpe dam had a slightly longer route and so would take off first and were to be at 53° 19′N 04° 00′E at Zero hour to cross the coast of the island of Vlieland at approximately the same time as the first of the southern wave crossed the coast at the Scheldt estuary.

Base

53°19′N	0400′E	33 miles north-west of Texel
53°20′N	04°54′E	5 miles west of Vlieland
52°53′N	05°22′E	Stavoren
52°21′N	05°37′E	Harderwijk
52°02′N	06°09′E	Doesburg [sic]
51°45′N	07°13′E	Haltern
51°44½′N	07°55½′E	1 mile south-east of Ahlen
51°29′N	08°04′E	Target X, Möhne Dam

Key waypoints on this route were the middle of Vlieland, Harderwijk, a large bend in the River IJssel 14¼ miles south-east of Apeldoorn, a large bend in the Rhine 9¼ miles south-east of Emmerich, a point on the Lippe midway between Dorsten and Haltern, and the city of Hamm.

When over the sea, Tempsford advised that 'aircraft should fly between 1,000' and 1,500' and if possible, get a "Gee" fix before approaching the island of Vlieland. This is very flat and can be crossed as low as 50'.' After crossing the island, aircraft could gain height to a maximum of 500–600 feet, since experience proved that map-reading below this height was very difficult. Pinpoints could then be obtained on the breakwaters on the middle of the dam across the mouth of the Zuider Zee, then at Stavoren, Harderwijk (where there was sometimes a flashing beacon), Apeldoorn, the River IJssel, thence to the Rhine and from then on as for Route 1.

Tempsford warned to check the tidal state at the Frisian Islands as this could alter their shape considerably. Vlieland, which is considerably narrower than either Terschelling or Texel, could be mistaken for either island at low tide. Navigators uncertain that they were approaching Vlieland should not attempt to search for the right island but continue since position could be confirmed either on the Zuider Zee dam or on the mainland had the wrong island been crossed. There were flak defences at either end of each of the three nearby Frisian islands. The best way to avoid them was to attempt to catch the defences unawares by crossing the middle of Vlieland. There was light flak at Harlingen; otherwise, there should be no danger from flak until the vicinity of Emmerich on the Rhine.

The third wave, the reserve, was to cross the Dutch coast at the Scheldt Estuary at 01.32, 2½ hours after the first two groups, following the same route as wave 1.

Return Routes: Three different return routes were briefed, theoretically to split the defences, each of which was calculated from a start point at the Möhne dam:

Route 1 Möhne dam
1 mile east-northeast of Ahlen
Ahsen
3 miles south-west of Haltern
Nordhorn
Genemuiden
Hoorn

| 52°56′N | 04°00′E | Over North Sea, 26 miles west of Leihoek |
| 53°01′N | 03°00′E | Over North Sea, 110 miles east of Lincs. coast |

Base

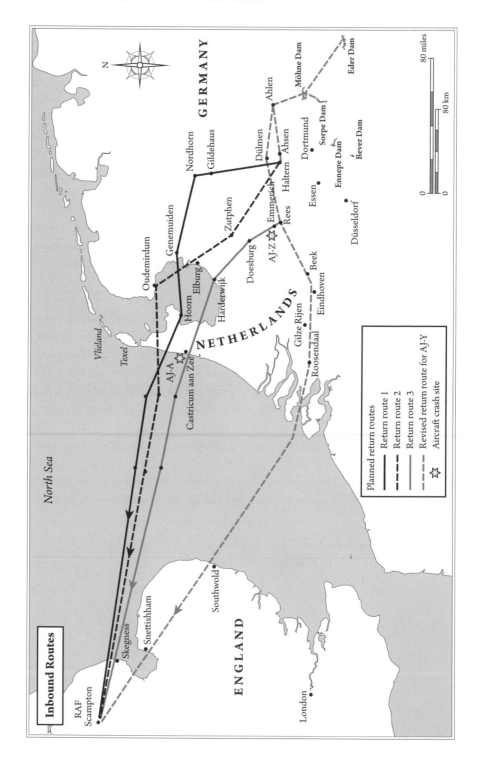

Route 2 Möhne dam
1 mile east-northeast of Ahlen
Ahsen
3 miles south-west of Haltern
1 mile north of Zutphen
Oudemirdum

52 50′N	04 00′E	Over North Sea, 29 miles west of Callantsoog
52°57′N	03°00′E	Over North Sea, 112 miles east of Lincs. coast

Base

Route 3 Möhne dam
1 mile east-northeast of Ahlen
Ahsen
1 mile south-west of Rees
1 mile north-east of Doesburg [*sic*]
Harderwijk

52°41′N	04°00′E	Over North Sea, 27 miles west of Castricum)
52°49′N	03°00′E	Over North Sea, 112 miles east of Lincs. coast

Base*

An eastbound reciprocal of the third return route had previously been considered as a third outbound route but rejected on account of a lack of significant coastal landmarks when approaching from the North Sea. An accurate position fix would only be possible using Gee, which could not be guaranteed owing to the risk of jamming or technical failure.

Navigators were given the planned route to target together with the Met forecast and predicted winds and then left to work out their individual flight plans, the flight out being worked on a true air speed of 180 mph, that for the return, without bomb and with a lighter fuel load, at 220 mph. For planning, the surface winds to 3°E were taken to be light and variable, northerly 5–10 mph from 3° to 5½°E, increasing to northerly 10–15 mph east of 5½°, becoming north to north-easterly in the target area, 20–35 mph.

---

* These routes are as given in the 'Chastise' Operation Order. Those given in Cochrane's post-Chastise report, dated 7 June 1943, suggest that many of the return routes flown were variations of these.

Interestingly some navigators recorded their targets as A, B and C, as had been designated in the original draft Operation Order, whereas others labelled them X, Y and Z, as recommended by Gibson. The reason is obscure, but it suggests that the flight plans may have been prepared in stages throughout the day and that the final change to X, Y and Z may not have taken place until the afternoon.

1530 approx. Reserve aircraft. On arrival at Scampton ATA pilot Hugh Bergel could see other similarly modified Lancasters, some with 'Upkeep' loaded, one of these rotating slowly. Curious and seeking a closer look, he was intercepted by a flight lieutenant and was told firmly that what he was seeing was highly secret and not to come any nearer. As he waited for the taxi Anson that would return him to Aston Down, Bergel pondered what he had seen but could make no sense of it. Meanwhile, groundcrew began to work on ED825. In the limited time available, they would have had to carry out the equivalent, of a post-flight check and rectification – although whether this allowed for repair of the faulty fuel feed is not known, refuel, and load 'Upkeep' and the Browning ammunition. During the check Corporal Hugh 'Duke' Munro, the squadron's radar specialist, discovered that a Bakelite insert was missing from the socket end of the 16-strand coaxial cable to the Gee set. No spare could be found and, knowing the urgency of the task and need for a reserve aircraft, Munro decided to expedite an unofficial solution. Carefully spacing out the individual small wire-end sockets, he mated them with the male plugs and hoped there would be no short-circuit. When tested, the joint held and the Gee set functioned.

Also, at some time during the day S/Ldr Maurice 'Shorty' Longbottom, one of the Vickers test pilots carrying out the trials programme at Reculver, arrived from Manston in Lancaster ED817 carrying with him another Vickers test pilot connected with the project, Robert Handasyde. Longbottom's log book shows that before making this flight to Scampton he had conducted two flights from Manston, one in Lancaster ED765 and another (possibly two) flights in a Mosquito. These were to demonstrate 'Upkeep' and 'Highball' to Sir Archibald Sinclair, the Secretary of State for Air, who was visiting Reculver on this day. If so then Longbottom and Handasyde are unlikely to have arrived at Scampton before noon, and although their flight is logged as Manston–Scampton–Manston there is no record of when they left to return to Manston, other than it being the same day. The reason for their flight is not recorded and cannot be surmised. However, the presence of a further 'Upkeep' Lancaster at Scampton that afternoon may have provided additional insurance against aircraft unserviceability.

1615 No. 5 Group sent a 'SECRET AND IMMEDIATE' telex message to G/C Whitworth at Scampton confirming: 'Code name for 5 Group Operation Order B.976 is "Chastise".' This was followed by the No. 5 Group's executive signal: 'Executive Operation "Chastise" 16/5/43. Zero hour 22.48B.' This was final confirmation that the operation was to go ahead and the signal for all aircrew to be assembled for the final briefing.

With Zero hour (the time at which the first aircraft would be approaching the enemy coast) now established, final timings could be calculated, including those for take-off. This triggered a further period of activity for Harry Humphries who had already completed the Night Flying Programme and organised the flying rations but was still waiting to notify the mess kitchens and transport section of the times for the provision of meals and crew buses. Eventually a runner arrived carrying a sealed envelope addressed in Gibson's hand:

> It gave take off hours and estimated time of return . . . From these times I had to work out such things as the buses to take the aircrews to their planes in good time to complete the preliminary crew drills and prevent unnecessary rush and a meal time to allow the boys to catch the buses. In between mealtimes and bus times I had to ensure that flying rations were available, and coffee which the aircrew carried in the aircraft whilst on operations. I had to be available to accept cash, wills, and letters to next of kin, should anyone wish to deposit such articles. Strangely enough, the men who did deposit anything with me always seemed to return to collect it.

At about the same time Air Commodore Satterly at No. 5 Group Headquarters spotted, or was advised of, a typographical error in the copies of the operation order which had been distributed. The three main targets, Möhne, Eder and Sorpe, had been denoted as X, Y and X rather than X, Y and Z. Corrections were duly despatched with 'IMMEDIATE' priority to HQ Bomber Command and to Whitworth to obviate any possible confusion.

1630 approx. The Tannoy ordered all No. 617 Squadron aircrew to the station briefing room on the upper floor of the dining block, across the road from Station Headquarters. The building's symmetrical front elevation with a projecting central unit and four stone pillars supporting a shallow curved canopy gave it the feel of an Odeon cinema. This impression was continued inside with a large atrium and art deco staircase up to the upper floor.

Entry was only permitted after a rigid inspection of identity cards. Tammy Simpson, Martin's gunner, recorded, 'It was the first time I can recall ever being asked to produce my identity card on a squadron.'

Exceptionally, Gibson's flight engineer John Pulford was not at Scampton for most of the day. He had been granted compassionate leave to attend, in his hometown of Hull, the funeral of his father, who had died on 7 May. Although Pulford had no idea of the target, or that he would be operating that night, he knew details of their training and had seen 'Upkeep'. This necessitated his having a police escort, causing much consternation to his mother and family who thought him to be in some kind of trouble. He left almost immediately after attending the service to be back at Scampton for final briefing.

Upstairs in the briefing room the aircrew seated themselves on wooden slatted benches at long trestle tables, facing a wall on which was pinned a large map of the UK and Europe, alongside a roll-up projection screen. The assembled group was brought to attention as Cochrane entered, accompanied by Gibson, Whitworth and Wallis. Walking down the central aisle, past the epidiascope used for projecting target photographs, the party made their way to the far end of the room and the crews were seated again. Gibson began proceedings by announcing that their targets were 'the great dams of Germany'. He then introduced Wallis who repeated what had been said to some at previous mini-briefings. Using a blackboard and cross-section drawing of the Möhne dam he described clearly and in some detail the development and *modus operandi* of 'Upkeep' and then went on to explain the importance of the reservoirs to German industrial output, notably steel production. At one point he reflected that since the Möhne had been inaugurated by the Kaiser in 1913 it was a 'good target'.

After Wallis, Cochrane stood up to address the crews. Exuding confidence that the operation would become successful, 'I know that this attack will succeed' and indeed become 'historic', he again emphasised the need for the strictest secrecy with regard to the nature of the weapon. While Cochrane spoke Wallis quietly expressed to Gibson his concerns for the crews: 'I hope they all come back,' whilst revealing his continued focus on the engineering aspects of the operation and the final proving of his thesis: 'I look upon this raid as my last great experiment to see if it can be done on the actual thing.'

Gibson then again outlined the structure of the operation, re-confirming the three waves and their targets. At this point it also appears from the post-raid report that crews of the reserve wave 'were given individual instructions at briefing which were liable to be amended by R/T or W/T during the sortie' in respect of their individual reserve targets (Lister, Ennepe, Diemel) and their positions in relation to the Möhne.

At this late stage Wallis's assistant, Herbert Jeffree, may have intervened to point out that it would be dangerous to return with an 'Upkeep' if its fuze had been armed on crossing the enemy coast, since there was no way of disarming it again in the air and that no 'Upkeeps' should be returned to base. However, this recollection was subsequently disputed by New Zealander Les Munro, who, as will be seen, flew one of two aircraft to return to Scampton with their weapon.

The weather forecast for the night was good. Home bases would have good conditions with moderate visibility. There would be broken cloud at medium level and broken strato-cumulus over northern Germany, Denmark and the German North Sea coast. Thunderstorms at present further south and over east Germany would die down and there then should be good conditions with moderate to good visibility, as over the rest of Germany, with slight strato-cumulus between 2,000 and 3,000 feet over the Frisian Islands and similar over the Ruhr, while in the target area of the dams a north-easterly wind was predicted.

As a further recap W/Cdr Dunn ran over signals procedures, and the formal part of the briefing was concluded at 1808 with the synchronisation of watches.

Tammy Simpson recalled:

> The briefing ... was very extensive. Toby [Foxlee, Martin's other gunner] and I chatted in a low voice as the opportunity arose, and we both agreed it would be a gunner's paradise for searchlight delousing. The weather forecast was for a very clear moonlight night.

Jim Clay, bomb aimer with F/Lt Les Munro's crew, noted: 'Everyone was in high spirits and ready to go.'

Flying Officer (F/O) 'Hobby' Hobday, navigator with Australian Les Knight, echoed the same recollection: '[This] was a marvellous thing to be on. It was so different from any bombing we had ever done before and much more exciting. We thought it was a great effort.'

Others were perhaps more thoughtful. John Hopgood was overheard by Gibson to say to his crew: 'The first aircraft to attack the dam will probably catch the gunners with their pants down. But the second to attack won't be so lucky – and that's us, fellers.'

The aircrew then split into various groups to review key points. Some gathered round the models, photographs and route maps, checking their memories and last-minute details. Dunn reminded the wireless operators in the three separate waves about their different responsibilities. Crews then headed to their respective messes for the pre-flight meal. As they came out into the early evening light those glancing towards the south-east would have noted the moon rising low over the horizon above Scampton's main gate.

Cochrane's comments regarding the need for security following the operation were well-founded. It had been intended for No. 618 Squadron to mount a 'Highball' attack against the German battleship *Tirpitz* within a day of the attack on the dams, but development problems, mainly concerning the Mosquito release gear, would prevent this. Nevertheless, it was hoped that 'Highball' might soon become operational for use against units of the German and Italian fleets. For fear of jeopardising 'Highball' or indeed any future 'Upkeep' operations, it was imperative that the enemy should learn as little as possible about the weapon, its principle of operation, performance and criteria for release. For these reasons a strict protocol had been devised by Bufton, in conjunction with Saundby of Bomber Command, to safeguard the security of the weapon.

Press representatives would not be permitted to quote any information from 5 Group, or its units and aircrew concerned with the operation. All press communiqués would be strictly controlled by the Air Ministry and would adhere to a cover plan already agreed. The story was that the operation employed a mine of great size. This had been dropped by a number of experienced crews who had been specially selected and trained for the operation, which demanded an extremely high standard of flying and the highest degree of accuracy in dropping the mine sufficiently close to the target to be effective. In the event the crews displayed the greatest skill in executing the operation as planned.

The crews were briefed accordingly to 'ensure that the highest standard of security is maintained for an indefinite period after Operation "Chastise" has been executed'.

Few foresaw that despite some of the 'Upkeep' details being revealed in the 1955 film, the weapon would remain classified until 1962.

1900 approx. Inevitably there was a growing tension as late afternoon transformed into early evening. In the mess it was hard to conceal the fact that 'something was on'. The presence of the AOC on the station was one thing, and those with an astute eye would have noticed that all of No. 617 Squadron's aircraft had been bombed up and fuelled for a long-distance flight. The mess waitresses could not fail to spot that 617's crews were having the standard pre-operation meal of bacon and two eggs. Nevertheless, all this went generally unremarked and an NCO who speculated about the operation in the mess after supper was quickly silenced by his companions.

Writing in *Enemy Coast Ahead* Gibson said:

We went up to the Mess and had some bacon and eggs. Dinghy
[S/Ldr Melvin Young, 'A' Flight Commander] said to me: 'Can I
have your egg if you don't come back?'

This was a well-known corny joke ... I said 'Sugar off' and told
him to do something very difficult to himself.

Harry Humphries noted:

In the officers' mess, there were a lot of strange faces; high ranking
Air Force Officers and several studious looking civilians – 'the
back room boys' – including the originator of the weapon which
breached the dam so successfully. I felt awfully small in the midst
of all this activity. I wanted to help everybody to do something, but
no help was needed. We had all done our little piece of the jigsaw
and we were ready. I went to my office at six p.m. and waited.

Despite his significant organisational role, Humphries still had no knowledge
of the target, or the nature of the operation, but could sense from the
atmosphere that this was something out of the ordinary.

The squadron's medical officer, F/O Malcolm Arthurton, shared a room
with David Shannon's rear gunner, Jack Buckley. Arthurton had flown on
a number of training flights to investigate the effects of low flying and air-
sickness, but an enquiry as to whether he might join the crew for this evening's
practice flight met with an evasive response. On then attempting to make an
external phone call, he found that no calls were permitted. It all pointed to
one thing: an operation was imminent.

After the meal the aircrew of the first two waves had only a brief time to
return to their quarters before setting off for the hangar crew rooms where
they would change into flying clothing and collect equipment and rations
necessary for the flight.

The five crews of the reserve wave, not due to depart until midnight, had
longer to wait. Freddie Tees, a gunner with P/O Ottley's crew had gone to the
sergeants' mess after the briefing. He had devoured the 'pre-op' meal with his
usual relish and listened to the chatter of the aircrew around him. He rejected
a suggestion that they should all go down and see the first aircraft off, going
instead to his billet to snatch a few hours' sleep, setting his alarm clock to call
him in time for his take-off preparations.

1945 Crews of the first two waves were beginning to drift down to the
squadron offices ranged alongside No. 2 Hangar, some walking or cycling,
a few in battered cars. S/Ldr Young busied himself tidying his office, while
Henry Maudslay conversed with his crew. Others sought out Humphries

to pass over final letters and keepsakes. The mood had perceptibly changed. The relief and anticipation generated at briefing was gradually subsiding as thoughts focused more sharply on the task ahead. Inevitably individuals reacted in their own way. Some crew members talked quietly together; others stood immersed in their own thoughts. Many cigarettes were lit while there were odd outbursts of loud voices and occasional nervous laughter. Ken Earnshaw, Hopgood's navigator, prophesied with uncanny prescience, that eight aircraft would not come back. Did he, like his pilot, believe that they would be one of those eight?

In the crew rooms they began to change into their flying kit, signing for their parachutes, escape kit and specialist equipment, checking helmets and masks for frayed or broken intercom cables. Pockets were emptied of anything that might provide information to the enemy; letters, old bus or cinema tickets and currency. Bomb aimers signed the Bombing Leader's notebook, confirming that they were conversant with the aircraft's load, and checked with their navigator that they had the necessary maps. Wireless operators collected blank log sheets for completion during the flight, a set of flimsies, thin paper sheets on which were typed call signs and code words, the separate secret bomber code for the night, and then signed for their Very pistol cartridges. Equipped and dressed they drifted outside, gathering in small groups or lying on the grass in front of the hangar.

Gibson provided his recollections in *Enemy Coast Ahead*:

> Standing around for an hour and a half before the take-off, every-one was tense and no one said very much. The long practice and the waiting and the business of being kept in the dark had keyed them up to a point where one could feel that they would have been better if they had stood on their toes and danced and shouted out loud, or even screamed to get rid of it, but they stood there with their hands in their pockets, smoking cigarettes and saying little. I said to Hoppy, 'Hoppy, tonight's the night; tomorrow we will get drunk.' We always said this, Hoppy and I, before going off on a mission.

Humphries recorded: 'This was *Der Tag* for 617 Squadron ... [and] from eight o'clock onwards the scenes outside the crew rooms were something to be remembered.' Gibson arrived with his entire crew packed into his car, radiating complete confidence.' To Humphries Gibson appeared 'fit and well and quite unperturbed', which later caused Gibson to comment: 'This was a complete lie.'

Sixty years later Humphries's recollection was still of an almost artificially relaxed atmosphere:

It was getting near zero hour. The stocky figure of Wing Commander Gibson could be seen descending from his car. I call it a car but it was so loaded with humanity at times that it resembled a Lincolnshire bus. He walked around among the boys, chatting, always smiling and if he was worried, he certainly didn't show it. I thought I had better say something to him before he took off and I walked over but before I could say a word, Trevor-Roper, his rear gunner, butted in.

'Hello short arse,' he greeted.

I flushed a little. Trev. always annoyed me, but I couldn't do much about it. Every time I retaliated, he just held me in one hand, a very big hand, and threatened to spank me with the other. I gave him a glance which should have withered him completely, but he just smiled right across his face. When Trevor-Roper smiled he just grinned from ear to ear and resembled a very sinister stage villain.

Responding to Humphries's question regarding any last-minute requirements, Gibson had one request: 'Plenty of beer in the mess when we return. We'll be having a party.'

David Shannon was the last of his crew to arrive, strolling from the locker room, keeping the transport waiting. Jack Buckley, fourteen years Shannon's senior, chided him as a father might his errant son, asking 'Have you cleaned your teeth, David?' The reason for Shannon's delayed arrival would later become known.

Shannon and Hopgood had become good friends during their days together under Gibson's command on No. 106 Squadron:

Hoppy grabbed me and we went round the back of the hangar to smoke a cigarette. He said, 'I think this is going to be a tough one and I don't think I'm coming back, Dave.' That shook me a bit. I said, 'Come off it, Hoppy. You'll beat these bastards; you've beaten them for so long, you're not going to get whipped tonight.'

Meanwhile Hopgood's rear gunner Tony Burcher, and bomb aimer John Fraser, sat on the grass immersed in their own thoughts, while the remainder of the crew played an impromptu game of cricket to pass the time. Les Munro sat in a chair flicking through a copy of the aircrew magazine *Tee-Em*. At about 2000 Gibson looked at his watch and signalled that it was time to head out to the aircraft. Bodies stirred and walked to the waiting transport, taking with them their associated impedimenta.

It was only a short journey to the dispersals. For some it was the first sight of 'Upkeep' beneath their aircraft. There was more light humour to ease the tension. Flight engineer Sgt Basil Feneron put his shoulder underneath and mock strained to lift Wallis's weapon. Warrant Officer Abram Garshowitz, wireless operator with Bill Astell's crew, chalked a variant of Churchill's famous phrase, 'Never has so much been expected of so few' on their mine, while further chalked graffiti adorned the fuselage adjacent to the rear door of Hopgood's M-Mother: 'Officers entrance only'.

Superstitions were evident too. Ivan Whittaker relieved himself over the tailwheel of P-Popsie. Mick Martin carried a small stuffed toy koala in his battledress pocket, while McCarthy's flight engineer, Bill Radcliffe, tucked his toy panda 'Chuck Chuck', down his flying boot. Tony Burcher had a stone given to him by young boy whose parents had been killed in an air raid, with the request that he should throw it out at the Germans during a raid. Instead, Burcher had kept the stone as a talisman. He also carried a more practical item. Hearing tales of food rationing in Britain, Burcher's mother in Australia sent him regular supplies of malted milk tablets. He had never carried them before, but this evening something made him slip the small bottle into an inside battledress pocket.

The aircrews' close rapport with the groundcrew made it hard to conceal that this was no training sortie. Corporal Munro, who had performed a late rectification on the reserve aircraft, later reflected:

> The interaction between ground crew and aircrew was such that your sixth sense told you that this was 'it', by the way the crews acted. If it's just another exercise, aircrews are quite relaxed and talkative. If it's the real thing, there is tension in the air, as well as a general quietness in communication.

The pre-boarding external check of the aircraft was all part of the ritual: checking the chocks were in position, pitot head, static vent covers and under-carriage jury struts removed and tyres were serviceable with no cuts or signs of creep; that the hinged leading edge and cowlings were secure with no sign of any fluid leaks. The flight engineer noted the fuel load from the Form 700, and if all was well the captain would then sign, accepting the aircraft as serviceable.

2010 approx. Gibson and his crew prepared to board G-George. An official RAF photographer, F/O W. Bellamy, was at dispersal to capture the moment. Two photographs were taken. The first showed Gibson and his Liverpudlian wireless operator F/Lt Robert Hutchison as the crew readied themselves in preparation for boarding. The photograph was recorded officially as 'W/Cdr Gibson is assisted with his parachute harness by one of his crew before take off.' However, the photograph shows Gibson adjusting his own chest-type parachute harness, clipping each of the four straps into the quick-release box. Also clearly visible is the Luftwaffe *Schwimmweste* life jacket with its top-up inflator tube, which Gibson wore in preference to the standard RAF-issue Mae West. The item had been acquired from an aircraft shot down by Gibson in 1941, while he was serving as a night-fighter pilot with No. 29 Beaufighter Squadron. Gibson's gaze is focussed on Hutchison's hand, which is clenched into a fist. It can only be conjecture, but it appears that Hutchison is about to toss a coin – possibly another example of aircrew banter to ease tension before take-off.

Moments later Cochrane arrived for a final word and to wish them well. He had been visiting the dispersals to talk to the groundcrews, expressing his appreciation for the effort they had made to prepare the aircraft for this evening, and hoping they would soon learn the full results of their labour.

Bellamy then took a second photograph as the crew boarded G-George, little knowing that it would become one of the enduring images of Bomber Command.

Gibson stands on the top of the short ladder leading to the aircraft's doorway. Lined up behind him are the rest of his crew, in set order to facilitate entry into the tight confines of the aircraft. Hutchison has his foot on the bottom step. Following him is front gunner F/Sgt George Deering. Closer to the camera P/O Fred Spafford, the bomb aimer, is ready to go into the nose of the aircraft once Gibson is seated at the controls. Next is Sgt John Pulford, who will unfold his collapsible flight engineer's seat alongside Gibson, followed up the aircraft by the navigator, P/O Torger Taerum, standing out of line, beneath the aircraft serial number. Finally, the oldest member of the crew, 28-year-old rear gunner F/Lt Richard Trevor-Roper from Shanklin, Isle of Wight, is last to board and will squirm his way over the tailplane spar and into his turret.

As if a microcosm of the force they represented, the crew comprised members from Britain and the Dominions. Four wore RAF blue, but Deering from Toronto (though of Scottish birth) and Taerum from Calgary were in the darker shade of the Royal Canadian Air Force, while near navy blue showed that Spafford, from Adelaide, was a member of the Royal Australian Air Force. In the dimming evening light the film barely picked out the differences in the colours. There was no need for thick flying jackets to keep out the penetrating cold experienced at altitude. It had been a warm day, and with the operation being flown at low level battledress would suffice. Most of them were wearing shoes, with only Pulford and Trevor-Roper opting for their familiar sheepskin-lined boots. Anticipating the physical effort required for this operation, Gibson wore no battledress blouse and flew in his shirt sleeves.

With them were essential items and tools of their trade. Gibson and Spafford carried their parachutes by the canvas lifting strap, taking care to avoid the metal D-ring, which would deploy the parachute if pulled. Pulford's canvas box contained a selection of basic tools and items with which it might be possible to make essential repairs, together with log sheets for recording engine temperatures and settings and oil and fuel consumption throughout the flight. Folded charts underneath Spafford's arm suggest that he preferred wider coverage than that provided by the narrow roller maps. Should they deviate from the prepared route there was less chance of going 'off the map'.

A similar scene was witnessed at the neighbouring dispersals as the other crews of the first and second waves climbed aboard, walking up the upward-sloping fuselage (at least the 'Upkeep' specials did not have the obstacle of the mid-upper turret), continuing their equipment checks as they went. Settling themselves into their respective positions, stowing their parachutes and kit, the crews waited for the signal to start up.

Chapter 7

Low Level to Germany

21.10 A red Very light soared up from Gibson's aircraft – the signal for the first wave aircraft to start engines. Across the airfield there was a spluttering cacophony as the Merlins fired one by one, with intermittent crescendos as magnetos were checked, before settling down to a steady rumble.

Harold Roddis, an 'A' Flight fitter, recounted:

> [The crews] always made time to have a chat and joke with us, but when the time came, they climbed the steps into the kite whilst we climbed on the mainwheels and plugged in the starter battery, and at a signal from the pilot primed and started the starboard inner and outer, then ducked under the fuselage and repeated this with the port inner and outer engines. We then unplugged the starter battery, pulled it to the edge of the dispersal and waited until the pilot and crew had carried out their checks and the F/E had checked his oil pressures etc. After they were satisfied that everything was OK, the pilot signalled 'chocks away' and we moved to the rear of the engines, grabbed the chock ropes and pulled these to the edge of dispersal and gave the all clear sign to the pilot.

2128 AJ-E F/Lt Barlow taxied E-Edward to the southern end of the runway strip in use and waited on the perimeter track before moving on to the grass and heading into wind adjacent to the runway controller's caravan, positioned to port at the start of the take-off run. After a brief pause Sgt Frank Wade, the runway controller, flashed a 'green' on his Aldis lamp. Barlow advanced the throttles. Slowly at first and then with gathering pace the Lancaster began to roll. At 21.28 (British Double Summer Time) E-Edward became airborne. One by one, three more aircraft began to move around the perimeter to the marshalling point where they awaited their signal to take off.

But already there was a problem. McCarthy should have been the first away – but while he was running up the engines of his aircraft, ED915 AJ-Q, a coolant leak developed on number four (starboard outer) engine, which was rapidly shut down by Bill Radcliffe, the flight engineer. With their aircraft unserviceable, there was only one option – take the reserve.

Fearful that another crew encountering a serviceability problem might beat them to it, McCarthy's crew began a rapid evacuation of Q-Queenie. Such was their haste that they threw essential portable equipment out of the window. In doing so the D-ring of McCarthy's parachute snagged on the window catch and the silk blossomed out over him as he stood below ready to catch it, enveloping him in its shrouds. After extricating himself with difficulty, McCarthy piled into a nearby vehicle with his crew and headed for ED825. There, another set-back awaited them. The aircraft only had one compass deviation card. Two were needed, one for the aircraft with 'Upkeep' aboard, the other without it. McCarthy got back into the vehicle and headed for the squadron offices alongside the hangar. As he stormed towards the instrument section he was intercepted by F/Sgt Powell, witnessed by Humphries:

> McCarthy spluttered. 'My bloody aircraft is u/s, I've got to take the spare. There's no compass deviation card. Where are those lazy, idle, incompetent compass adjusters?' We calmed him while many willing people searched for the missing compass card. Mac was in a mess. He stood six feet one inch and weighed about 15 stone. The excitement and exertion had really disturbed his equanimity. His shirt was wringing wet and he gulped in great breaths of air. His huge hands were clenching and unclenching spasmodically.
>
> 'Calm down old boy,' I said. 'You'll make it.'
>
> Flight Sergeant Powell came running towards us with the all-important card in his hand. 'Here you are sir,' he said as the sound of aircraft engines starting up could be heard.

Word had reached the hangar that a replacement parachute was needed. Within minutes one was found and passed to McCarthy, who sped off back to his aircraft. Meanwhile another crew member was less than happy about the change of aircraft. To improve his vision rear gunner Dave Rodger had removed the central Perspex panel from his turret on Queenie. Now, taking advantage of the imposed delay and assisted by willing ground crew, he set about modifying the reserve aircraft.

While McCarthy's issues were being dealt with, the remainder of the northern wave were moving forward and taking off individually in turn. After Barlow, Munro at 2129, then Byers at 2130, followed by Rice at 2131. The sun was beginning to set and by now F/O Bellamy had travelled to the far end of the runway where his camera captured the silhouette of a departing aircraft against the western horizon.

2135 AJ-N Crews of the southern wave aircraft were settling in and testing equipment. Aboard Les Knight's N-Nuts, still at dispersal, navigator F/O Hobby Hobday instigated a time check to synchronise watches and the aircraft clock.

In the minutes following Rice's departure, Gibson, Hopgood and Martin completed their final cockpit checks. The groundcrews pulled the wooden blocks away and ran out to the edge of dispersal ahead of the wing tips where pilots could see they were clear. Releasing the brake lever, with the inner engines running at about 800–1,000 rpm and using bursts of the outer engines, they began to taxi from dispersal, steering with brakes and differential throttle. Rudder and aileron trimmers were set to zero, with a little up elevator trimmer to help the aircraft climb after take-off.

Their departure was to be less conventional. Scampton's grass surface permitted a loose formation take-off, with Martin and Hopgood behind to port and starboard respectively. This speeded departure and meant that the aircraft were able to set course with the minimum of delay. The squadron had adopted this tactic during the later stages of their training, so it attracted no undue attention. In any case there wasn't the usual group of WAAFs and ground staff by the controller's caravan to wave good luck to the departing crews, while those in the know, including Humphries and Powell, observed discreetly from the hangars or the watch office.

After Gibson arrived at the end of the runway the controller's green Aldis flashed. He then made a short taxi forward to ensure the tailwheel was straight and waited whilst the other two aircraft formed up on either side. Final take-off checks were completed: propeller pitch fully fine, mixture controls to 'Rich', fuel pumps on, brakes on and flaps set at 25 degrees. The engine noise increased as the throttles were opened. Leading initially with the port engines and helped by a subconscious application of starboard rudder to counteract any tendency to swing, the pilots set the aircraft rolling. With a full load, each aircraft gained pace slowly at first, across Scampton's undulating grass, the controls becoming more responsive as the speed increased. At an indicated airspeed of 110 mph, with the engine gauges showing +9 psi boost and some 2,850 rpm, contact with the ground became tentative as the wings took the load. After using the maximum available run and with the northern boundary hedge looming perilously close the three aircraft lifted slowly into the air; then a dab on the lever to brake the wheels as they folded into the inboard nacelles and the airspeed could build up. With a slight reduction in boost and revs the flaps were raised in increments, whilst the aircraft were kept down to little more than tree top height. It was 21.39.

2142 AJ-G   As Gibson, Hopgood and Martin eased into a circuit of the airfield, Munro, followed by the other three, each a minute apart and flying at 100 feet, prepared to set course. Immediately after take-off the navigators switched on their Gee sets. It would take five minutes for the valve technology to reach operating temperature and only then would they be able to see and adjust the traces on their screens. There was no wind, but Munro requested a drift check to make certain before making good a track of 84 degrees.

2144   Over at 'A' Flight dispersal, groundcrews pulled the chocks clear of the wheels of AJ-A, AJ-J and AJ-L which, with bursts of power, began to taxi to the take-off point, forming up in their vic led by Young, with Maltby to starboard and Shannon to port. Frank Wade flashed his green. In unison the throttles of twelve Merlin engines were opened, and the aircraft strained against their brakes. Then they rolled forward, sluggishly at first but gathering speed across the uneven ground. Gradually the wings took the load and they lifted off, wheels seemingly barely clearing the northern boundary hedge. In the watch office the duty officer logged their departure: 2147.

2148 AJ-J   A minute later, as they turned for their initial circuit of the airfield, Maltby's navigator, Sgt Vivian Nicholson, switched on the IFF (Identification Friend of Foe), identifying them as 'friendly' on their transit to the coast.

As he did so Gibson's formation straightened up from their circuit. It was now time to set course for the Suffolk coast. Flying at 200 feet, at a ground-speed of 174 mph, the pilots turned onto a course of 125 degrees. As they raced low over the Lincolnshire countryside Tammy Simpson, Martin's rear gunner, viewed the receding airfield through his sight to report a 1-degree drift to starboard. Martin duly applied a touch of port rudder.

2150 AJ-W   Checking his API, Les Munro's navigator, F/O Rumbles, reported that they were now two-thirds of the way to their crossing point on the Lincolnshire coast. Off the starboard bow, the bomb aimer, Sgt Jim Clay, may have identified St Michael's church on the rising ground at Burwell. Four minutes later they crossed over the beach at Sutton on Sea, on track but a little behind schedule. Munro increased speed to 180 mph.

2155 AJ-Z, AJ-B, AJ-N   As Munro crossed the Lincolnshire coast, the sun was just sinking below the horizon and back at Scampton the final three aircraft of the southern wave left their dispersals to taxi to the southern

W/Cdr Guy Gibson (*front right*), seen here with aircrew of No. 106 Sqn and his dog. The black Labrador, acquired in 1941 while Gibson was based at West Malling with No. 29 Sqn, wears a mock Iron Cross name tag.

Above: Barnes Wallis, Assistant Chief Designer of Aircraft for Vickers-Armstrong. Originally a marine engineer, he switched to airship design during World War I, and then to aircraft in the 1930s. One of the country's foremost aeronautical engineers, with ideas far ahead of his time, he was knighted in 1968.

Both right: Wellington BJ895 makes an early high-level drop of a 'Golf Mine' over the Fleet, December 1942. Chesil Beach can be seen in the background.

ACM Sir Arthur Harris, AOC-in-C, Bomber Command. A believer in area bombing, he was initially sceptical of attacks against 'panacea' targets and opposed the creation of specialist squadrons.

G/Capt Sidney Bufton, Director of Bomber Operations at the Air Ministry. An advocate of the Pathfinder Force and a protagonist of the attack on the Dams, he was often at odds with Harris.

Above: AM Sir Ralph Cochrane, Air Officer Commanding No. 5 Group, was responsible for implementing Operation 'Chastise'. He had been a WWI airship commander and between the wars war served as a pilot in Harris's squadron.

Left: G/Capt John 'Charles' Whitworth, Scampton's Station Commander, had flown Whitleys during the early part of the war and later became technical advisor for the film *The Dam Busters*.

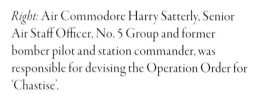

Right: Air Commodore Harry Satterly, Senior Air Staff Officer, No. 5 Group and former bomber pilot and station commander, was responsible for devising the Operation Order for 'Chastise'.

Target No.
I (j) 9

MÖHNE DAM — GÜNNE near SOEST (GERMANY)
G.S.G.S. 4416. Sheet Q2. Lat. 51° 29' N.
RB 226214. Long. 08° 04' E.

Illustration No.
I (j) 9/1

Pre-war photograph, date unknown

Re-issued January 1945

LOW OBLIQUE VIEW, LOOKING S.S.W.
Photographed before breaching of dam on 16/17 May 1943 when Power Station
on right of picture was demolished.

A.I.3c (1)

TYPE B

From the Möhne dam target folder: a ground view of the dam showing the towers which served
as the bomb aimers' aiming marks. The low rolling hills are in contrast to those at the Eder.

A pre-war view of the Möhne dam from the parapet showing
its landscaped setting and (*left*) the 6,000-kW power station
destroyed when F/Lt Hopgood's 'Upkeep' overshot the dam.

A section of the briefing model of the Möhne Dam showing the twin anti-torpedo nets and the flak positions on the towers. The dummy trees placed as camouflage are marked as '?' – unidentified.

A pre-war photograph of the Sorpe Dam from the west bank of the reservoir. The solidity and thickness of this earth-banked construction is readily apparent, necessitating a different form of attack.

Right: Lancaster ED825 'modified to carry a certain item of store' seen during performance trials at Boscombe Down. This was the reserve aircraft taken by F/Lt Joe McCarthy to the Sorpe Dam.

Bottom right: ED817, the second of the 'Upkeep' trials Lancasters, seen here after the raid when it joined No. 617 Squadron as replacement for P/O Bill Ottley's ill-fated ED910 AJ-C.

Below: Most probably taken after the Dams Raid, F/Sgt Bill Townsend's Lancaster ED886 AJ-O, with 'Squanderbug' nose insignia, in formation with a standard Lancaster.

'Upkeep' loaded on W/Cdr Gibson's ED932 AJ-G, showing the spring-tensioned calliper arms with a belt drive to the pulley on the hydraulic motor for spinning the weapon prior to release.

A Lancaster makes a practice run towards shore at Reculver, May 1943. Pilots had to counter the aircraft's tendency to climb as 'Upkeep' was released to avoid presenting a better target to the defences.

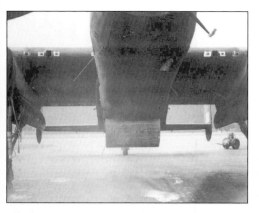

Above: A front view of AJ-G. The wing leading edge carries barrage balloon cable cutters. Beneath the front fuselage are (*left*) the VHF aerial and (*right*) the shielded lamp of the spotlight altimeter.

Right: F/Sgt George 'Chiefy' Powell. Ground staff, both administrative and engineering, played a vital role in the formation of the squadron and maintaining its operational efficiency.

F/Lt Harry Humphries, squadron adjutant, responsible for much of the routine administration and record-keeping, without which the squadron could not function, and of great assistance to Gibson and his flight commanders.

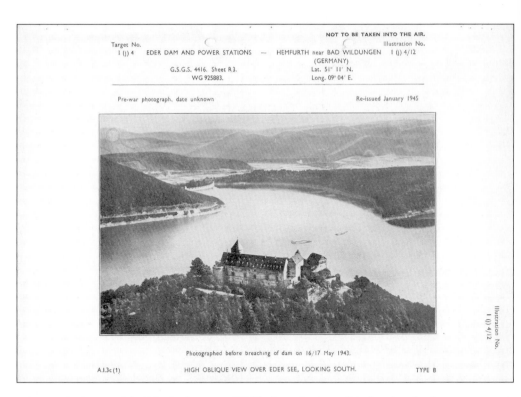

Target No.

Illustration No.

1 (j) 4   EDER DAM AND POWER STATIONS   —   HEMFURTH near BAD WILDUNGEN   1 (j) 4/12
(GERMANY)

G.S.G.S. 4416. Sheet R3.
WG 925883.

Lat. 51° 11' N.
Long. 09° 04' E.

Pre-war photograph, date unknown

Re-issued January 1945

Photographed before breaching of dam on 16/17 May 1943.

A.1.3c (1)   HIGH OBLIQUE VIEW OVER EDER SEE, LOOKING SOUTH.   TYPE B

Illustration No. 1 (i) 4/12

An attacker's view of the Eder looking over Waldeck castle. Aircraft had to dive for the promontory (*right*) and then line up on the dam (*upper left*), before banking away right down the valley.

The Eder dam looking across the lake toward Waldeck Castle. The valley down which attacking aircraft had to dive can be seen to the left of the castle. The difficulty of the terrain is readily apparent.

A pre-war view of the Eder dam from the Michelskopf, annotated to highlight the two power stations. Pre-war postcards such as this and the one opposite provided much of the crews' briefing material.

A bomb aimer's target map of the Eder Reservoir with key topographical features indicated. The maps were shaded and printed in limited colours to be clearly visible under restricted cockpit lighting conditions.

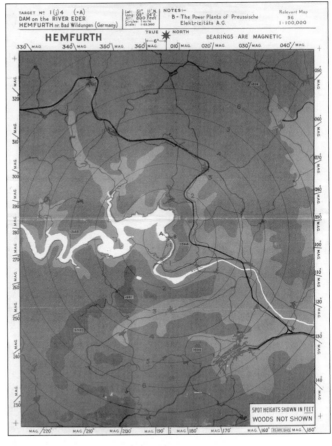

T. TOWNSEND C.GM.D.F.M.   617 SQUADRON

Above & left: F/Sgt Bill Townsend, whose skilful evasion of the enemy defences as dawn approached brought his crew safely home – the last aircraft to return.

Below left: Australian F/Lt David Shannon, aged 20, was the first to attempt the difficult dog-leg approach to the Eder, finally releasing his weapon to strike the right-hand side of the dam.

Above & right: Australian P/O Les Knight piloted AJ-N which finally breached the Eder dam. Official War Artist Cuthbert Orde visited Scampton after the raid to make the striking drawings shown here and opposite.

P/O. L. G. KNIGHT DSO.   617 SQUADRON

Left: After seeing the crest start to crumble as he made his attack, F/Lt David Maltby released his 'Upkeep' slightly to port to widen the breach.

Right: The official photographer captures F/Lt Hutchison (*left*) and W/Cdr Gibson shortly before boarding G-George for Operation 'Chastise'.

F/Lt Joe McCarthy, an American who had joined the RCAF before America's entry into the war, proudly displays his joint Canada/USA shoulder flash. McCarthy's was the only aircraft of the northern wave to reach his target – the Sorpe dam.

F/Lt 'Mick' Martin, an Australian serving in the RAF, would later pioneer the squadron's low-level target-marking with W/Cdr Leonard Cheshire.

Martin's bomb aimer, Australian F/Lt Bob Hay. As Squadron Bombing Leader he accompanied Gibson to view dropping trials at Reculver.

Above: The breached Möhne dam in a German photograph taken the morning after the raid. The reservoir is still emptying, but already barrage balloons are being flown to deter any further low-level attacks.

Right: The remains of the home of the Director of the Kaiser lighting factory in Neheim. All the occupants escaped as the waters rose, apart from the Russian cook who was too frightened to leave.

Australian F/Lt Robert 'Norm' Barlow (*above*) and his crew were killed when they flew into a high-tension line near Rees. Their 'Upkeep' (*above left*) survived the crash and subsequent fire. German officials inspected the weapon after it had been defuzed and it was then taken to the Ordnance Disposal site at Kalkum for further examination.

Right: F/Lt Bill Astell. Like Barlow, Astell was brought down by a collision with high-tension cables.
Above: The height of the pylon at Marbeck struck by ED864 AJ-B emphasises the danger to low-flying bombers.

S/Ldr Henry Maudslay, B Flight Commander, survived the attack on the Eder, only to stray off track on the return flight and be shot down by flak defending the river port of Emmerich.

Damage to the parapet wall of the Eder Dam caused by the detonation of Maudslay's 'Upkeep', testimony to the difficulties encountered by the crews attacking this target.

Originally buried in Düsseldorf, Henry Maudslay and his crew now rest in Reichswald Forest War Cemetery, Kleve, along with the crews of Astell, Barlow and Ottley.

The crews lost on Operation 'Chastise' are all commemorated by memorials at their crash sites. The memorial to Maudslay and his crew at Netterden was unveiled on 17 May 2019.

Taken at 5.45 on the morning of 17 May, Neheim is seen to have been cut in half by the Möhne's raging floodwaters, which were now beginning to recede.

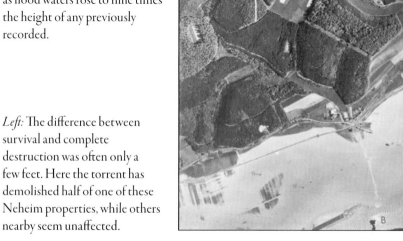

A broken bridge, shattered masonry, twisted rail track and the detritus of destruction all illustrate the severe disruption to communications caused by the floods throughout the Ruhr and Eder Valleys.

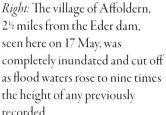

Right: The village of Affoldern, 2½ miles from the Eder dam, seen here on 17 May, was completely inundated and cut off as flood waters rose to nine times the height of any previously recorded.

Left: The difference between survival and complete destruction was often only a few feet. Here the torrent has demolished half of one of these Neheim properties, while others nearby seem unaffected.

Above: Gibson's crew at debriefing: *Standing looking on:* Harris and Cochrane.
Visible seated L–R: Intelligence Officer, Spafford, Taerum and (*nearest camera*) Trevor-Roper.
W/Cdr Gibson's face is partly visible two to the right of Trevor-Roper, in shadow.
On the table are the contents of an Eder briefing folder.

Above right: Scampton, 27 May 1943. HM King George VI escorted by Whitworth and Gibson,
talks to F/Sgt Ken Brown. Behind Gibson's shoulder in the background, Barnes Wallis.

Right: In all, thirty-four awards, including Gibson's Victoria Cross, were made to 'Chastise'
survivors. In London, 22 June, to attend the squadron's investiture at Buckingham Palace are
(*L–R*) Jack Leggo, Tammy Simpson, Bob Hay, Toby Foxlee and 'Mick' Martin.

F/Lt John Hopgood. Though injured on the way to the target, Hopgood pressed home his attack.

Canadian bomb aimer F/Sgt John Fraser survived after 'the shortest parachute jump in history'.

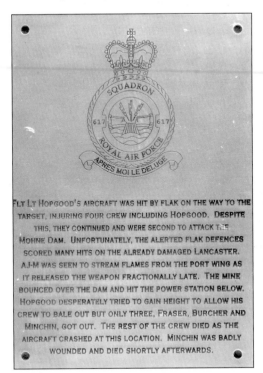

SQUADRON
617 617
ROYAL AIR FORCE
APRES MOI LE DELUGE

FLT LT HOPGOOD'S AIRCRAFT WAS HIT BY FLAK ON THE WAY TO THE TARGET, INJURING FOUR CREW INCLUDING HOPGOOD. DESPITE THIS, THEY CONTINUED AND WERE SECOND TO ATTACK THE MOHNE DAM. UNFORTUNATELY, THE ALERTED FLAK DEFENCES SCORED MANY HITS ON THE ALREADY DAMAGED LANCASTER. AJ-M WAS SEEN TO STREAM FLAMES FROM THE PORT WING AS IT RELEASED THE WEAPON FRACTIONALLY LATE. THE MINE BOUNCED OVER THE DAM AND HIT THE POWER STATION BELOW. HOPGOOD DESPERATELY TRIED TO GAIN HEIGHT TO ALLOW HIS CREW TO BALE OUT BUT ONLY THREE, FRASER, BURCHER AND MINCHIN, GOT OUT. THE REST OF THE CREW DIED AS THE AIRCRAFT CRASHED AT THIS LOCATION. MINCHIN WAS BADLY WOUNDED AND DIED SHORTLY AFTERWARDS.

John Hopgood's gallantry is commemorated on this plaque at the crash site south of Ostonnen.

Australian rear gunner Tony Burcher was blown out of AJ-M as it exploded, injuring his back. After two years as a prisoner of war he was liberated and eventually returned to flying duties.

ICI
REPOSENT
54
PRISONNIERS
DE
GUERRE
FRANCAIS

4ᵉᵐᵉ R.A. MAINE
414 Cⁱᵉ

NOYES
DANS LA
RUPTURE
DES BARRAGES
DE   LA
RUHR
LE¹ᵉ MAI 1943

Many of those who drowned that night are buried in the Möhnefriedhof in Neheim. There are sections commemorating Dutch, Polish and Russian foreign workers, together with this memorial marking the graves of fifty-four French prisoners.

Looking north up the Möhne Valley from Neheim. Rescue and salvage teams begin clearing the rubble and debris, a scene repeated at numerous locations along the Ruhr and Eder valleys.

The blast furnaces of the Henrichschutte steelworks at Hattingen seen at midday on 17 May across the flooded River Ruhr.

Above left, before: The settlement of Himmelpforten and its Porta Coeli church.

Above: Today only the foundations of Himmelpforten remain. The cross on the site of the church altar indicates the height of the wall of water that swept down the valley.

Left: One of the first victims of the flood. Pastor Berkenkopf, the incumbent at Porta Coeli, who died when his church was swept away.

The breach in the Eder dam continued to discharge for the next forty-eight hours.
The power stations appear intact but had been damaged by blast, debris and flooding.

The Orangerie and the Marble Bathhouse in Kassel inundated by floods from the Eder.
Sufficient warning allowed the city's inhabitants to seek safety on higher ground.

Above: An RAF reconnaissance photo of Fröndenberg reveals 1: submerged roads; 2: flooded electricity works; 3 & 4: destroyed road and rail bridges, 5: wrecked railway carriages and 6: submerged sidings.

K 1564
RAILWAY VIADUCT near HERDECKE
Enlargement to 1/9000 of part
of ...0/0 of 1/599
...

No. 24.733.

Left: The collapse of the Herdecke railway viaduct moments before a train was due to cross is revealed by its shadow on the floodwaters. The railway line still hangs intact, bridging the gap.

P/O Geoff Rice struck the water of the Zuider Zee while crossing the Waddenzee, losing his 'Upkeep', but was able to maintain control and return his damaged aircraft to Scampton.

AJ-W ED921 was hit by a flak shell while crossing Vlieland, wrecking the compass and intercom. The damage forced New Zealander F/Lt Les Munro to abort the mission and return to base.

F/Sgt Cyril Anderson and his crew whilst with No. 49 Sqn.
L–R: John Nugent, Gilbert Green, Douglas Bickle,
Arthur Buck, Cyril Anderson and Robert Paterson.

Above: P/O Warner Ottley, killed along with five of his crew on Operation 'Chastise'.

Left: Warner Ottley's grave in Reichswald Forest War Cemetery, where all his dead crewmates are also buried.

Ottley's AJ-C was shot down by flak defending the rail yards at Hamm. A simple wooden cross on the edge of woodland at Heesen marks where six men died and one miraculously survived.

Sgt Fred Tees, rear gunner of AJ-C, survived the crash when his turret was blown from the airframe. When he died in 1982 his ashes were scattered alongside the rest of his crew. Reunited after thirty-nine years.

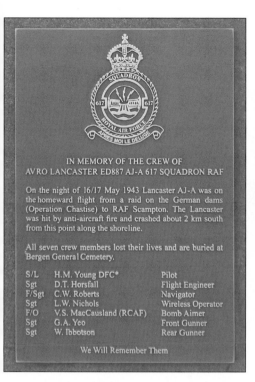

IN MEMORY OF THE CREW OF
AVRO LANCASTER ED887 AJ-A 617 SQUADRON RAF

On the night of 16/17 May 1943 Lancaster AJ-A was on
the homeward flight from a raid on the German dams
(Operation Chastise) to RAF Scampton. The Lancaster
was hit by anti-aircraft fire and crashed about 2 km south
from this point along the shoreline.

All seven crew members lost their lives and are buried at
Bergen General Cemetery.

S/L	H.M. Young DFC*	Pilot
Sgt	D.T. Horsfall	Flight Engineer
F/Sgt	C.W. Roberts	Navigator
Sgt	L.W. Nichols	Wireless Operator
F/O	V.S. MacCausland (RCAF)	Bomb Aimer
Sgt	G.A. Yeo	Front Gunner
Sgt	W. Ibbotson	Rear Gunner

We Will Remember Them

S/Ldr Young and his crew were shot down into the sea just as they crossed the Dutch coast, homebound. Their loss is commemorated by a plaque on the beach near where their aircraft came down.

S/Ldr Melvin Young, A Flight Commander, who accompanied Gibson to the Eder as deputy leader. Young had successfully survived two previous ditchings but this time there would be no return.

The wreckage of Young's Lancaster, ED887 AJ-A, washed up on a sandbar at Castricum.
The remains were finally broken up by North Sea storms many years later.

A carved stone at the Möhne dam commemorates those civilians and forced labourers who lost their lives in the *'Möhnekatastrophe'*. The path of the flood can also be traced by other memorials erected by local communities to mark the tragic events of 17 May 1943.

A memorial to the first casualties of Operation 'Chastise'. P/O Byers's Lancaster AJ-K was lost while crossing the Waddenzee. Only F/Sgt McDowell's body was recovered and is interred in Harlingen cemetery where the crew are commemorated by this plaque unveiled in 2022.

end of the runway, led by Maudslay with Astell to starboard and Knight to port.

2158 As Maudslay's vic waited for the controller's 'green', Young's formation completed their circuit at 150 feet, reflecting his tendency to fly a little higher, and turned onto their course of 125 degrees for Southwold. A minute later their receding rumble was replaced by that of Maudslay getting airborne.

Harry Humphries watched each aircraft from the window of his office, then went outside to see them setting course after a circuit of the airfield. Chiefy Powell joined him: 'Grand night sir,' he said, 'I do hope they finish the job. They have worked so hard.'

2200 AJ-W Over the sea and aware of their late arrival at the coast, Munro's navigator took another reading from his API. The wind from the east had strengthened marginally and they were still behind schedule so Munro increased their speed by a further 5 mph.

2201 AJ-T By now all of the main force should have been away, but it was not until 2201 that McCarthy finally became airborne, 34 minutes later than scheduled.

2205 AJ-G Gibson's trio had cut across The Wash and were now approaching Snettisham, confirmed by a visual identification. Thirty-five miles behind them Young's vic was over Woodhall Spa. Three minutes later Maudslay's formation set course from Scampton along the same heading.

2210 Over The Wash, Maltby descended to 60 feet to test his spotlights and calibrate his barometric altimeter. Meanwhile, over the North Sea, Munro's and Rice's navigators checked their APIs – the former being 50 miles east of Mablethorpe with a south-easterly wind nudging them a little northward. Rice was on the same course, if slightly to the north, 13 miles behind.

2215 AJ-T As McCarthy approached the coast, Clay identified Sutton on Sea, one mile to the north. The flight engineer, Bill Radcliffe, a former engine mechanic, was normally conservative about throttle usage to maximise fuel economy, but tonight was an exception as they sought to make up their lost time.

2220 AJ-G Gibson led his formation across the flat expanse of East Anglia, passing Dereham to port. The opening of *Enemy Coast Ahead* provides an evocative recollection in his own words. It is a masterpiece of description:

> The moon was full; everywhere its pleasant, watery haze spread over the peaceful English countryside, rendering it colourless.

But there is not much colour in Lincolnshire, anyway. The city of Lincoln was silent – that city which so many bomber boys know so well, a city full of homely people. People who have got so used to the Air Force that they have begun almost to forget them. Lincoln with its great cathedral sticking up on a hill, a landmark for miles around. Little villages in the flat Fenland slept peacefully. Here nice simple folk live in their bastions on the East Anglian coast. The last farmer had long since gone to bed, the fire in the village pub had died down to an ember. The bar, which a few hours ago was full of noisy chattering people, was silent. There were no enemy aircraft about, and the scene was peaceful. In fact, this sort of scene might not have changed for a hundred years or so. But this night was different – at least different for 133 men: 133 young fliers, and I was one of those men. This was the big thing. This was it.

We were flying not very high, about one hundred feet, and not very far apart. I suppose to a layman it was a wonderful sight these great powerful Lancasters in formation, flown by boys who knew their job. Below us, and also practically beside us, at 200 miles an hour flashed past trees, fields, church spires and England.

We were off on a journey for which we had long waited, a journey that had been carefully planned, carefully trained for, a mission which was going to do a lot of good if it succeeded; and everything had been worked out so that it should succeed. We were off to the Dams.

Those who have seen a Lancaster cockpit in the light of the moon, flying just above the earth, will know what I mean when I say it is very hard to describe. The pilot sits on the left on a raised comfortably padded seat fitted with arm-rests. He usually flies the thing with his left hand, re-setting the gyro and other instruments with his right, but most pilots use both hands when over enemy territory or when the going is tough. You have to be quite strong to fly a Lancaster.

In front of him the instruments sit winking. On the Sperry panel, or the blind-flying panel as bomber pilots call it, now and then a red light, indicating that some mechanism needs adjusting, will suddenly flash on. The pilot of a bomber must know everything. He must know the duties of the rest of the crew inside out and should be able to take any one of them over should the occasion arise. The flight-engineer is the pilot's mate and sits beside him watching the engine instruments. Most flight-engineers are ground mechanics of Bomber Command who have volunteered to fly on operations, and a grand job of work they do too.

It is warm inside and both pilot and flight-engineer are very lightly clad, their oxygen masks hanging on one strap from the comer of the face. These masks are necessary evils. When over enemy territory they are worn continuously, not only because oxygen is required but because the pilot has no time to take his hand off the wheel and put the microphone up to his face. The result is that one gets quite chapped after six hours with the thing on. Many times the question is asked, 'Why can't we have throat microphones like the Americans?'

Between the two front windows is a large instrument, perhaps the most important of all, the repeating compass, worked by a master unit at the back. The pilot's eyes constantly perform a non-stop circle from the repeater to the A.S.I. [Air Speed Indicator], from the A.S.I. to the horizon, from the horizon to the moon, from the moon to what he can see on the ground and then back to the repeater. No wonder they are red-rimmed when he returns.

Such is the scene. The glass house. Soft moonlight. Two silent figures, young, unbearded, new to the world yet full of skill, full of pride in their squadron, determined to do a good job and bring the ship home. A silent scene, whose only incidental music is provided by the background hiss of air and the hearty roar of four Merlin engines.

In my Lancaster it was pretty warm even though Hutch had turned off the heat. I was in my shirt sleeves and my Mae West. Incidentally, my Mae West was a German one, pinched off some fellow shot down back in 1940, and the envy of the whole squadron. The windows were open and a jet of cool air was blowing in, making a tremendous screeching noise. I yelled to Pulford, the flight-engineer, at the top of my voice, 'Close that window for Christ's sake.'

Pulford, a Londoner, and a sincere and plodding type, was pushing and struggling and at last got the thing closed; like the silence at the end of a crash the noise snapped off and we were in comparative silence. Then I spoke to Terry. 'Where are we now, Nav.?'

'I think we are about a mile to port. I'll just check. What do you think, Spam?

Spam was the bomb-aimer and it was some time before he answered because he had been taking off his parachute harness and was now picking up his position from a roller map. It looked like a roll of lavatory paper. But no matter what it looked like it had to do a pretty important job; the job of that roll and Spam and Terry was to get us to the target. 'Yeah, you're right, Terry, we are a little over a mile to port; there's the railway going to King's Lynn.

Spam, the Australian, was the best bomb-aimer there is, but he was not too hot at map-reading, and Terry looked over my shoulder to check him up. Later he popped back into his cabin to make a quick calculation. Then I was told to alter course three degrees to starboard and by the slightest pressure on the rudder the great Lancaster almost imperceptibly pointed her grim blunt nose a little further south, and on either side the boys did the same.

Just after passing Wymondham, Taerum called out: 'Ten minutes to the coast. We will be able to get a pretty good check over there. We go slap over Yarmouth.' (Gibson states Yarmouth in his text, but the route in fact passed between Southwold and Yarmouth.)

Behind them, Young's formation pinpointed West Raynham, placing them a little north of Gibson's route, possibly allowing for the easterly wind which was now being detected.

2225 Meanwhile, some of the aircraft of the northern wave, which should have been heading due east over the North Sea, were beginning to detect a slight drift to port. Munro was now 100 miles from the Dutch island of Vlieland, still slightly south of the track being flown by Rice who had not detected the drift, despite dropping flame floats for the rear gunner to take drift sightings.

2225 AJ-T All was not going well for McCarthy, now 16 miles east of Mablethorpe. For the past quarter of an hour his wireless operator, Len Eaton had been trying to coax his TR 1154/55 W/T set into life. Without it they could not transmit to or receive messages from No. 5 Group Headquarters. McCarthy decided to continue without it, instructing Eaton not to log the unserviceability until later in the flight in order to avoid any suggestion on return that with such a problem at this early stage he should have turned back.

2230 AJ-G As Gibson's formation crossed the coast at 200 feet just north of Southwold a minor change of course was required to accommodate the north-easterly wind that was drifting them to starboard. After this the aircraft descended to 60 feet above the sea. In *Enemy Coast Ahead* Gibson maintains that he tried to engage the autopilot of G-George – although at such a low level this seems unlikely – only to find that it wasn't working.

The aircraft were still maintaining radio silence, but Martin nosed alongside Gibson, his wireless operator Len Chambers flashing a message in Morse. Hutchison read it and reported to Gibson: ' He says we are going to get damn drunk tomorrow night.' Gibson told Hutchison to respond in kind. In *Enemy Coast Ahead* Gibson adds that shortly afterwards they passed over a small convoy. Exchanging identification signals, Hutchison again flashed an enigmatic: 'We are going to get damn drunk tomorrow night.'

The navigators were well into their routine. Visual map-reading and dead-reckoning were now supplemented by Gee. In Maltby's aircraft Sgt Vivian Nicholson had just used his set to fix their position six miles south of Norwich, still flying on a course a mile or so north of that taken by Gibson.

2235 AJ-Z   Meanwhile the final vic of the southern wave, led by Maudslay, was just passing south of Dereham following the track flown by Young's formation ahead of them. Three and a half minutes later, Young, Maltby and Shannon crossed over the Suffolk coast north of Southwold pier. This final landfall was used to check and re-set the API ready for the sea crossing. Like Gibson's formation before them, they nudged 5 degrees to port to accommodate the wind.

2240 AJ-W   Some 52 miles west of Vlieland Munro was making good progress, with Byers three miles ahead. Despite his late departure, McCarthy was now over a third of the way across the North Sea, but several miles north of the planned route.

2245 AJ-W   Munro had now reached an intermediate waypoint 40 miles off Vlieland. Jock Rumbles, his navigator, called for a small change of course to port to take them to their entry point across the Frisian Islands. Since they were a little ahead of schedule, speed was reduced to 165 mph.

2250 AJ-G   Gibson's vic had completed two-thirds of the sea crossing and by now crews had tested their spotlights. At various stages they also dropped flame floats to check for drift.

> As England receded far behind our tails, Terry [Taerum] suddenly said: 'There's no wind tonight, Skip, so we shouldn't have any drift – but we'll just check, so I'll throw out a flame-float.' Then he yelled to Trev behind: 'Will you get a drift, Trev?'
>
> A little later Trev's voice was heard from the back. 'O.K. There's no drift, the flame-float is about ten miles behind; it's still straight behind my guns.'

Gibson was writing for a public audience and the final comment may be rather more literary licence than fact. Other aircraft were recording a drift to starboard of varying strength as they crossed the sea. At 2248 Knight's navigator, who preferred Gee fixes to the use of flame floats over the sea, calculated a 7 mph wind from the north and an entry by Martin's navigator three minutes later records a heading of 116 degrees to make good a track of 120 degrees, again indicating starboard drift.

Young's formation were now 24 miles south-east of Southwold, a little south of track and a quarter of the way across the sea. Twenty-one miles behind them dead on track 3 miles out from the coast the self-destruct pistol of Maudslay's 'Upkeep' had now been armed, as should have been the others, although some crews left this action until reaching the enemy coast.

Meanwhile Fighter Command Mosquitos were taking off to patrol the German night-fighter airfields at Deelen, Venlo, Eindhoven, Soesterberg, Schiphol and Gilze Rijen.

2255   Trailing the northern wave, McCarthy was continuing 5 miles north of the planned route and was 80 miles from Vlieland. AJ-H and W armed their self-destruct pistols as they approached the coast of the island. One minute ahead of them and with the element of surprise, Barlow was the first to run the gauntlet. He appears to have slipped past the island unscathed, but in doing so alerted the gun crews so that they were ready for the following aircraft.

Looking to starboard, Jim Clay, Munro's bomb aimer, saw an aircraft passing over Texel to the south of the briefed route, having possibly miscalculated drift or mistaken his turning point over the sea: 'The sun had set when we reached the enemy coast but there was a little gloomy moonlight. I thought I saw someone to starboard skim the water and send up a plume of spray – it could have been Geoff Rice or Barlow or Byers.' The post-Chastise report of 7 June 1943 was also uncertain as to the identity of this aircraft:

> E or K is thought to have been shot down from 300 feet off Texel by light flak at 22.57 hours. If this aircraft was one of the second Wave then; (i) it was flying higher than detailed (possibly to obtain a pinpoint on the coast) or (ii) it was either off track to the south of the leg from Base or had altered course from the D[ead]R[eckoning] position 5320N – 0454E too early so crossing the Texel area west of track.

It was Byers in AJ-K. He appears to have realised that he was off track and after assuming he was out of range climbed to 450 feet in order to establish his position. By doing so he made himself more visible to the defences which included naval flak units 1. and 3./Marine-Flakabteilung (Naval Anti-Aircraft Battalion) 201 and 3./808 MFA, equipped with 10.5-cm flak with a low-elevation range of about a mile. The aircraft was hit and plunged into the Waddenzee. Byers and his crew all perished. The only crew member recovered was rear gunner F/Sgt James McDowell whose body was washed up on 22 May and buried in Harlingen. The remainder of the crew are commemorated on the Air Forces Memorial at Runnymede. A memorial commemorating ED934 and its crew was also unveiled in Harlingen on 19 June 2022.

2256 AJ-W Within minutes Munro had correctly identified Vlieland and cut across the narrow centre of the island. He recalled: 'Having gained height to clear the dunes on reaching the coast, I was in the process of losing that height and had not reached the water when hit by a single 20 cm light flak round which entered the rear of the aircraft.'

Clay was certain that they had been hit by a flak ship, but the front gunner, Sgt Howarth, later maintained that it was a ground battery. Munro subsequently agreed, saying that there was only one line of tracer and that a flak ship would have had more guns. The flak came from the port bow hitting the aircraft on the port side with a single round which passed into the rear fuselage, where it destroyed the dead reckoning compass master unit, the VHF and intercom and damaged the hydraulic piping to the tail turret. Shouting above the engines, Munro instructed Warrant Officer Percy Pigeon, the wireless operator, to go back and see if the intercom could be repaired. Without intercom there was no possibility of crew coordination for their own attack

2259 A minute behind Munro, Geoff Rice in H-Harry reached Vlieland and turned south-east to cross the island. He was lucky and made the crossing unscathed despite also having to pull up to clear the land before dropping back down again and heading for their next turning point at Stavoren.

Back at Scampton, following the departure of the two main waves there was little for those on the ground to do but wait in anticipation.

Some had gone back to the Officers' Mess where Jeffree, Wallis's assistant, had been buying drinks for those whom Wallis had not had a chance to thank. After a normal main-force take off, Humphries too would have gone back to the mess, but tonight was different. He felt compelled to remain for a while around the offices with Powell and Jim Heveron, the orderly room sergeant. His stomach had an empty feeling of uncertainty and trepidation. Eventually he went back to the mess and found Section Officer Fay Gillon, a WAAF intelligence officer who possibly knew where the squadron were going, but if she did, she did not say. They both sat there drinking, acutely aware of the electric atmosphere they were experiencing.

Over in his billet, Freddie Tees had slept through the first two waves' take offs and when duly summoned by his alarm, dressed carefully in all the clothing he needed to stay warm and alert in his turret. Making his way to the crew locker room in good time, he donned his parachute harness and Mae West. He checked his parachute pack carefully before going out to the aircraft.

Cochrane and Wallis had already departed for No. 5 Group Headquarters at Grantham. There they would be in direct Morse contact with the aircraft, enabling Cochrane to build a picture of the attack's progress, vital for the later tactical deployment of the reserve wave. At this point he could have no indication that by the time he reached Grantham only one of the five aircraft detailed to attack the Sorpe would still be en route to this objective.

To continue with Gibson's account:

> We had been flying for about an hour and ten minutes in complete silence, each one busy with his thoughts, while the waves were slopping by a few feet below with monotonous regularity. And the moon dancing in those waves had become almost a hypnotising crystal. As Terry spoke, he jerked us into action. He said, 'Five minutes to go to the Dutch coast, Skip.' I said, 'Good,' and looked ahead. Pulford turned on the spotlights and told me to go down much lower; we were about 100 feet off the water. Jim Deering, in the front turret, began to swing it from either way [sic], ready to deal with any flak ships which might be watching for mine-layers off the coast. Hutch sat in his wireless cabin ready to send a flak warning to the rest of the boys who might run into trouble behind us. Trevor took off his Mae West and squeezed himself back into the rear turret. On either side the boys tucked their blunt-nose Lancs. in even closer than they were before, while the crews inside them were probably doing the same sort of things as my own. Someone began whistling nervously over the intercom.
>
> Someone else said, 'Shut up.' Then Spam said, 'There's the coast.'
>
> I said, 'No, it's not; that's just low cloud and shadows on the sea from the moon.'
>
> But he was right, and I was wrong, and soon we could see the Dutch islands approaching. They looked low and flat and evil in the full moon, squirting flak in many directions because their radar would now know we were coming. But we knew all about their defences, and as we drew near this squat and unfriendly expanse, we began to look for the necessary landmarks which would indicate

how to get through that barrage. We began to behave like a ship threading its way through a minefield, in danger of destruction on either side, but safe if we were lucky and on the right track. Terry came up beside me to check up on Spam. He opened the side windows and looked out to scan the coast with his night glasses. 'Can't see much,' he said. 'We're too low, but I reckon we must be on track because there's so little wind.'

Based on Taerum's reported comment, G-George would be fifteen miles inland, roughly half way between the last waypoint and the Dutch coast. Again, if Gibson's recollection is correct, the final observation was wide of the mark. By the time the formation was 7 miles from the Scheldt estuary a Gee fix at 2300 by Martin's navigator confirmed that they were three miles south of their planned route at this critical point in the flight. The route in had been devised to pass along the channel between Schouwen and North Beveland (Walcheren), but the northerly wind, stronger than anticipated, was taking them over the latter.

The aircraft of Young's formation were now approaching the intermediate waypoint at 51°52′N 03°00′E. At 2300 Sgt Nicholson, Maltby's navigator, obtained a fix placing them slightly south of their planned route, on a heading of 117 degrees and some 30 miles from the channel taking them south of Zierkzee. A minute later Maudslay's formation was 60 miles from the coast, but about 1½ miles north of the planned route, probably to allow for the wind that was driving them south.

Curiously the post-raid report claims that, at this point along the route, up to 03°00′E, the prevailing winds, recorded as being up to 10 mph, and ranging in direction from 360 degrees to 100 degrees (i.e. northerly to east by south) were 'nowhere near strong enough to cause any big navigational issues'.

According to the official post-raid analysis, Gibson, Hopgood and Martin reached the enemy coast at 2305. Contrary to Tempsford's recommendation to climb to check position and then dive to cross the enemy coast at speed outbound, Cochrane, Satterly and Gibson had decided it was better to reduce the risk of detection and keep low, at the expense of absolute accuracy.

Gibson described the moment:

'Stand by, front gunner; we're going over.'
    'O.K. All lights off. No talking. Here we go.'
    With a roar we hurtled over the Western Wall; for a moment we held our breath. Then I gave a sigh of relief; no one had fired a shot. We had taken them by surprise.

2306   But within two minutes they were back over water the wind having taken them over North Beveland instead of between the islands. Fortunately, with the element of surprise, the defences were caught unawares. Realising that they were off track Gibson climbed to 300 feet to check their position. He was fortunately able to identify a windmill and some radio masts. Diving back down, he eased the Lancaster's nose to port to bring them back nearer to track while Taerum calculated a revised course to take them north of Bergen op Zoom. Fortunately, while crossing the coast the aircraft had adopted a more open formation, making a less compact target, so there was little problem for Martin, flying to port and a little behind Gibson. There was minor concern as Gibson's Lancaster slid across his path, but the manoeuvre definitely made keeping station more difficult for Hopgood, to starboard and on the outside of the turn, and momentarily his aircraft fell a little behind. Two minutes ahead the Schelde Rijnkanaal crossed their path in an elongated 'S' running north to south providing a useful datum. Four miles further and their route passed some three miles south of the polder on the outskirts of Steenbergen where 19 months hence Gibson's life would come to an abrupt end.

Meanwhile the northern wave continued to experience trouble. Although Geoff Rice in H-Harry had experienced navigation issues across the North Sea, he had identified and crossed Vlieland successfully. Since Munro had been flying a holding orbit after being hit, rather than being a minute behind him, Rice was now ahead, flying almost directly towards the moon. He climbed a little to establish his position then began to descend again. Ahead lay the Afluidsdijk, the causeway barrier separating the Waddenzee from the IJsselmeer, its western end cutting across the reflected moonpath. Beautiful as the scene was it was also deceptive.

About three miles from the approaching barrier, Sgt Edward Smith, Rice's flight engineer, suddenly noticed that the altimeter was reading zero. He was about to call a warning when the aircraft struck the sea. As Rice instinctively pulled back on the column to pull the Lancaster off the water a second blow was felt. Water sprayed up through the floor and over the navigator's charts while more was scooped up by the rear end of the bomb bay, to pour out round the rear turret causing Sgt Stephen Burns the rear gunner to exclaim 'Christ, it's wet at the back!' Another crew member was heard to call, 'You've lost the mine.'

The first impact had torn the 'Upkeep' from the calliper arms, removing the starboard one in the process. The weapon had then struck the fixed tailwheel, forcing it upwards through the tailplane spar and wrecking the Elsan chemical toilet mounted ahead of it, its fluid contents adding to the discomfort of the rear gunner.

The self-destruct pistol of Rice's 'Upkeep' had been armed by the time the aircraft hit the sea and the weapon should therefore have self-destructed, even if there was insufficient depth of water to activate the hydrostatic pistols. As far as can be ascertained the weapon did not detonate, the pistol possibly suffering damage owing to the bomb being ripped from the aircraft, rather than released in the normal manner.

Rice's reflex reaction which saved the aircraft, had also given sufficient height for it and its otherwise preoccupied crew to clear the 25-foot-high barrier in their path. A rapid damage assessment was made. The aircraft was still flying and the controls did not seem unduly affected, but with the mine confirmed lost there was clearly no point in continuing.

2306 In AJ-W Percy Pigeon returned from his inspection of the damage and reported that it was irreparable. After circling for a while Munro took the only reasonable choice, to abort the operation, his decision communicated to the others by means of a scribbled note. Navigator Frank Rumbles logged: '2306: Hit by flak at 2256. Course 327 degrees. A/c to fly reciprocal. Intercom dead.' Selecting a direct reciprocal when they had recently been fired upon, had its risks, but given that the DR compass had been wrecked and Munro was now relying on his P4 compass in the cockpit it was the most prudent action.

After hitting the water, Rice also began by flying on a reciprocal after which the evidence is ambiguous. Some accounts state that he made an exit between Vlieland and Texel, and despite the defences of all the islands being alerted and searchlights sweeping to close the channel, the crew of AJ-H slipped through without further damage. However, Macfarlane's navigation log recorded a reciprocal return to the inbound turning point over the North Sea about 5 miles off the east coast of Vlieland before turning due west at 2316.

2310 On the southern route, in Maudslay's formation, Hobby Hobday, Les Knight's navigator, suspected that his API had stopped working. This was confirmed by a Gee fix which placed them 29 miles from the Scheldt estuary and about 3 miles north of their planned route, despite the northerly wind that had taken Gibson's formation south of their entry point.

2312 Two minutes later, and 28 miles ahead, Young's formation were approaching the turning point at the Scheldt. There they would make a gentle port turn onto a course of 98 degrees, allowing for the northerly wind to make a track of 105 degrees to Roosendaal.

2313 A minute later, McCarthy, the last of the northern wave, was approaching Vlieland. By now he had made up 13 of the 34 minutes lost by his delayed departure, flying at 200 mph rather than the briefed 180. The island's defences were alert after firing at Byers, Munro and Rice. As the Lancaster approached a searchlight lit up and two of MFA 246's guns opened up forcing McCarthy to take evasive action: 'Very hot reception from natives when we crossed the coastline. They knew the track we were coming in on, so their guns were pretty well trained when they heard my motors. But, thank God, there were two large sand dunes right on the coast which I sank in between.'

2315   Once past the island McCarthy headed south-east across the Waddenzee, taking a slightly more easterly track than Rice. At this point a further threat materialised. The approaching Lancasters were too low for radar detection, but once they had been spotted visually the alarm was raised and the Luftwaffe night-fighter base at Leeuwaarden, 32 miles to the east, scrambled Messerschmitt 110s of IV./NJG 1 to investigate. They were seemingly unaware of the low-level nature of the attackers' route, however. McCarthy noted that he could clearly see the fighters 'floating along at a thousand feet above us' as they headed for their designated patrol area over the Den Helder peninsula.

Munro and Rice had made good their escape and were now over the North Sea. Like McCarthy, by flying at 100 feet, they remained undetected by ground radar which might have vectored the fighters onto a lone Lancaster. Although the fighters' radar would also have been ineffective at such low altitude due to ground returns, they could have been able to detect the aircraft in the clear moonlight had ground radar been able to direct them within visual range. For them it would be a fruitless patrol.

As he tracked south to Stavoren McCarthy observed two fires burning on the ground, one to starboard and the other ahead. He mused about their origins, surmising that they did not appear to be burning aircraft and that they were most likely farm fires.

2315 approx.   Gibson and Martin were at the end of the 36-mile leg approaching Roosendaal, by which time Hopgood had probably regained his position in the formation. They were looking for a Y-shaped railway junction, at which point course was again to be altered slightly to port, from 105 to 95 degrees, setting them up for the critical long leg between the two major night-fighter airfields of Gilze Rijen and Eindhoven.

2321   Nine minutes behind Young, and one minute ahead of their planned time, it was now Maudslay's turn to run the gauntlet as they crossed the coast at the Scheldt. Once again all went well and despite being the third formation to pass the batteries of MFA 810 they appear to have encountered no enemy opposition.

2325 Gibson's formation was now 40 miles east of Roosendaal, approaching the north-west of Eindhoven, having slipped past Gilze Rijen six minutes earlier. At this point, over to starboard, the Wilhelmina Kanaal was joined by the Beatrix Kanaal, while ahead the Boxtel to Eindhoven railway line ran north-west to south-east across their path crossing over the Wilhelmina Kanaal. A mile and a half further the planned route followed the canal. These made ideal pinpoints, with the canal becoming a visual marker leading straight to their next turning point at Beek.

At the same time, Young, Maltby and Shannon reached their turning point at Roosendaal. Here, Maltby's navigator Nicholson noted 'Leader turns too soon.'

Surprisingly, since Young was senior flight commander and formation leader, his navigator, F/Sgt Charles Roberts appears to have had little operational experience, having only flown two sorties, both while at his conversion unit. Possibly for this reason, Young had a tendency to fly at 300–500 feet rather than the specified 100 feet. This made identification of navigational landmarks much easier and at a greater distance but caused much consternation to Shannon and Maltby. Seeing the approaching junction soon Young may well have instigated the turn too early. This might have been a costly error. The first 24 miles of the next leg would take them south of the defences of Breda and Tilburg and also the Luftwaffe airfield at Gilze Rijen to port, skirting these by only about three miles. An early turn would begin a course closer to these concentrations.

Maudslay's formation was now crossing over to the mainland near the small harbour of Stavenisse and appears to have closed the gap slightly with Young's formation.

Over the Dutch mainland visibility was excellent with a nearly full moon low above the horizon forty-five degrees off to starboard, illuminating roads, rail lines, buildings and canals, making map-reading easy. In Young's formation, Len Sumpter, David Shannon's bomb aimer, monitored the route using folded charts on which power lines were highlighted in red, whereas Edward Johnson, in the nose of N-Nuts of Maudslay's vic, preferred the convenience of his home-made roller map, backed up by Hobday's Gee fixes, which would continue to beyond the Rhine.

2326 McCarthy pinpointed the lighthouse at Stavoren and adjusted his course, heading for the southern shore of the IJsselmeer. In trying to obtain a position fix MacLean discovered that the Gee set was no longer operating – though it is not known if this was due to jamming or whether 'Duke' Munro's improvised repair had only given temporary respite. To add to his concerns, knowing that night fighters were in the vicinity, an electrical fault suddenly caused a cockpit light to come on, which could not be extinguished until Bill Radcliffe destroyed it with a blow from the emergency axe.

Ahead of him, Barlow, the other remaining member of the northern wave, who should have reached this position some 12 minutes earlier, was now approaching the next pinpoint at Harderwijk.

2328   Passing north of Eindhoven, Gibson's formation watched the Wilhelmina Kanaal slide in from underneath their starboard wing, their paths converging until they were running directly along it, approaching the distinctive T-shaped canal junction at Beek. Today the junction is less rural and has an extra arm added on the far side, but in 1943 the Wilhelmina Kanaal came to an abrupt end as the Zuid-Wilhelmsvaart Kanaal cut across. A gentle turn to port brought them to a course of 63 degrees to take them to the Rhine.

2330   Light flak and machine guns defending the vicinity of Gilze Rijen airfield, along with heavy flak from Klein Tilburg and Nerhoven are reported by Dutch witnesses to have opened fire on a British aircraft flying very low. Two or three searchlights were also visible. It is possible that this could have been Young or one of his formation who may have been in the locality at this time, possibly as a result of the early turn.

Back at Scampton, preparations were in progress for the despatch of the final wave. The five remaining crews, of Ottley, Burpee, Brown, Townsend and Anderson, boarded their aircraft. Settling into his position in AJ-Y, Sgt Bickle, Anderson's wireless operator, made the initial entry in his log: 'On Watch' and spent the next ten minutes checking his equipment.

2330   Air-raid sirens, possibly in response to the Mosquitos making attacks on Düsseldorf and Cologne, were sounded to warn the people of the eastern Ruhr of enemy air activity. Some of the inhabitants of the villages of Gunne, Niederense and Himmelpforten and the town of Neheim Husten in the valley below the Möhne dam took to their shelters while others preferred to monitor the situation. Well-used to such alerts, they realised that most of these heralded attacks on the major industrial conurbations in the region rather than their immediate locality.

Fifty miles away, the inhabitants of the village of Hemfurth, a mile downstream from the Eder dam, were leaving a civil defence meeting. During this the question of the vulnerability of the dam was again raised. That morning the water level indicator on the dam had shown the reservoir to be at maximum capacity, 200.20 million cubic metres and the reservoir was only 4 cm from its overflow limit. Those attending were assured by the senior officials from Korbach, the regional centre eleven miles away, that the dam's location in a steep-sided valley would render any attack unsuccessful, if not quite impossible.

2331 AJ-G The ground rose slightly from Beek for the next 9 miles, falling gradually away again into the Meuse valley. In Gibson's formation during the descent after a slight rise, F/Lt Bob Hay, Mick Martin's bomb aimer, picked up the glint of the moon on the rail line running from Boxmeer to Oostum. Beyond it a further reflection indicated the snake of the river, two miles beyond.

Twenty miles from the coast McCarthy's 'Upkeep' was armed in readiness for their arrival over land at Harderwijk. (New land has been reclaimed since 1943 and this position is now 5 miles north of Lelystad.) With the wind now coming from the port beam McCarthy was travelling at some 30 mph faster than the briefed speed and making good his lost time. By the time he reached Harderwijk at about 2336 he was only six minutes behind schedule.

2334 AJ-Z Maudslay's formation identified the rail junction at Roosendaal and set course for Beek. The third formation to follow this route, they had no knowledge that the defences of Gilze Rijen had already been in action. Despite this their navigation appears to have been accurate and their route took them far enough south of the defences not to cause any problem.

2335 AJ-A Continuing almost due east, ten minutes after Roosendaal and south-east of Tilburg, Young's formation picked up the Wilhelmina Kanaal, crossing their path north-west to south-east.

2342 AJ-J The formation had reached the canal junction at Beek. Maltby's navigator, Sgt Nicholson, could no longer rely on Gee for fixes, recording 'Gee jammed something chronic' in his log. From now on navigation would be reliant on map reading, dead reckoning and the API.

2344 AJ-W On his homeward track, after being hit by flak over Vlieland, Munro was now approximately halfway across the North Sea, 89 miles from Mablethorpe.

2349 AJ-T McCarthy reached the Het Zwarte Schaar, the distinctive ox-bow bend in the River IJssel at Doesburg and nosed ED825 to starboard, heading for the point on the Rhine at Rees where the northern route linked up with that from the south to head east round the north of the Ruhr defences.

This is the point at which the route had been changed at briefing to take the aircraft further north of the Ruhr defences. From the point at which the north and south routes met at a bend in the Rhine one mile south-west of Rees the route had originally turned east south-east to Ahsen. Following Hopgood's intervention at briefing, the aircraft continued north-east from Rees before turning east just south of Borken towards Dülmen.

Barlow, the first to leave Scampton, had been scheduled to reach Doesburg two hours after take off, but subsequent timings suggest that he arrived there at about 2342, some 16 minutes behind schedule. The reason for this is unknown, possibly due to stronger winds en route, though some sources suggest that he may have been damaged by flak over Vlieland or during his run down from the IJsselmeer. On this basis he would have reached Rees at 2349 where he should have turned onto a heading of 84 degrees to take him to the revised waypoint of the lakes at Dülmen.

2350 The residents of the small commune of Haldern-Herken, three miles north-northeast of Rees, heard the sound of an approaching low-flying aircraft. Local resident Johanna Effing recounts:

> There was a loud bang. Thereupon we left the house basement in Haldern-Herken and saw that the field in front of us was ablaze. A plane flying from a westerly direction had struck the top of a pylon carrying a 100,000 volt line and crashed into the field. A large bomb had rolled fifty metres away from the wreckage and the crash site.

Barlow's Lancaster had been snared by a major hazard to low-flying aircraft, a high voltage line. At night it was almost impossible to see the cables. At best the pylons might be spotted, but then a split-second decision had to be made. Apply power and pull up to go over them, but risk 'mushing' into them – the aircraft in climbing attitude but still flying horizontally – or push the nose down and hope that there was enough clearance between the ground and the sag of the cable to pass through safely. Many bomb aimers had highlighted the paths of known power lines crossing the route but here another factor may come into play. German evidence confirms that the Lancaster was approaching from the west but Haldern-Herken is not on either the planned or amended route. To overfly it Barlow would have had to divert eastwards early from the Doesburg–Rees leg onto a course taking him direct to the lakes at Dülmen, or Ahlen, in which case he would have met the line obliquely, or significantly miscalculate his turn at Rees, making a track of 30 rather than 84 degrees, which would have taken him to the power line at a near right-angle. The former might be explained by an attempt to make up some lost time, the latter, though less likely, by a navigational problem.

The Lancaster took the top off one pylon and damaged a second, before coming down in a field, killing all on board as it erupted in flames. Despite the risk from exploding ammunition the locals emerged and gathered round. Amongst them was the mayor of nearby Haldern, Herr Lehmann. Inspecting the wreckage he climbed onto what he took to be a large cylindrical fuel tank embedded nearly two feet into the ground, and self-importantly announced: 'I'll notify the Chief Administrative Officer that he needn't send any more petrol coupons for the rest of the war; we've got enough fuel in this tank.'

Within half an hour members of the local Hitler Youth fire service arrived, with a Luftwaffe representative. Recognising that the 'fuel tank' was a large bomb they evacuated people to a safe distance; on receiving this news Herr Lehmann is reported to have 'felt quite sick'. As the embers died down and daylight broke officials searched for the remains of the crew. Amongst the finds were personal items including wallets, gold rings, watches and a torch on which the owner had scratched what was believed to be a tally of 32 operations. There were no survivors. All seven of the crew were originally buried in the Nord Friedhof, Düsseldorf, before being re-interred in the newly created Reichswald Forest War Cemetery, near Kleve, in October 1946.

In theory the weapon should have been detonated by the self-destruct fuze embodied for exactly this sort of eventuality. Whether or not the fuze had been armed on crossing the coast, as briefed, or whether the pistol was damaged or jammed by the impact is unknown. Nevertheless, the Germans had just been presented with an intact example of one of the Allies' most secret weapons. They were quick to analyse it. A team from *Sprengkommando* (bomb disposal team) 1./IV Ratingen-Düsseldorf, including a number of political prisoners co-opted as a labour force, arrived under the command of Hauptmann Heinz Schweitzer and residents were told to open their windows while the weapon was rendered safe. Removal of the end plate revealed the explosive filling, which was then extracted and burned off in the open. Once safe, 'Upkeep' was loaded onto a lorry and taken to a Luftwaffe establishment at Kalkum, north Düsseldorf. There it was viewed by Reichsminister Albert Speer (who was also General Inspector for Water and Energy) and further dissected, and reconstruction of the suspension and release gear attempted so far as it could be ascertained from the charred wreckage. By 26 May a set of drawings had been made by engineer Siegfried Werner. These are now the most complete set to survive of 'Upkeep', since extant Vickers drawings relate only to components and details.

While there is no indication that Barlow's impact with the power line was witnessed by any other aircraft, a fire on the ground as seen by McCarthy, was also noted in this area by Knight's gunner Harry O'Brien and may have been Barlow's burning wreckage.

Gibson's formation continued its north-easterly course across the eastern Netherlands towards the Rhine. He recalled:

> We flew on. Germany seemed dead. Not a sign of movement, of light or a moving creature stirred the ground. There was no flak, there was nothing. Just us.
>
> And so we came to the Rhine. This is virtually the entrance to the Ruhr Valley; the barrier our armies must cross before they march into the big towns of Essen and Dortmund. It looked white and calm and sinister in the moonlight. But it presented no difficulties to us. As it came up, Spam said,
>
> 'We are six miles south. Better turn right [*sic* – Gibson meant to write 'left'], Skip. Duisburg is not far away.'
>
> As soon as he mentioned Duisburg my hands acted before my brain, for they were more used to this sort of thing, and the Lanc. banked steeply to follow the Rhine up to our crossing point. For Duisburg is not a healthy place to fly over at 100 feet. There are hundreds of guns there, both light and heavy, apart from all those searchlights, and the defences have had plenty of experience . . .
>
> As we flew up: 'How did that happen?'
>
> 'Don't know, Skip. Compass u/s?'
>
> 'Couldn't be.'
>
> 'Hold on, I will just check my figures.'
>
> Later: 'I'm afraid I mis-read my writing, Skip. The course I gave you should have been another ten degrees to port.'
>
> 'O.K., Terry. That might have been an expensive mistake.'
>
> During our steep turn the boys had lost contact, but now they were just beginning to form up again; it was my fault the turn had been too steep, but the name Duisburg or Essen, or any of the rest of them, always does that to me. As we flew along the Rhine there were barges on the river equipped with quick-firing guns and they shot at us as we flew over, but our gunners gave back as good as they got; then we found what we wanted, a sort of small inland harbour, and we turned slowly towards the east. Terry said monotonously, 'Thirty minutes to go and we are there.'

A course ten degrees to starboard of that required from Beek would have resulted in arrival at the Rhine in the Xanten–Wesel area, some eight miles south-southeast of Rees, although 19 miles from Duisburg. The Rhine here has a similar configuration to that at Rees which may have given rise to confusion. Their route would have been of similar duration and crossed railways and towns similar to the planned route, so such an error may have gone unnoticed. Had they reached Xanten a steep turn to port onto a heading of some 350 degrees would have been required backtracking them to Rees. Yet against this is the fact that the three aircraft were maintaining formation, each guided by its own navigator, and also that Martin's navigator, F/Lt Jack Leggo, was the squadron navigation officer. Gibson's departure from the route should have been apparent as the other two aircraft started to edge away from his track, so Gibson's recollection may have some degree of embellishment.

The Dam Busters records that: 'just short of the river [Rhine] some twelve light flak guns opened up without warning; the aircraft gunners squirted back at the roots of the tracer,' but this may have been confusion on the part of Brickhill with other flak encountered later by 'Chastise' aircraft north of the Ruhr, although German records do indicate light flak activity a mile or so north-west of Wesel on this night.

2356 Young's formation appears to have reduced the gap with Gibson's formation as they reached the Rhine, which again may be accounted for by Gibson's possible navigation error. This point at Rees was the start of the adjustment made to take the route northward to avoid the flak near Huls and they turned onto a track of 73 degrees, heading for the lakes at Dülmen. A minute later, at 2357, McCarthy too arrived at Rees and turned to follow them.

Meanwhile, Munro and Rice continued their return to Scampton – the former now being 55 miles east, and Rice further out at 91 miles east-northeast of Mablethorpe.

Midnight Cochrane and Wallis arrived at No. 5 Group Headquarters after their drive from Scampton and entered the underground operations room to be met by Satterly. Wally Dunn was there, seated on the platform running along the length of one side, along with other members of the duty staff. Opposite him was a blackboard containing the details of aircraft operating that night with a large map of Europe dominating the end wall, marked with the routes being taken by the 'Chastise' force. There was the usual air of quiet efficiency, though the presence of so many senior officers and Dunn's direct contact with the aircraft by W/T indicated that this was no normal night's activity. With the entrance of Cochrane and Wallis the tension seemed to mount as they waited for information. While the others conducted conversations in hushed tones, an increasingly tense Wallis began to pace up and down.

Likewise at Scampton, a similar waiting game was being played, though with a lesser number in the know. Summers and Jeffree had retired to the mess where the bar was again opened. Meanwhile, out on the grass verge outside No. 2 Hangar overlooked by Gibson's office, F/Sgt Powell carried out the burial of the squadron commander's dog, which he and Corporal John Bryden had brought from the main gate guardroom, its body wrapped in a parachute. There has been much debate about the position of the grave and indeed even as to whether the dog was buried there. It seems inconceivable that Powell would not have carried out Gibson's request, and over the subsequent 80 years the grave marker has been replaced at least four times (most recently in 2021) making the exact location difficult to confirm.

Over Germany more opposition was being encountered. At midnight, four minutes after crossing the Rhine, Young's formation was transiting south of Bochum-Borken when Maltby's navigator recorded 'Flak fired at aircraft. Evasive action taken.'

0004 AJ-G Gibson, Hopgood and Martin had crossed the Coesfeld–Dorsten rail line and were now approaching the lakes at Dülmen. Some 27 miles behind them Maltby pinpointed the railway 'between the Rhine and the lakes at Dülmen', presumably that between Borken and Dorsten, running north–south near Dingden. Knight recorded reaching Rees one minute ahead of schedule. There, Maudslay's formation turned onto a course of 85 degrees to follow Young's vic towards Dülmen, taking them into the area north of the Ruhr highlighted by Hopgood at briefing.

McCarthy's aircraft had slotted in between Young's and Maudslay's formations. From now on he would play a lone game of hide and seek with the defences.

0004½ Gibson's formation reached the lakes south-west of Dülmen and adjusted course slightly towards the next waypoint at Ahlen. Various elements of the attacking force appear to have run into isolated pockets of defence between the Rhine and this location, but to little serious effect. Now, at the Dülmen lakes, Gibson's formation encountered significant and unexpected opposition from an intense concentration of both searchlights and flak.

Gibson and Martin reacted immediately as their gunners returned fire. The Lancaster was reasonably manoeuvrable for its size though considerable practice was required to take violent evasion at ground level. The controls were positive and moderately heavy under normal cruising conditions, though aileron control lagged when evasive manoeuvres were attempted, especially with a fully loaded aircraft.

Understandably accounts of this encounter are varied – in *Enemy Coast Ahead*, Gibson maintained that they had flown over 'a brand new aerodrome which was heavily defended and which had not been marked on our combat charts', although such an aerodrome cannot be identified. Tony Burcher, flying as rear gunner in Hopgood's aircraft, gave several accounts, both oral and written, in which he described events from his perspective. These differ in points of detail, and it has to be borne in mind that, aside from his own immediate personal experience, information about what was happening to the rest of the crew was restricted to intercom communication and what he could determine from his restricted vision at the tail of the aircraft.

Intense light flak opened up as the three aircraft were suddenly illuminated and held by a number of searchlights. The gunners returned fire, in an attempt to douse the lights. The bulb on Burcher's reflector sight blew, although dazzle from the beams made sighting almost impossible. Some of the lights were extinguished but not before M-Mother had been hit a number of times. Burcher smelled the cordite and then felt the pain as shell splinters injured him in the groin and stomach. The aircraft jolted and swung violently as the flak struck home. Over the intercom he heard Sgt Brennan, the flight engineer, report that a port engine was on fire, and Hopgood's instruction to shut it down and feather the propeller. Confirmation that this action had been taken came with the loss of hydraulic power to his turret, which from now on could only be operated by hand cranking, a cumbersome and laborious exercise. In another account, to the Australian War Memorial in 1993, Burcher said that the issue was a glycol leak and denied that the prop was feathered, though the engine had lost a lot of power.

When the aircraft was clear of the area Hopgood called each member of the crew to assess the damage sustained. Burcher reported his injuries, Sgt Minchin, the wireless operator, reported that he had been hit in the leg (though in another account Burcher states that this injury may have been sustained during the bombing run). There was no reply from Gregory in the front turret, leading Burcher to assume that he was either dead or mortally wounded. Conversation from the cockpit also indicated that Hopgood had been injured, suffering a head wound which was bleeding profusely. Hopgood told Brennan to hold a handkerchief against it.

Gibson and Martin escaped without damage. Ironically this encounter would have been avoided had the route not been moved north following Hopgood's concern about the flak at Huls. The original route from one mile east of Rees to Ahsen on the Wesel–Datteln Canal, and then to Ahlen, would have taken the aircraft south around the Dülmen flak, although there is no guarantee that they would have not encountered other flak positions.

0007 AJ-G   Hutchison transmitted a warning of the Dülmen flak to No. 5 Group Headquarters by W/T, giving its location as 51°48′N 07°12′E. However, it would not be re-broadcast to the remainder of the force for another four minutes.

0009 AJ-A   Because of this delay it appears that Young's formation also ran into the flak at Dülmen. Sgt Nicholson, Maltby's navigator, recorded: 'Position G (Lakes) . . . turning point identified OK . . . Evasive action taken.' By this stage it appears that Young's formation had closed a little on the leader, possibly having taken a slightly different course from the Rhine, the gap between the two leading formations now being only 5 minutes. At the same time, in the third wave, Knight's navigator recorded their position just south-east of Rhede and instructed his captain to turn towards Dülmen.

0009 AJ-C   Scampton: As the leading aircraft threaded their way through the northern Ruhr defences, back at Scampton the crews of the reserve wave had boarded their aircraft . First away was AJ-C, piloted by P/O Warner 'Bill' Ottley.

At the appointed hour Ottley started engines and completed the pre-flight checks. All was well and soon C-Charlie was taxying out to the take-off point. When they arrived there, Freddie Tees could see the silhouettes of the other reserve aircraft, engines rumbling as they waited their turn. The runway controller flashed his green Aldis signal from the control cabin, giving permission to take off and bidding them farewell. There were no spectators to watch the reserve take off. The night had turned chilly with a hint of air frost. Cochrane, Satterly and Wallis were monitoring progress from Grantham and station personnel not on duty were all abed. Some of the lighter sleepers may have stirred at the sound of the straining engines. Otherwise, for Freddie, it was yet another operational take-off. Who knew what awaited them once they had crossed the enemy coast?

0010 AJ-T   McCarthy reached his next waypoint – described as a 'lake' 36 miles from Rees. This would equate to the lakes at Dülmen, where Gibson's formation had run into heavy opposition. The warning of this opposition had not yet been re-broadcast. Had McCarthy been flying the same route as Gibson it would seem reasonable that he too would have encountered these defences, but he does not appear to have done so, suggesting that he may have taken a slightly more southerly route and that the lake was that at Haltern, 3 miles south of the Dülmen flak.

0011   P/O Lewis Burpee in AJ-S was next to set out.

Thirty miles away, at No. 5 Group, Wally Dunn re-broadcast Gibson's warning of flak at Dülmen to all aircraft, on full power. Cochrane, Satterly and Wallis would shortly be joined by Harris, who had been driven up from his headquarters at High Wycombe. Entering the Operations Room, he enquired as to any news of the force. Cochrane replied, saying that other than Gibson's flak warning nothing had been heard – but that the attack on the Möhne dam was scheduled to begin very shortly. Meanwhile Wallis had ceased his pacing and was now sitting on the steps leading up to Dunn's platform as the tension mounted.

0012   At Scampton, AJ-F was next away. Prior to take off its Canadian captain, F/Sgt Ken Brown, had smoked his customary two cigarettes before boarding, replacement gunner Daniel Allatson taking his position in the front turret.

A short while before, while Brown had been waiting for the crew bus to take them to dispersal, fellow Canadian Lewis Burpee had wandered across to him, holding out his hand and said pointedly, 'Goodbye, Ken,' to which Brown replied in the same vein. Later Brown recalled 'I didn't expect he'd come back. Some people felt that way.'

0014   F/Sgt Bill Townsend followed two minutes later in AJ-O. The Lancaster accelerated sluggishly across Scampton's rough grass surface. With little wind the runway seemed far too short as Townsend hauled the heavily laden aircraft over the boundary hedge with inches to spare. F/Sgt Cyril Anderson, in AJ-Y was the fifth of the reserve wave and last of the 19 aircraft away at 0015. Silence descended over the airfield.

Each of the reserve wave would fly the southern route taken two and a half hours earlier by Gibson and the eight other leading aircraft.

0015   Gibson's formation were approaching Ahlen, where their turning point was marked by a large colliery spoil tip, the Osthalder. At 514 feet above sea level it stood out sharply, rising 288 feet above the flat surrounding countryside, its rounded twin peaks providing a distinctive landmark. The route took them about a mile to the north of it, with the Ahlen marshalling yards to port, and then swung south-east to the Möhne.

Young's formation was now past the defended area which had damaged Hopgood, and Maudslay's trio were still heading towards this potential hot spot. The latter may have been following a course slightly to the north of that taken by Young's formation. Maudslay, Knight and Astell were now strung farther apart. A slight change of speed by Knight may not have been reciprocated by Maudslay, and Astell appears to have been uncertain of a pinpoint, either at the Rhine or a little further on. He hesitated to turn at a waypoint and fell behind. The three aircraft were now in effect separated and proceeding in line as individuals.

Two miles west of the settlement of Marbeck, between Borken and Raesfeld, Maudslay was leading, followed by Knight while Astell trailed about a mile behind. Looking back from the astrodome of AJ-N, Knight's wireless operator Bob Kellow, saw what he interpreted to be two lines of tracer intersecting on a Lancaster which burst into flames before crashing into the ground with a tremendous explosion. It was assumed that he had witnessed Astell being shot down by light flak, and the subsequent post-Chastise report of 7 June recorded:

> Aircraft 'B' is thought to have been shot down 8 miles north-west of Dorsten at 00.15 hours by light flak. This aircraft was observed by 'N' and reported dead astern when shot down. This suggests that both aircraft were flying along the same track and that 'N' gave to the ground defences a warning of hostile aircraft soon enough for them to intercept 'B'.

This was not the case. Like Barlow twenty-five minutes earlier, Astell had collided with a power line.

The crash occurred near a farm belonging to a Herr Tucking who had been woken by the sound of aircraft. With the Battle of the Ruhr having commenced in March 1943, this was not unusual, but these sounds were different, approaching at low height and passing seemingly only feet over his farmhouse roof. Having run downstairs in his nightclothes, Herr Tucking went outside in time to witness the third aircraft, Astell's, strike the top of an electricity pylon 200 yards away with a large bang, carrying away the top section of the structure and the cables. There was a gigantic flash and the Lancaster immediately caught fire. It passed over Herr Tucking's house and that of his neighbour, Herr Thesing, to crash in a field just beyond a crossroads, where it exploded. Out of the flames came a rolling ball of fire, the burning 'Upkeep', which travelled some 150 yards further, detonating with tremendous force some ninety seconds later. The explosion created a large crater and broke windows and stripped the roofs of three neighbouring buildings.

It was half an hour before onlookers could approach the burning wreckage, and then only with care due to exploding ammunition, but there was nothing that could be done for the crew. By 0400 the local police had received a detailed report of the crash The crew's bodies were recovered from the wreckage and taken to Borken where they were subsequently interred in the City Cemetery. Their bodies were exhumed in February 1947 and concentrated along with other British and Commonwealth war dead in Reichswald Forest War Cemetery.

There is an intriguing post-script to the loss of AJ-B. Sensing Barnes Wallis's anxiety during a particularly difficult period of the development of 'Upkeep' one of his colleagues sent him, for support, a copy of a prayer to

St Joseph, the patron saint of craftsmen and engineers. Adjacent to the crash site stood a roadside shrine, also dedicated to St Joseph. Despite its proximity, and the surrounding devastation, the shrine and the statue of its saint were quite undamaged.

Although there is no doubt now that Astell came down at Marbeck, earlier documents offer conflicting accounts of these events. The No. 617 Squadron Operations Record Book suggests erroneously that Astell, rather than Maudslay, was leading the formation at this time and 'appeared uncertain of his whereabouts, and on reaching a canal crossing actually crossed at the correct place, turned south down the canal as though searching for a pinpoint. He fell about half a mile behind his accompanying aircraft doing this and got slightly off track.' The use of the term 'canal' and 'turned south' would place the break-up of the formation back at the junction at Beek, unless 'canal' refers erroneously to the Rhine. It also raises the question as to whether the other two had become separated from Maudslay at an earlier stage. Other records suggest that Astell was shot down over an airfield, although no airfield existed in this area. At least one post-war account appears to have confused the loss of Astell with the later loss of P/O Lewis Burpee who crashed on the perimeter of Gilze Rijen airfield.

0016 AJ-W   A minute after the fate of Astell and his crew had been decided, Operation 'Chastise' was coming to a close, but in a less violent manner, for F/Lt Munro now crossing the coast inbound over Mablethorpe on his enforced return to Scampton. As he did so, Sgt John Nugent, navigator aboard F/Sgt Anderson's Y-Yorker, departing that airfield, recorded 'Airborne' in his log before giving his captain the course to steer for Southwold.

0019   Maudslay and Knight successfully skirted the flak position at Dülmen lake and set course for Ahlen. Thirty miles ahead of them, Young, Shannon and Maltby had reached this turning point, which took them safely beyond the heavily defended marshalling yards of Hamm, and swung south-east onto a course taking them between Soest and Werl, direct to the centre of the northern arm of the Möhne lake.

Gibson's formation had already completed this turn, passing west of Soest, easily identified by its four distinctive church spires. They continued on their south-easterly heading to crest the Haarstrang, the ridge immediately to the north of the Möhne lake. As they did so they passed close to the 54-foot-high Bismarckturm (Bismarck Tower), the last of many constructed to commemorate the German Chancellor. Located on the crest, this provided excellent views to the north across to Soest and Werl and to the south over the Möhne lake. It was now in use as an observation post for the Luftwaffe.

Lookouts on duty there spotted the approaching Lancasters and raised the alarm as they began circling the upper reaches of the lake. On board AJ-G, Hutchison would have already started the motor to spin 'Upkeep' to the required 500 rpm.

On the dam, the gunners of 3. Batterie, Flak Regiment 840, commanded by Lt Jorg Widmann, had been alerted by a call from their headquarters at Schloss Schwansbell near Lünen and were busy preparing their weapons. Each 20-mm Flak 38 had a crew of six commanded by an *Unteroffizier*.

Chapter 8

Attack

On arriving at the Möhne lake Gibson turned to starboard to reconnoitre the dam, remaining out of range of the known flak positions and also ensuring that he gave no clue to the line of attack. The sound of the engines echoing off the hills gave the flak little indication of the location of the aircraft, and the gunners began firing a '*Sperrefeuer*' – a barrage on pre-arranged bearings designed to deter any would-be attacker. The reflection of their red and green tracer from the surface of the lake gave the impression of more intense defences.

0020 AJ-T McCarthy reached the Osthalder at Ahlen and set course for the Möhne. F/Sgt Len Eaton, was fixing the TR 9 set beneath MacLean's navigation table. With his TR 1154/55 W/T set out of action, it was McCarthy's only means of communication with the ground – but then only at limited range.

In the 6,000-kW power house below the Möhne dam Ferdinand Nolle, a special constable based in Gunne, was assisting the duty engineer Clemens Kohler with his record-keeping. As the flak guns on the dam began firing Nolle made his way up to the dam intending to meet his relief Wilhelm Strotkamp, who was late, having been watching the circling aircraft. Nolle warned his colleague not to venture into the dam's inspection galleries, then the two men went on to the roadway to watch before going into the duty room at the northern end of the dam.

0021 AJ-N & AJ-Z Knight and Maudslay reached a curve in the Dortmund–Ems Canal two miles north of Ludinghausen, having just crossed the Dülmen–Ludinghausen railway line. They were now seven minutes from their next turning point at Ahlen. Three minutes later Knight made a minor course correction to maintain track to this point.

Shortly after this Gibson called to check on the nine aircraft of his force. All responded except Astell.

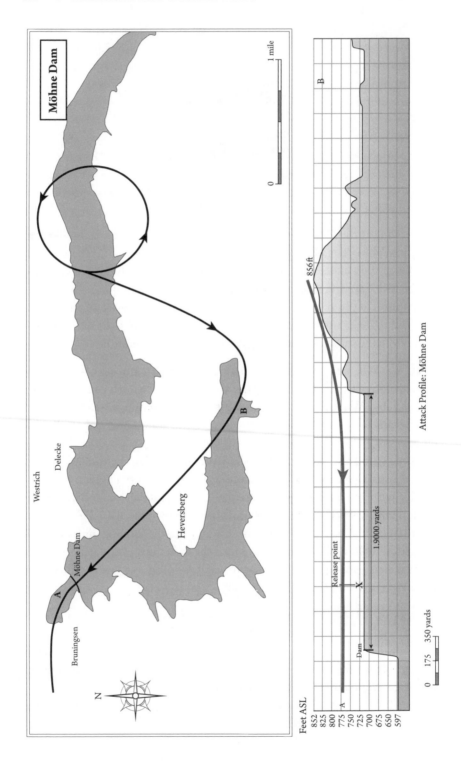

Möhne Dam

Westrich

Delecke

Heversberg

Bruningsen

Möhne Dam

A

B

N

0   1 mile

Feet ASL

852
825
800
775
750
725
700
675
650
597

A

Release point

X

1.9000 yards

Dam

856ft

B

Attack Profile: Möhne Dam

0   175   350 yards

0025 approx. Gibson called the other aircraft informing them that he was going in to attack and instructing Hopgood to be ready to take over if anything happened. Hopgood responded with 'OK Leader. Good luck.'

The line of attack at the Möhne has become a matter of some debate. The distance from the Möhne dam to the shore of the Heversberg is approximately 1,900 yards, thus giving a maximum run of 1,450 yards to the release point.

Earlier accounts of the operation suggested that the attacking aircraft ran in along the northern arm of the lake on a roughly westerly heading, hurdled a small spit on the northern side of the Heversberg and then turned to starboard to line up at 90 degrees to the dam. This would then leave approximately 950 yards, approximately 10 seconds' flying time, after the turn in which to level the wings and attain straight and level flight at the required speed before reaching the release point. Given the difficulty of maintaining height in a banking turn, and a tendency to err on the high side until the wings were level (since the inboard wingtip will be lower than the cockpit) this was a very difficult manoeuvre to execute with a degree of precision in a heavy aircraft. In addition, there was the danger that the aircraft might be silhouetted against the sky or that moonlight reflected off the wings during the turn could reveal the aircraft to observers on the ground. An added difficulty would be timing the turn without the target being visible until virtually the point at which the turn would have to commence.

Later researchers have demonstrated that a straight run in over the Heversberg on a north-westerly heading would permit the aircraft to settle down over the southern arm of the lake, descending consistently to achieve the required height and speed for the final approach. A minimum and easily controlled pull-up and descent would be necessary to get over the Heversberg (approximately 150 feet above lake level), but this could be engineered with the minimum of control input and without the added complication of having to re-establish height, speed, heading and level wings within a very short space of time. The aircraft could thus arrive at the start of its final approach a greater distance from the target, well set up on the correct heading, with only final height and speed adjustments being necessary. A compromise would be to approach along the line of the Heversberg and then turn in to the target to achieve an approach starting nearer to that possible from a straight run, but still with the complication of having to establish the release criteria following a banked turn onto target.

All told, the second, straight run from the south-east, appears to have been the line adopted as the least demanding, though by no means easy to achieve at night in a heavy aircraft in the face of fierce opposition.

0026 Young, and Maltby arrived at the Möhne dam. In AJ-J Sgt Nicholson noted 'Flak not too light' in his log (possibly having witnessed the main stream of the flak being directed during Gibson's and possibly Hopgood's attacks), and recorded the wind over the target, from east-northeast at 10 mph.

Shannon appears to have arrived sometime after the other two. As he did so, he flew within range of the flak on the right-hand tower and his Lancaster was 'hosepiped' by the gunners, to the verbal consternation of his bomb aimer, Len Sumpter, as the Lancaster suffered its only damage on the operation – a small hole in the fuselage. Sumpter noted the steepness of the hills and Danny Walker, his navigator, recalled that light flak would be 'beautiful in all its different colours if it were not so dangerous'.

0027 By the time McCarthy reached the vicinity of the Möhne and turned south-west for the final ten-mile leg to the Sorpe, Gibson was about to open the attack on the Möhne. This had been recognised and accommodated in Appendix A to the 'Chastise' Operation Order detailing the route with the comment: 'Second Wave is to be routed to Target Z via Target X, but is to keep sufficiently clear to avoid interfering with aircraft attacking Target X.' As in the case of the Möhne force the appendix also stipulated a maximum height of 1,000 feet for the final stages to the target, in this case Ahlen–Möhne–Sorpe, presumably to accommodate the dangers of rising ground.

0027 Gibson began his run, coming in over the wooded Heversberg, the crew engaging in their well-practised teamwork essential to deliver 'Upkeep' to the target.

To begin with, Gibson had the element of surprise, then, from the northern tower of the dam, twenty-four-year-old Corporal Karl Schutte, commanding the gun crew on the northern tower, and his men suddenly spotted the Lancaster's approaching Aldis lights. 'The English must be mad. They've switched on their landing lights!' With a definite target to aim at, the gunners swung their guns and lowered their sights onto the approaching aircraft. Some witnesses suggest that the aircraft was first spotted on account of its front gunner opening fire, rather than the spotlights which were only seen as the aircraft reached the dam.

0028 Gibson's 'Upkeep' was seen to bounce three times before sinking. The aircraft crossed the dam, the three guns in fields adjacent to the compensating basin opening fire as it came into view. As the aircraft passed out of range the explosion of 'Upkeep' caused the lake to boil and erupt with a column of water a thousand feet high, which rose and hung in the sky, stained red on one side by the Very light fired to indicate the weapon's release.

However, the range had been too great The 'Upkeep' had sunk and detonated some 60 yards away from the dam wall. It is also possible that it struck the torpedo net. Ferdinand Nolle recalled: 'The reel of steel cable holding it unwound at high speed. It couldn't have been fixed properly.'

A seismograph at Göttingen University recorded readings (amount of movement and duration) of 0.6 mm and 40.8 secs. This record of the first detonation is timed as 00.27. (Some records state that Gibson commenced his run at 0028 – almost certainly attributable to minor discrepancies in time-keeping.)

In the power house, Clemens Kohler had heard aircraft circling the lake, one of them coming closer. A thought suddenly occurred to him. British bombers did not normally come over the Ruhr in moonlight, and the reservoir was now at almost full capacity. Deeply troubled, he called the offices of the Vereinigte Elektrizitätswerke Westfalen (United Electricity Company of Westphalia) in Neheim. 'The aircraft are attacking the dam.' The official at the other end of the line registered disbelief and dismissed his alarm. The noise outside grew louder. Kohler ran to the door and went outside to witness a scene of terror: Gibson's Lancaster roared over the dam 200 feet above him, guns were firing and then a huge explosion sent a tremendous cascade of water over the dam. The air and ground seemed to shake with the cacophony of battle. Waiting no longer, Kohler ran through the descending spray up the side of the valley. Halfway up, drenched to the skin, he stopped to rest beneath a tree, staring with fear and fascination at the wall of the dam.

0028 Maudslay and Knight reached the turning point at Ahlen and turned south-east for the Möhne, six minutes away. As they did so, Les Munro arrived over Scampton and circled the airfield in preparation for landing.

0030 Flak defending Gilze Rijen is reported to have fired on low-flying aircraft. Since none of the first wave was in the vicinity this was possibly one of the early Mosquito intruders.

0030 McCarthy arrived in the vicinity of the Sorpe. Thick mist was filling the valleys and it was difficult to identify the reservoir. Once he had located the dam he then circled to assess the situation and devise the best attack run. 'Upkeep' had to be released during a run parallel to the dam, at the mid-point of the wall. This necessitated a steep dive from about 1,000 feet over the village of Langscheid to the north of the lake, levelling out at about 850 feet after half a mile, to release 'Upkeep'.

On assessing the site, McCarthy's first reaction was: 'Jeez! How do we get down there?'

Getting away after release was no easier, pulling back on the controls in order to effect a climb-out over the hills on the far shore to reach a safety height of 1,000 feet in a distance of some 1,000 yards.

The task was made more complicated by the presence of the steeple of St Antonius church which lay almost on the ideal approach path, but McCarthy soon realised that he could use this as a datum. He tried an approach, but both Sgt George Johnson, the bomb aimer, and McCarthy were unhappy with the line or altitude and he pulled the Lancaster up into a turning climb to port and prepared for another attempt. Thankfully there were no defences with which to contend, but it was not going to be easy.

0031 Three minutes after Munro's arrival back at base, Rice approached the Scampton circuit. Concerned as to the extent of the damage to H-Harry, he instructed Sgt Smith the flight engineer to check the contents of the hydraulic system lest there was insufficient to operate the undercarriage and flaps. Smith confirmed Rice's fears, so he decided to operate the undercarriage using the emergency compressed air system. This was designed to permit the lowering of both undercarriage and flaps (providing the former was done first with the flap operating lever in neutral) but previous experience had shown that this was not always so. Concerned that there would be insufficient emergency air pressure, Rice warned Scampton control of the situation. 'Aircraft damaged – possibly no flaps' and requested an approach heading to give the maximum landing run.

0033 approx. Maudslay and Knight arrived in the vicinity of the Möhne lake. It was five minutes since Gibson had made his attack and he judged that the lake's surface was now sufficiently settled for a second attack. He called up Hopgood to make his run. Hopgood's concern that the gunners would be ready for the second aircraft proved only too true. As he made his run the other crews could see the enemy fire rapidly concentrate on his approaching Lancaster. With Gregory out of action there was no return fire from his front turret and nothing to distract the defending flak. Gibson noted a hit on the port wing, adding to the earlier damage sustained at Dülmen, then the starboard wing was hit. Amidst this confusion, and clearly with no chance of a second run at the target, F/Sgt John Fraser released the 'Upkeep' fractionally too late. The weapon bounced over the dam parapet to land near the power station recently vacated by Clemens Kohler.

Tammy Simpson, Martin's rear gunner, watched as M-Mother crossed the dam, the intensifying flames suggesting a fuel-fed fire. Shannon's navigator, F/O Walker, thought that he saw a 'sheet of orange flame from the side of the fuselage'. It was clear that the aircraft was doomed. Hopgood banked the aircraft to starboard, away from the line of the Möhne valley, heading north-west towards the village of Ostonnen and struggling to gain height and give his crew a chance to escape. The Lancaster had reached 500 feet when it exploded, the blazing wreckage coming down in fields three-quarters of a mile south of Ostonnen.

When Hopgood prepared the crew to attack, he warned Burcher that the defences were putting up a great barrage ahead. Burcher heard Ken Earnshaw instructing Hoppy to go lower and heard John Fraser call 'Bomb gone!' At that moment there was a terrific impact and flames began to stream past Burcher's turret. He cranked his turret fore and aft enabling him to get into the fuselage to retrieve his parachute. Clipping it on, he plugged back into the intercom only to hear Hopgood's 'Abandon aircraft'. Looking down the aircraft Burcher saw Sgt Minchin, the wireless operator, crawling down the fuselage, his leg shattered. Helping him to the rear door, Burcher ensured the wireless operator's chute was attached and holding Minchin's D-ring, pushed him out, but did not see the parachute open. Calling Hopgood he announced, 'Rear gunner abandoning aircraft.' As Hopgood replied 'For Christ's sake get out . . .' the aircraft exploded. Burcher was blown out of the doorway, striking his back on the tailplane. Despite the low altitude his parachute deployed, billowing sufficiently to cushion his landing.

In the nose of the aircraft, immediately after releasing 'Upkeep' John Fraser had pulled back the cushion covering the nose exit. Pulling the emergency release, he jettisoned the hatch only to see the ground perilously close. Realising there was no time to lose he pulled his D-ring inside the aircraft, bundling the spilling silk into his arms and rolled through the opening. As he fell free he saw the tail wheel of the Lancaster whip past his head as the ground rushed to meet him. He felt a tremendous jolt as his chute deployed and broke his fall; in the same instant his boots seemed to hit the treetops. He later claimed it as the lowest parachute jump in history.

For the four remaining crew members, there was no escape. Their bodies were recovered from the remains of AJ-M the following morning, its tail fins being the largest recognisable section. Of the three crew members who had left the doomed aircraft, the severely injured Sgt Minchin did not survive. His body was found by the Germans in a field the following morning. Those who died were originally buried in the Soest-Ostonnen Cemetery and later exhumed and re-interred in Rheinberg War Cemetery in August 1948.

Burcher and Fraser – the only two of the crew who had not joined in the game of cricket before boarding – were more fortunate. Burcher, his spine fractured by the Lancaster's tailplane, managed to drag himself to a culvert where he remained for a while. In great pain he then decided to make his way towards the sound of a nearby railway line but was seen and apprehended by a member of the Hitler Youth and a policeman. Taken to a nearby house, he asked for a glass of water, only to be told 'Thanks to you and your comrades, there is no water!'

Fraser came down between Ostonnen and Sieveringen. He later gave an account of evading for a period, although German reports suggest that he was soon apprehended, again having made his way to the railway. Both crewmen spent the remainder of the war as PoW. After a medical examination, Burcher was encased in a concrete cast, plaster of Paris being unobtainable. Unconventional and uncomfortable, the treatment nevertheless proved effective, allowing him to re-commence flying duties post-war.

Corporal Schutte saw his crew's fire striking the approaching Lancaster, setting an engine on fire, the flames increasing as the bomber reached the dam. A great cheer rose from the gun crew. Their elation was cut short by a tremendous explosion as the power station disintegrated; Schutte was knocked to the ground, a thick cloud of smoke filled the valley below the dam and the blast wave stripped part of the roof of the north tower, cutting the phone lines, collapsing the access stairs and stranding the gun crew on top.

From his position on the valley side beyond the dam Clemens Kohler watched Hopgood's burning aircraft curve round on its fiery course northwards. He later claimed that two gunners were blown off 'the towers' and lay wounded on the crown of the dam, although at this stage of the attack only the gun on the south tower was lifted from its mount and put out of action, and its crew were unharmed. Immediately Lt Widmann began to organise the transfer of ammunition from the south tower to the remaining two functioning guns on the dam.

0035 There was no need to allow time for the water to calm down. Although Hopgood's bomb had caused a considerable amount of smoke around the target, Gibson called in Martin to make his run. Realising that the defences now appreciated the line of attack, Gibson made the decision to fly in ahead and slightly to starboard of Martin to distract the gunners and reduce the amount of fire directed at him. By running in to starboard he was placing himself over what were now the dam's only active defences.

As Martin ran in he could clearly see the northern tower (and thus its gun crew were able to see him), but from a mile away the southern tower was partly obscured by smoke, making it difficult to assess range accurately. Despite Gibson's efforts, the flak found Martin. At the very last moment Bob Hay, the bomb aimer, got sight of both towers and released the 'Upkeep'. Simultaneously the Lancaster was hit by a 20-mm shell in the starboard wing near the empty outer fuel tank. Fortunately, there was no fire. The upper skin of the wing was rippled, and the underside tank access panel blown away, but the aircraft still handled normally and the crew did not discover the extent of the damage until they returned to Scampton.

Martin's 'Upkeep' was released at a speed of 217 mph, on a heading of 335 degrees, spinning at 480 rpm. The smoke prevented Tammy Simpson in the rear turret from seeing the number of bounces, or seemingly that it had veered off towards the western side of the reservoir, its detonation soaking the gunners on the left-hand tower. The reason for this is uncertain. On occasion during trials 'Upkeep' had been found to deviate to the left at the end of its run, but equally if the wings were not level at the time of release, one end of the cylinder might dig in causing a deviation of course. The simultaneous impact of the flak shell and the moment of release may have created such a situation.

As Martin pulled away the crew's concerns focused on clearing the area, assessing the results of their attack and then taking stock of the damage to their aircraft. Possibly as a result of this and Gibson's keenness to press on with the attack, the message telling Grantham of the result of their drop would not be sent for a further thirteen minutes.

The enormous column of water thrown up by the detonation of each 'Upkeep' was accompanied by a tremendous blast wave. The force of this blew out all the windows in the nearby Seehof Restaurant and also the guard post at the end of the dam where Strotkamp was now taking shelter. So great was the force of the blast that on one occasion he was thrown bodily across the room into the wall.

0036 AJ-W Munro touched down at Scampton. With all means of communication wrecked he was unaware of Rice's presence in the circuit and had no option but to make a straight-in approach, without being able to announce his arrival. Taxying to dispersal he was met by Heveron and Powell who were concerned when they saw what they mistook to be battle damage beneath the aircraft, only to be reassured by Caple that what they could see were the fuel jettison pipes – Munro had jettisoned fuel to lighten the aircraft for landing. On leaving the aircraft Munro was more concerned about having to abort the operation than the danger of landing with an 'Upkeep' aboard.

0037 Hutchison's confirmation of Gibson's attack sent by W/T was received at Grantham. It was an optimistic assessment: 'GONER 68A'. ['Special weapon released. Exploded five yards from the dam. No apparent breach.'] The Morse crackled into Dunn's telephone receiver. They could all hear it and it was slow enough for Cochrane to read. Dunn spoke it in plain language for the others.

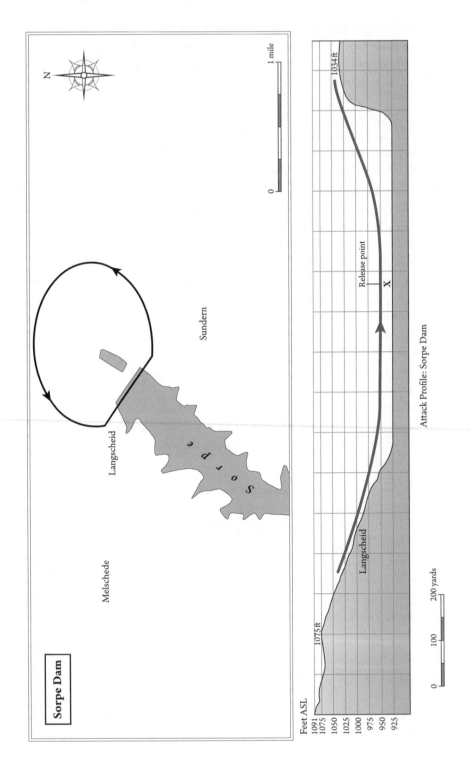

Sorpe Dam

N

Melschede

Langscheid

Sundern

S o r p e

0   1 mile

Attack Profile: Sorpe Dam

Feet ASL
1091
1075
1050
1025
1000
975
950
925

1075 ft

1034 ft

Release point

X

Langscheid

0   100   200 yards

'I'd hoped one bomb might do it.' said Wallis.

'It's probably weakened it' came Cochrane's encouraging reply.

0038 The Göttingen University seismograph recorded readings of 0.8 mm, 14.9 secs for Martin's 'Upkeep'. There was no record of the explosion of Hopgood's 'Upkeep' on the power station since its detonation in air rather than water gave little or no seismic shock. On the northern tower Karl Schutte assessed the situation. Their gun barrel had become red hot and would have to be changed if they were to continue firing.

0043 Visibility at low level was further hampered by spray from the explosions which was settling on the Perspex. Gibson called Young in to attack. Martin flew in on his left while Gibson flew on the far side of the dam to engage the gunners near the compensating basin, flicking his navigation lights on and off in order to attract as many of the guns as possible.

German witnesses observed that before Young's run, one of the aircraft made a reconnaissance to assess the result of the previous attack: Karl Schutte: 'The noise of engines rose again ... It seemed to me that [the aircraft] were circling the fire. We all opened fire, which the aircraft returned.'

Then Young made his run.

> At that moment the third [*sic*] aircraft began its attack. We began firing at it and hit it with a number of shots – but it was only 20 mm and what could that do to a large aircraft? Any damage would be pure chance. The gunners on board the aircraft were firing at us. We saw a necklace of tracer coming towards our tower. Everyone wanted to get out of the way of these enormous glow-worms, but we had our duty to keep firing.

Young's 'Upkeep' was released and was seen to make 'three good bounces', sinking in contact with the wall – possibly the first one to do so. With the proximity of the detonation's waterspout to the dam, an even greater amount of water was seen to overtop the parapet, and for a moment both Young and Gibson believed that the dam had breached, only to find it still intact as the water subsided.

As with Burcher, Schutte subsequently gave many accounts of his experiences. In another he recalled:

> There was an aircraft in front of our eyes, but we could not see it release a bomb. Fortunately, it flew right over the dam.
>
> We knew nothing more. The aircraft had attacked, shining lights. What had happened? Had our firing hindered the bomb

aimer? Already the guns in the valley were firing at him – and then suddenly our gun stopped.

Schutte's crew had maintained a rapid rate of fire, but the heat generated by this inevitably took its toll. While they were firing at Gibson, flying to draw the fire from Young, their gun suffered a stoppage. Desperately trying to clear it they removed the magazine and loading mechanism, only to discover that a round had damaged the breech. A minute later, at Göttingen, the seismograph recorded 0.2 mm, 2.6 secs.

Sitting underneath a tree on the valley side beyond the dam, Clemens Kohler could see something that the aircrew could not. Cracks were beginning to form in the parapet, from which fine jets of water were spraying, visible in the moonlight. As he watched the fissures seemed to increase. The dam could not withstand many more attacks such as these. It seemed too late now to save the inhabitants of the valley from a terrible inundation.

0046   Meanwhile ten miles away from this intense action, after a quarter of an hour at the Sorpe dam McCarthy was still trying to make an effective run. He tried nine times between 0030 and 0045 without success. Not only was positioning the aircraft to run parallel to the dam difficult, but estimating the mid-point of the wall, when the far end was indistinct and there were no other visual clues was even harder. The crew were becoming increasingly uneasy about remaining over the target for such a time. Dave Rodger the rear gunner, who was experiencing what must have been to him an extreme roller-coaster ride, was particularly vociferous with comments which Johnson took to heart – recalling them over seventy years later: 'Won't somebody get that bomb out of here!'

Finally, after the tenth run, Johnson was sufficiently satisfied to release their mine from 30 feet at a ground speed of 170 mph flying on a heading of 140 degrees. The aircraft lifted rapidly as its load fell away and fell into the water close to the centre of the dam. The suddenness of this effect caught the crew unawares and Rodger in the rear turret, already anxious about the time spent in the target area, called to McCarthy to 'get the hell down' – concerned that they would make a perfect target for fighters. As they turned the 'Upkeep' exploded and Rodger could see the column of water against the moon. As they came back to take a look, flying through the descending spray they could see that the crest had crumbled for some 15–20 feet.

After the tension of the previous quarter of an hour elation and relief was felt throughout the crew. McCarthy gave vent with such vocal expression that Don MacLean the navigator issued a rebuke, telling him to concentrate on his flying. Such was their preoccupation that the message telling of their successful drop was not sent until 0300, by which time they were almost home.

As at the Möhne, the attack was witnessed by the engineer on duty in the power house below the dam. Joseph Kesting heard the sound of the Lancaster and went outside to see it flying along the length of the dam from the distance of Langscheid. It was so low and close that he could make out the RAF roundels. Then another aircraft (or so he thought – it was McCarthy making another run) came and dropped what he described as 'an object like a large septic tank' over the crest and into the water. There was a tremendous explosion and a great column of water rose, descending on the air side of the dam. Kesting's impression was that the attack was being made on the power house.

0047 Rice had arrived back at Scampton at 0031 but unsure of the condition of his aircraft he circled at 1,000 feet for 20 minutes, during which time he burned off extra fuel and the crew settled themselves into crash positions. Unaware of Munro's proximity, or that he was making a 'straight in' approach, Scampton control was unable to warn Rice of the other's presence. As Rice prepared to land, Munro's Lancaster cut across below him on its final approach baulking his attempt to land and forcing him to make another circuit.

Aware of the damage around the rear fuselage and loss of his tailwheel, Rice brought the Lancaster in for a 'wheeler' landing, holding the tail up for as long as possible until the fins contacted the grass, bringing the aircraft to a grinding halt. Unable to taxi back to dispersal the crew climbed out, being met by Whitworth who drove out to inspect the wrecked Lancaster and took them to debriefing. After telling their story, Rice remained in the briefing room awaiting the return of the other crews.

0048 At No. 5 Group Headquarters the tension was mounting. It had been thirteen minutes since they had heard of Gibson's drop. Then silence. The minutes passed and the tension mounted. The next message received was hardly reassuring. Aboard AJ-A Sgt Nichols sent the message 'GONER 78A' – an explosion in contact with the dam, but no breach.

Not only had an apparent direct hit failed to breach the dam, but Cochrane and Satterly, who were aware of the order of attack, were left pondering the fate of Hopgood and Martin who were scheduled to attack before Young. Wallis's confidence that a single hit would destroy the dam seemed flawed and even cumulative damage appeared ineffective.

By now visibility had improved and both towers were clearly visible. Gibson instructed Maltby to attack, calling on Martin to come in over the lake and orbit to port of Maltby's run, firing at the defences while he did likewise, orbiting to starboard. Once again Gibson took what he believed to be the more heavily defended side of the target, though by this time only the gun on the northern parapet roadway and those by the compensating basin were serviceable.

0048 AJ-C Meanwhile, the head of the reserve wave was about to cross the Suffolk Coast at Southwold.

0049 As Maltby approached the dam on a heading of 330 degrees at 223 mph he could see debris on the parapet. But there was something else. It was beginning to crumble in the centre. Sensing that the wall was breaking he nudged the Lancaster's nose slightly to port. Their 'Upkeep', released at 0049, bounced four times and sank in contact with the dam, again exactly as Wallis had envisaged.

The Lancaster swept over the dam. Schutte was able to make out figures in the cockpit and felt that it passed almost with arm's reach. With no other means of retaliation, the gun crew resorted to their carbines and rifles in an effort to bring it down. A futile gesture, but all that they could do.

As Maltby turned away and looked back, the 'Upkeep' exploded: 'Our load sent up water and mud to a height of a thousand feet. The spout of water was silhouetted against the moon. It rose with tremendous speed and then gently fell back. You could see the shock wave at the base of the jet.'

Sgt Nicholson, AJ-J's navigator recorded in his log: 'Bomb dropped. Wizard.'

As the dam continued to crumble, the seismograph at Göttingen recorded: 0.8 mm, 57 secs.

0050 In Neheim many were sheltering in their cellars. Some residents had heard the flak fire from the direction of the lake. The local police station had received an unofficial warning about the flood, but these as well as other private phone calls were not taken seriously. After hearing about these warnings, the city architect, Kraft, asked if it was true that the dam was broken. The police lieutenant on duty replied that the security service at the dam would have reported to the local police department if it was. But they hadn't.

Neheim was only informed officially after Nazi Party officials had contacted the district government in Arnsberg confirming the dam's destruction. Only then, when Arnsberg called Neheim at 00.50, was action taken. Over twenty valuable minutes had been lost since Kohler had tried to warn the village.

0050 Lawrence Nichols, Young's wireless operator, inexplicably sent 'GONER 78A' to Grantham.

0051   A minute later, No. 5 Group received 'GONER 58A' from P-Popsie. This was thirteen minutes after Martin had made his run, suggesting either that he was assessing damage to the Lancaster, or was pre-occupied with providing cover for Young and Maltby. At the same time, having completed his attack on the Sorpe McCarthy turned onto a north-easterly heading, at 100 feet and with a ground speed of 220 mph, heading back to the Möhne, unaware of the progress of the attacks there.

0052   On the roof of the dam's northern tower, Schutte was in no doubt what was happening. As the spray from Maltby's attack subsided he could see that the wall was breached and shouted to the battery commander, Leutnant Widmann: 'The dam has gone!' Widmann, on the roadway on the shore side of the tower whose view was obstructed, replied, 'No it hasn't.'

Likewise, there was uncertainty in the air. Gibson, over the lake, may have been heading east at this time, without a clear view of the dam. Anxious to complete the attack he called up David Shannon telling him to start his run. As Shannon acknowledged there was an elated call from Martin who was crossing the air side of the dam: 'I think it's gone! Look at it for Christ's sake!'

Simpson, Martin's rear gunner recalled: 'I saw . . . the whole face of the dam between the two towers burst outwards and a wall of water disgorged itself. It was an awe-inspiring sight, and then there was complete silence.'

Shannon was just about to line up for his run when Gibson called him: 'It's alright, Dave. Skip it!', Shannon broke away while Gibson approached the dam and saw the water pouring through the breach, 'looking like stirred porridge in the moonlight'. Later he wrote: 'This was a tremendous sight which probably no man will ever see again.' There was now only one gun firing from the dam and this was quickly silenced as the seven remaining aircraft came in to take a look.

From his position high on the side of the valley, Clemens Kohler had watched after the detonation of Maltby's bomb, as the wall between the towers bulged and then burst releasing a jet of water which shot out, crashing to the ground with a tremendous roar and thunder.

Max Schulze-Sölde, an artist whose works were banned as 'degenerate' by the Nazi regime, was watching from his home nearby. He witnessed a 'giant smoke mushroom' close to the dam wall:

> Only a few seconds later the sound of the tremendous detonation reaches us. The air pressure is so strong that it penetrates through the open door into the interior of the house. Suddenly an eerie roar rises up to me from the valley; the small lake in front of the wall [the compensating basin] is getting wider and wider, the landscape

seems to have changed strangely. Powerful waves glitter silvery in the moonlight. The wall is broken!

The remains of the power house were swept away in an instant by the tidal wave which began its unstoppable progress down the valley, inundating the 888,000-gallon compensating basin in a matter of a minute or so. Within minutes any further observation was obscured by a heavy rolling cloud of spray and mist, but the tremendous roar remained, testimony of the destructive force released.

Wilhelm Strotkamp saw the dam wall shake as though in an earthquake, and now reported to his superiors in Soest that the dam had been breached, telling them to warn settlements further down the valley since direct communication with Neheim was impossible.

An employee of the Ruhr Talsperreverein living in a house below the basin reported:

> We heard the planes roar overhead and over us and wanted to rush out of the house. The explosion of the second bomb [Hopgood's], shook the structure of our half-timbered house. At this moment, my watch must have stopped – it was 00.30. Then a new terrible explosion blew my wife and I together. We heard the sound of the water and ran up to the nearby height ... My wife with our three-year-old boy in her arms, me with our other four children behind. My eldest daughter (16) was caught on a barbed wire fence. When I tried to free her, the tidal wave overwhelmed us. I lost my daughter in a whirlpool. The water washed me ashore in a side valley. When I regained consciousness, my daughter was gone.

Also in the area at this time was Joe McCarthy making his way back from the Sorpe. McCarthy's briefed route home was via the Möhne, then to Ahlen, the lakes at Dülmen, then on to Rees. His navigator Don MacLean recorded their arrival at the Möhne in his log: '0054 Target X. s/c Ahlen'. This is two minutes before Hutchison's message to Grantham; they must have reached the area only minutes after the dam had been breached, but already the geography had changed. Bomb aimer 'Johnny' Johnson recalls that map reading was pointless since 'the entire area looked like an inland sea. Any features that I might have tried to pick out were now submerged.'

0054 AJ-J Without lingering too long in the target area Maltby headed for home. Sgt Nicholson re-set the API to provide an established datum and gave a course of 338 degrees for their first turning point, the spoil heap 19 miles away at Ahlen.

0055 Grantham received 'GONER 78A' from Maltby: Bomb exploded in contact with dam wall. No apparent breach.

0056 Within a minute Dunn was receiving a further message, this time from Hutchison:

NIGGER

To avoid any misunderstanding this codeword was repeated by No. 5 Group, using full power, to Gibson's aircraft. Hutchison replied:

CORRECT

0056 AJ-P Martin too appears to have lingered only a little in the area of the Möhne, before he set course for Ahlen from Delecke point on the northern shore of the reservoir.

0057 AJ-T Early during their return leg, McCarthy's front gunner, Sgt Batson, asked permission to open up on a train seen on a line crossing their path, possibly on the line between Soest and Werl. After receiving McCarthy's assent the crew were severely shaken when the train turned out to be heavily defended, returning fire with a vengeance. The aircraft jolted as it was hit, though there was no apparent damage and the aircraft continued to handle normally. Dave Rodger in the rear turret opened fire as the tracks passed behind them. The exchange continued for a mile or so until Rodger stopped, at which point the German also stopped firing. He was later to reflect. 'I wish I'd stopped a heck of a lot sooner.'

McCarthy recalled that no sooner were they out of range of the train than the northern horizon ahead suddenly illuminated with searchlights and a considerable amount of flak. He was heading straight for a marshalling yard with a large town or city beyond. He was on a direct course for Hamm, rather than skirting east of it to Ahlen.

Malte Schrader commanded a 37-mm anti-aircraft battery detailed for the protection of the Hamm railway installations. Earlier in the evening the local defences had been alerted by the first waves of Lancasters as they passed north of the town heading for Ahlen. Now looking south-east, he saw a large four-engine aircraft flying extremely low towards the railyards. Safety guards erected to prevent low elevation guns from damaging nearby property delayed his opening fire, but once these were overcome the air was rent by the staccato sound of Hamm's defences going into action.

Keeping the aircraft as low as possible – 'We were so low that they didn't need to fire at us, they only needed to switch the points' – McCarthy hauled the Lancaster into a 180-degree turn and then flew several circular orbits out of range while MacLean sought to rectify the situation. After a brief discussion between pilot and navigator it was concluded that the aircraft had been flying some 19 degrees west of the intended track. McCarthy made allowance and headed for Ahlen. The track time between the Möhne and Ahlen should have been five minutes, but it appears that they arrived at Ahlen at 0104, ten minutes after leaving the Möhne.

This error is evidence that the problems with regard to the compass deviation card encountered with the hasty switch of aircraft had not been fully resolved. It is possible that ED825 took off with a card which recorded only deviation with the 'Upkeep' on board, and not the figures for use after release, which would have been those used for the aircraft's delivery flight the previous afternoon.

0058 After the crews at the Möhne had watched the unfolding drama for about three minutes, Gibson ordered the remaining aircraft still with their 'Upkeeps', Shannon, Maudslay and Knight, to accompany him to the Eder, along with Young who would act as deputy leader should anything happen to Gibson. They each set course individually from the southern tip of the rapidly emptying Möhne lake, heading south-east on a track of 114 degrees, at a ground speed of 180 mph.

0100 Despite the alert issued by the Flak Headquarters at Schloss Schwansbell, the attack on the Möhne dam took them completely by surprise. The first they were aware of the disaster came shortly before one o'clock when Lt Widmann phoned and reported: 'Several attacks by enemy Lancasters on the dam wall. The dam is breached in the middle. Water is pouring down the valley. One aircraft shot down. One tower's gun put out of action. Two guns damaged, one with jammed breech.' Widmann soon managed to get a second message to Lünen: 'The hole in the dam is growing as more of the wall breaks away. Water is cascading down the valley. It's a catastrophe! The whole dam is shaking!'

Then the line went dead.

0100 approx. Three miles downstream from the Möhne on the southern edge of the village of Niederense was the former monastery of Himmelpforten. The 'Porta Coeli' church shared its name with the Cistercian monastery there, which was founded in 1246 and dissolved in 1804. For almost 700 years, the buildings of Himmelpforten had survived all the storms of time, but now they were struck by the full force of the water from the breached dam. The occupants of the manor house air-raid shelter sought sanctuary on the higher Gutswald; three were carried away by the flood. The others reached the forest from where they watched and listened to the breaking of walls and splintering of beams as the towering waves overwhelmed their community. Soon only the church spire remained above the waves, standing for about 10 minutes before collapsing into the torrent with a final toll of the bell. Pastor Joseph Berkenkopf, who had delivered the sermon for Mother's Day only the day before, and twenty-five others were killed. Himmelpforten was never rebuilt. A wooden statue of St Francis from the church was eventually recovered in Schwerte, 27 miles downstream. Today, on the site of the high altar, a tall steel cross the height of the tidal wave, serves as a reminder of a night of terror.

The water continued its relentless progress down the valley. Where the valley narrowed, the height of the wave increased, reaching 45 feet in parts.

0100 AJ-J Maltby reached his turning point at Ahlen and turned south-west along the originally planned route to Ahsen, thus passing closer to the Ruhr but avoiding the guns near Dülmen.

0100 AJ-C During the leg across the North Sea, Freddie Tees carried out the usual test on his Brownings and was satisfied that both turret and guns were in full order and ready for the battle ahead. Intercom talk was kept to the essential minimum; the laconic conversation needed to effect a change of course, or a direction from the pilot to the flight engineer in relation to engine settings, oil temperature checks and fuel system management. Otherwise, each crew member was left to his own thoughts

0103 AJ-P Martin too would have been in the Ahlen area. Cochrane's post-raid report records that from there all three return routes followed the reciprocal of the amended outbound route north of the Ruhr, via the unexpected flak position near the lakes at Dülmen, and it is possible that Martin followed this, giving the defended area a wider berth. Otherwise, other returning aircraft may have reverted to the original return route as detailed in the Operation Order, heading west-southwest to Ahsen and then south of Haltern before heading north-west, towards the Dutch–German border.

As Martin's gunner Tammy Simpson recalled:

> Mick turned for base, flying, if anything, even lower than when we flew in on the way to the target. The trip home was quite uneventful as far as any opposition or searchlights were concerned. I guess it was just as well because, unbeknown to me, and I did not know until the next day, the only ammunition left for me was a couple of feet for each gun. Not much was said on the way home. I knew that with Jack [Leggo, the navigator], Bob [Hay, bomb aimer] and Mick, the aircraft wouldn't have been more than a hundred yards off track all the way home.

0104 AJ-T McCarthy reached the turning point at Ahlen and altered course for the lakes near Dülmen. Realising that his compass was unreliable, McCarthy and MacLean decided that rather than follow the alternative route home which had been briefed and risk getting off track again amongst possible defended areas, it would be prudent to re-trace the reciprocal of their inward route to the Zuider Zee. It was the most reliable and quickest way to bring them over water, thus minimising exposure to any ground defences, and by staying low McCarthy reckoned he would be immune from any fighter activity. Bill Radcliffe the flight engineer, who was normally conservative with regard to his treatment of the engines and fuel consumption, threw caution to the winds. Their priority now was to cross enemy territory and reach the coast in the shortest possible time.

0108 Maltby's AJ-J reached the Ahsen–Haltern area, passing the briefed Ahsen waypoint, but turning before the next point south-west of Haltern, and then heading almost due north towards Nordhorn. While on this leg – possibly over the wooded area near Haltern, or near Dülmen – the Lancaster passed over a defended area and was forced to take evasive action.

0108 The chief of police in Soest had seen several aircraft flying towards the Möhne lake and heard the dam's defences in action. Contacting the battery commander at Gunne, he learned of the attack on the dam and drove there anxious to see for himself, finding on arrival that it was already breached. Since the guardroom telephones were out of action, he established an emergency command post in the Hotel Möhnestrasse, on the northern bank of the valley overlooking the dam, to summon assistance but there was little else of immediate practical use that could be done.

0110 approx. AJ-C P/O Ottley, leading the reserve wave, reached the Dutch coast at the Scheldt Estuary and set course for Roosendaal.

0112 Gibson, Young, Shannon, Maudslay and Knight were nearing the Eder. A minute earlier the air-raid warning centre in Kassel had received notification that the Möhne dam had been attacked and hit and now they received a report from the observer post at Waldeck that there were low-flying aircraft in the vicinity of the Eder lake. Unaware of the attack on the Möhne, the local population were unperturbed as they began to hear the sound of approaching aircraft.

0014 AJ-T McCarthy had reached the lakes between Dülmen and Haltern, and set course on the next leg, cutting back across the north of the Ruhr to the turning point on the Rhine just south of Rees.

0117   Gibson and the other four aircraft were completing their uneventful transit to the vicinity of the Eder lake but locating the dam was proving difficult. The terrain was much hillier and more wooded than that around the Möhne, with numerous small settlements but few easily identifiable landmarks. To make matters worse early morning mist was now filling the valleys. Gibson's first contact with the Eder lake was too far west. It took him a further five minutes of searching its serpentine length to locate the dam at its eastern end. Fortunately, the area immediately around the dam was relatively clear, but apart from Young, there was no sign of the other three aircraft carrying 'Upkeep'. German reports suggest that, having eventually found the dam, Gibson fired red Very cartridges to indicate its location to other aircraft in the vicinity. If so, it appears they went unseen at this time.

0120 approx.   Maltby's AJ-J pinpointed Gildehaus, east of Bad Bentheim, crossing a series of distinctive railway lines, on its approach to Nordhorn.

0122 AJ-J   On reaching Nordhorn, identified by the Vechte river, canal and lake and distinctive church spire, Maltby turned to port on an west-northwesterly heading for the town of Genemuiden on the south-east shore of the Zuider Zee. At about the same time Martin was skirting the flak at Dülmen before heading on a north-westerly course that would skirt Winterswijk and take him to Zutphen.

0125   The 30-foot-high tidal wave reached Neheim at about 0120, some thirty minutes after the wall had broken. The inhabitants were quite unprepared. At first, there was the sound of what seemed like an express train, followed by shouts 'The water is coming!' On the northern side of the city, the Möhneweisen camp on the banks of the Möhne river, housing forced-labour workers from Eastern Europe, was one of the first parts to be inundated. Some of the guards unlocked the barracks to let the workers free. Some climbed the fences, rather that wait for the compound gate to be opened. While a number headed for higher ground, others went the wrong way, only to drown. Some of the wooden barrack blocks were swept away intact, 'floating like arks'. The cries of survivors inside were still being heard 2 miles away as the 'arks' passed through Herdringen, only to cease abruptly as the huts smashed against the abutments of a bridge three-quarters of a mile downstream; drowned prisoners were carried with the raging torrent, some for over 30 miles, as far as Schwerte.

Being close to the source of the disaster, and with little warning, it is not surprising that Neheim suffered the greatest human loss. The burial registers of Neheim recorded the demise of 529 unnamed labourers. Subsequent

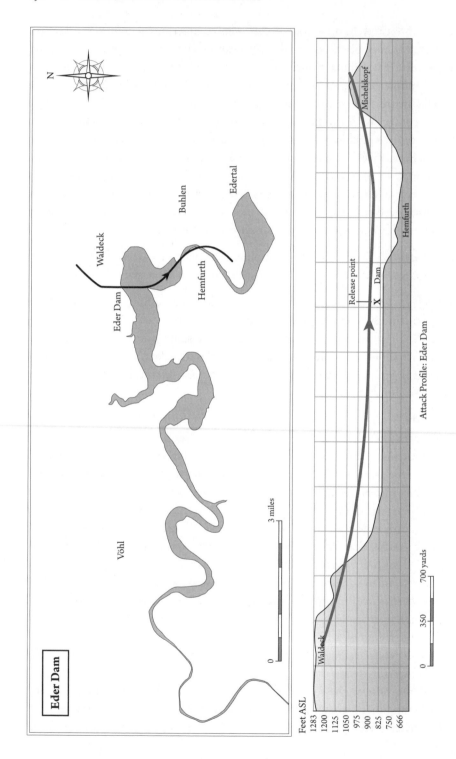

Eder Dam

N

Vöhl

Waldeck

Eder Dam

Buhlen

Hemfurth

Edertal

0   3 miles

Feet ASL

1283
1200
1125
1050
975
900
825
750
666

Waldeck

Release point

Michelskopf

X Dam

Hemfurth

Attack Profile: Eder Dam

0   350   700 yards

burials comprised 59 French prisoners of war, 9 Belgian prisoners of war, 14 Dutch civilian workers and 49 unnamed persons. Over 250 female slave workers remained unaccounted for. Although an accurate number will never be known it is believed that at least 859 died, among them 147 Germans and 712 foreign workers. Over a thousand people were made homeless and over 5,000 homes damaged to a greater or lesser degree.

At 0125 the electricity substation near the Möhne bridge short-circuited with a brilliant flash. Then the concrete bridge itself collapsed into the maelstrom.

0125 AJ-L Shannon, who had flown from the Möhne with his 'Upkeep' still spinning, experienced the same problems as Gibson. He first flew west along the lake in search of the target, and then, while backtracking east, thought that he had located the target area, but was in the vicinity of Rehback, some two miles west of the dam. It has been suggested that he mistook an old quarry face on the eastern side of a bend in the lake for the dam wall. This seems strange, since the rock face, which might have been mistaken for the air side of the dam wall faces north-west, rather than south-east but this may indicate some of the problems of visibility and orientation faced by the crews, caused by the patches of low-lying mist.

Shannon was about to make a run towards the position where he took the dam to be when Gibson called up saying that he was over the dam and would fire red Very lights to indicate his location. As these went up Shannon realised his error and headed east to join Gibson. The others also heard Gibson and saw the lights. Within a few minutes all were making a left-hand orbit of the target, of about a mile radius, passing from the north of Waldeck, over the dam and then back round over the village of Buhlen, about a mile east-northeast of the dam.

Since there had been no model to study at the briefing, this was the crews' first full appreciation of the difficulties facing them. There was no flak – the dam was defended only by two sentries armed with rifles patrolling its crest – but the dam's location and the surrounding terrain presented a formidable challenge. The reservoir was cradled by steep-sided hills. A prominent spit of land, the Hammerbergspitze, projected into the lake from the southern shore 1,200 yards from the dam and precluded a steady straight approach. Then, 1,400 yards beyond the dam, a ridge, the Michelskopf, some 400 feet above lake level, prevented a straight getaway. Any attack run would have to take the profile of a roller coaster dogleg: a dive down to the spit, followed by a turn to port near lake level, giving a run of some 700 yards in which to achieve the correct height and speed before the point of release. Immediately after this the aircraft would need to increase power and start its turning climb to starboard to follow the curve of the valley downstream.

0125 approx. Werner Salz, an engineer in the Hemfurth power stations below the Eder dam had returned from working a late shift and retired to bed, only to be woken soon by the air-raid siren. Shortly afterwards he heard the sound of approaching aircraft, which appeared to be circling the village and the dam. Going outside onto high ground he witnessed a number of large four-engined aircraft flying very low, their crews visible in their cockpits.

0128 AJ-J Over the Netherlands, on his return track between Nordhorn and Genemuiden, Maltby passed to the south of Hardenberg, identified as they crossed a canal, river and railway running parallel in a north-east to south-west direction. Martin would also have been tracking along this leg, between Dülmen and Nordhorn during this period.

0130 The reserve wave had now reached the Scheldt estuary. Brown in AJ-F reached the coast at this time, with Townsend following a minute later. The flak positions in this area had been alerted by the first nine aircraft and were still at the ready. It is reported that a low-flying aircraft was engaged by the 37-mm light flak of Flak Abteilung 665 near Molenschot, but the shells missed, some damaging nearby Dutch houses. Searchlights then came into play as other batteries near Verhoven opened fire, again without result. This engagement has been attributed to aircraft of the final wave, but this cannot be confirmed, as the timing would appear to be too early and may be a mis-recording of 0150.

0132 AJ-T McCarthy should have reached the Rhine at Rees. His 36-mile route from the lakes near Haltern/Dülmen should have taken approximately 10 minutes' flying time at a speed of 220 mph, but this timing adds another 8 minutes or 28 miles onto this leg and cannot be due to a reduction of speed. Uncertain of his exact position, McCarthy opted to return via his inbound route since the pinpoints along this were familiar.

0132 At the Eder dam, in response to a call from the local air-raid defence controller, the duty corporal for the 3rd Company, 603rd Regional Defence Battalion at Hemfurth confirmed that three enemy aircraft were circling around the Eder dam. News of the events at the Möhne had already been circulated and the controller then put a call through to Colonel Burk, the commanding officer of a nearby SS training regiment, warning of the possibility of an imminent flood disaster. Burk immediately prepared a task force of trucks and men for despatch to the area if required.

While the controller was making his call to Burk a further message arrived from Hemfurth. The aircraft had released flares and had switched on search-lights.

Time was running short. Gibson called Shannon in to make his first run. The approach to lake level descended a ravine to the west of the Schloss Waldeck, perched on the summit of a 1,200-foot promontory on the north shore of the lake, so that the aircraft was already descending below the level of the castle before it reached the shoreline. This way in would permit a slightly curving path, setting the aircraft up for the final turn to port which would bring the aircraft to the correct heading for the dam. Careful throttle management was required to avoid an excessive build-up of speed.

The wings had to be level at the point of release, 450 yards from the dam, with the aircraft travelling at some 220 mph on a track at 90 degrees to the dam wall. Immediately after release power was applied and the stick pulled back, banking to starboard, thus turning and climbing parallel to the rising ground to port, which as the turn progressed fell away to the end of the spur thus increasing separation distance between the aircraft and ground.

Shannon curved in from north of the lake, behind the Schloss Waldeck. Sparks showered from his exhausts as Sgt Henderson, the flight engineer, pulled the throttles back in an effort to lose speed. On lining up on the dam Shannon found he was not low enough and travelling too fast. 'Sorry, Leader. Made a mess of that. I'll try again.'

0136 approx. AJ-L Shannon had made two further attempts, again without success. Accounts of this stage of the attack indicate not only the degree of difficulty, but also the frustration and growing tension. This cannot have been helped by the knowledge that there were only three 'Upkeeps'. In theory aircraft of the mobile reserve could be detailed to proceed to the Eder but time was pressing and understandably focus must have been on breaching the Eder with the force immediately available.

Gibson instructed Shannon to hold off for a while. The Waldeck observation post notified the Kassel air-raid warning centre that aircraft were circling over the reservoir.

0136½ AJ-J While Shannon was struggling at the Eder, Maltby was about to leave the Netherlands slightly north of track, crossing the polderland on a course of 282 degrees and pinpointing a group of lakes 6 miles north-west of Meppel.

0137 Fifty miles to the south, McCarthy crossed the Het Zwarte Schaar river bend at Doesburg, with the steeple of the Martinkerk visible on the horizon to port. Still keeping low and pushing 220 mph he was now only 40 miles from the coast at Harderwijk and the relative security above the IJsselmeer.

Accounts of events at the Eder vary. Having told Shannon to hold off, Gibson then called in Squadron Leader Henry Maudslay. Maudslay may then have made two attempts before Shannon tried again, trying a new line of approach. This seems to have tried to avoid crossing over the Hammerberg spit, but instead passing close to its tip. While this made it easier to achieve the desired height and speed, it did not guarantee an accurate 90-degree line of approach to the centre of the dam wall. It seems that Shannon made two further runs of this nature, releasing on the second. As his bomb aimer, F/Sgt Len Sumpter, called 'Bomb gone' Henderson applied full power and Shannon hauled the Lancaster up and round, the approaching slope of the Michelskopf illuminated in the beam of the landing light which he had switched on as a further aid.

Whether as a result of taking a deliberate line to starboard, or not being able to tighten his turn sufficiently to line up on the centre of the dam between the towers, Shannon's final run released 'Upkeep' on a heading of 150 degrees – some 30 degrees to starboard off a direct line. The 'Upkeep' was seen to bounce twice, suggesting release at a range less than 450 yards, before striking the dam and glancing off at an angle. It then continued to run into the shallow water at the southern end of the dam – seemingly between the bank and the southern tower where it detonated with the usual plume of water, this time interspersed with mud and debris.

Gibson and Knight, who witnessed the run, did not report any visible damage to the dam, but according to Shannon, he saw a hole appear about 9 feet wide below the level of the parapet. This does not accord with any other report. At the time of the attack the lake was over topping the upper spillways and it is possible that he mistook this or water running past one of the main sluice openings lower down the wall.

As with the attacks on the Möhne, the shock of 'Upkeep's' detonation was recorded by the seismograph at the Göttingen Institute, timed at 0137: 0.4 mm, duration 34.0 secs.

0140 AJ-T   In the vicinity of Apeldoorn, just before reaching the Zuider Zee, a flak gun opened up on McCarthy. Despite their extremely low altitude it very nearly got their range, giving rear gunner Dave Rodger the momentary thought that their time was up, then they were safely past and heading for the coast at Harderwijk.

Wickede, a town of some 3,300 residents, had listened to the dull thuds of the 'Upkeep' detonations 8 miles away at the Möhne dam. Then they ceased and most people returned to their beds, only to be woken at 01.40 by a loud rushing sound. Looking out they saw the full moon becoming obscured by a strange rising mist. Shortly afterwards water started to pour into the streets, flooding lower floors and rising higher. In haste, occupants grabbed what they could and made for the upper floors, or roofs. Some were less fortunate as their wooden-framed buildings, unable to withstand the torrent, started to collapse beneath them, forcing them to swim or cling to whatever might help them stay afloat. For many, there was no escape. At least 118 inhabitants drowned. In the following days the authorities struggled to identify the dead, the task compounded by bodies carried down from Neheim, while others from Wickede were recovered as far away as Essen.

The supply line between the Ruhr and the Eastern Front was seriously interrupted when the bridge at Wickede carrying the main railway line from the Ruhr industrial area to Kassel across the river was destroyed, and the embankment carrying the track between Wickede and Neheim badly damaged.

0141 The reserve wave were now passing Roosendaal. It is not known whether they had been forced south by the stronger winds as had Gibson's formation earlier, but if this was the case then a lesser adjustment to port than planned would have been required to take them on their next heading towards Beek.

Martin in AJ-P was now approaching the lake west of Meppel (close to the same area crossed by Maltby some minutes earlier). There he turned to port and headed out across the Zuider Zee, following the planned route to the Den Helder peninsula.

0141 At the Eder, Gibson was becoming increasingly concerned with the amount of time being spent developing the attack. Though the threat of fighters at low level and in such confined airspace was small, there was always the danger that they might be assembling to pick them off as they headed for home. The last thing that anyone wanted was to be caught at dawn or even later, still over enemy territory. Inexplicably, the Waldeck observer post made no report to Kassel at the time of Shannon's attack, but at 0141 reported that the aerial situation remained unchanged. Aircraft were still circling over the reservoir.

0142 approx. Gibson ordered the next attack. S/Ldr Henry Maudslay came in again but still had problems meeting the parameters of height and speed.

The tension was mounting and at one point a degree of frustration could be detected in the exchanges between Gibson and Maudslay over the VHF as a further run was made, again without success. In *Enemy Coast Ahead*, Gibson says that having made his two abortive attempts Maudslay then called up and announced that he was going to make his final run. This view is echoed by Fred Sutherland, Knight's front gunner, who says that after Maudslay had made two abortive runs: 'Gibson was getting a bit irritated. He said, "Henry, that's very nice flying, but you will have to do better than that." Henry said, "Sorry sir. I will try again."'

Maudslay came in again. To one observer something appeared to be hanging down from Maudslay's aircraft, thought to be indicative of damage sustained on the flight to the target. Reverting to Gibson's account of Maudslay's final run, although there is no specific detail, he does allude to a possible problem:

> We could see him running in. Suddenly he pulled away; something seemed to be wrong, but he turned quickly, climbed up over the mountain and put his nose down, literally flinging his machine down the valley. This time he was running straight and true for the middle of the wall. We saw his spotlights together, so he must have been at sixty feet. We saw the red ball of his Very light shooting out behind his tail and we knew he had dropped his weapon. A split second later we saw someone [*sic*] else; Henry Maudslay had dropped his mine too late. It had hit the top of the parapet and had exploded immediately on impact with a slow yellow vivid flame which lit up the whole valley like daylight for just a few seconds. We could see him quite clearly banking steeply a few feet above it. Perhaps the blast was doing that. It all seemed so sudden, and the flame seemed so very cruel. Someone said, 'He has blown himself up.'

Knight's crew saw it slightly differently, placing the explosion slightly behind Maudslay's aircraft, while Shannon, possibly with the explosion between him and the Lancaster, was not in a position to see any detail, only record the flash of the detonation.

Gibson immediately called Maudslay over the VHF: 'Hello Z-Zebra. Are you alright?' There was no answer. He called again, to which there was a faint reply, heard by each of the other crews: 'I think so. Stand by.' After that, silence.

In his de-briefing report, Gibson stated: 'The mine overshot and struck the parapet, detonating instantaneously. The pilot was spoken to afterwards by R/T and was heard to reply once, when he sounded very weak.'

Nothing further was heard or seen of this aircraft by the accompanying crews, although, contrary to witness reports at the Eder, Maudslay and his crew had survived the explosion and were beginning to make good their return course to Scampton.

Maudslay's 'Upkeep' had detonated on the parapet of the dam, above the third main discharge sluice to the east of the centre of the dam. It destroyed some 150 feet of the stone balustrade and hurled masonry and fragments over the dam, some of them going through the power station roof, and causing the 60,000-volt powerline crossing the valley to short circuit with a brilliant flash.

0143 The observer post at Waldeck reported that two four-engined aircraft were over the dam, and two minutes later reported smoke rising above the dam – presumably that created by the parapet detonation of Maudslay's 'Upkeep'.

0145 As at the other two main targets, the attacks on the Eder were witnessed by the engineer on duty in one of the two power stations below the dam, Karl Albrecht: 'At first, we'd assumed that the bombers were using the lake as an assembly point. The first bomb fell at about half-past one but did not damage the wall much, though it damaged power house No. 1.' He also reported that there were 'two brilliant flares burning beneath the dam on the island between the two power houses', which he presumed were to act as an aiming guide for the bombers.

With no knowledge of 'Upkeep' and its method of delivery, such an assumption was perfectly logical. In reality these lights, below parapet level, would be unlikely to be seen by an aircraft approaching low over the lake. The reference is probably to the Very cartridges fired by Shannon and Maudslay as they released their weapons and passed over the dam, or possibly to the cartridges initially fired by Gibson to help the remainder of the force to locate the target.

0145 No. 5 Group re-broadcast the flak warning issued by Gibson for the defences near the lakes at Dülmen. The reserve wave were now threading their way through the Scheldt estuary. Aboard each aircraft the wireless operator logged the message and passed it to the navigator. In the rear turret of Ottley's aircraft, Freddie Tees had been conducting a methodical search of the night sky since approaching the Dutch coast. He did not expect to encounter night fighters at such low level, but habit made him do so. At one point during the flight, he noted that they were lower than the height of a passing church steeple.

With Knight having the final 'Upkeep' and with growing concern about the likelihood of success at this target, Gibson appears to have instructed Hutchison to attempt to make contact with Astell, using W/T. Gibson would have tried earlier, using VHF (R/T) when checking the force at the

Möhne. At that time Astell had failed to answer and this later attempt was made probably as an insurance against Astell's VHF being unserviceable. If this were the case, then there might have been another aircraft available to attack.

0148 Hutchison made a further attempt to raise Astell by W/T. Again there was only silence.

0150 A further attempt was made to contact Astell, but he had now been dead for over an hour and a half.

0152 AJ-P Martin, following the flight plan, made a landfall at Hoorn on the east coast of the Den Helder peninsula before heading for the North Sea coast, 21 miles away.

0152 Gibson called on Knight to attack. Having watched attempts by the others, Knight had reassessed the approach route. It appears that he made a straighter approach, possibly descending to the northern shore of the lake down a valley further west of that alongside Waldeck Castle, possibly that about a mile west-south-west, on the other side of the Katzenstein, and crossing the Hammerberg further east at a point where the spit was nearer lake level and which also gave him a marginally longer run to the dam. Even so, as with Shannon and Maudslay, Knight found it extremely difficult to achieve the coincident height, heading, speed and range. He and his crew were dissatisfied with their first attempt, their speed being too high, and called a dummy run.

Up to this point there had been a lot of chatter over the intercom and VHF as the other crews tried to give advice. 'Come in down the moon and aim for the point, and then turn left,' as cited by Gibson, suggests that Knight's first attempt was his modified route, and that someone, most likely Shannon, was suggesting the ravine route that he had used with the sharper turn to port, flying almost directly into the moon, which by this time was at 175 degrees (i.e. almost due south) and 15 degrees above the horizon. The continued advice was becoming a distraction and Knight told Bob Kellow, his wireless operator, to switch the VHF off.

For his next attempt Knight stuck to his preferred run, with the moon on his starboard beam. As they descended towards the lake Ray Grayston, the flight engineer, pulled the throttles right back to idle in an effort to prevent the speed from building up. Crossing the spit, Knight then found it easier to line up on the dam; they were at the right height and speed, on a heading of 135 degrees, 15 degrees to port of Shannon's run in. After about seven seconds the bomb aimer, Edward Johnson, was able to call 'Bomb gone!' and Grayston pushed the throttles 'through the gate', providing maximum power and enabling Knight to begin his climbing turn to starboard to clear the ridge beyond the dam.

Gibson, who was flying slightly above and about 400–500 yards to starboard of Knight, watched the run. 'Upkeep' bounced three times, reaching the wall slightly to the right of centre before sinking in contact, exactly as Wallis had intended. A perfect shot. The seconds ticked by and N-Nuts crossed over the dam, its red Very light soaring up behind indicating 'weapon released'.

With no defences to contend with, Harry O'Brien in the rear turret stared in anticipation at the dam wall, waiting for the detonation. The involuntary lift of the aircraft combined with Knight's pull on the controls seemed to make the Lancaster stand on its tail. The distorted perspective was further exaggerated as the 'Upkeep' detonated and a plume of water rose 800–1,000 feet into the air, as if rushing to meet him.

Looking back from the astrodome and bracing himself against the gyrations of the aircraft, Bob Kellow recalled:

> When we passed over the dam wall at the Eder we had to clear a large hill directly ahead of us. After the mine had been dropped Les [Knight] pulled the nose up quite steeply in order to clear this hill and in doing so I could look back and down at the dam wall. It was still intact for a short while, then as if some huge fist had been jabbed at the wall, a large almost round black hole appeared, and water gushed as from a large hose.

A hole had been punched through the wall, about 30 feet from the crest (which coincided with the depth of detonation as set by the hydrostatic pistols). The parapet and roadway remained intact above it for a brief period before collapsing into the swirling water.

In Shannon's aircraft, bomb aimer Len Sumpter, first heard 'a hell of a bang' and then their Yorkshire rear gunner, Jack Buckley, who was in a position to see the dam, shouted: 'It's gone!'

0153 A fourth and final attempt was then made by Hutchison to contact Astell. This seems strange given that it coincides with Knight making his final and successful attack. This call may have been made either before the breach was confirmed, or if this was already apparent, then any response from Astell might have resulted in him being diverted to the Sorpe. However, the reasons for making this attempt to contact him can only be speculation.

Werner Salz, the dam engineer, had heard the detonations as the 'Upkeeps' exploded. The third was particularly intense, the shock wave being felt through the ground beneath his feet. Realising that the dam must have been hit he began to run towards Hemfurth to find that water had already reached the houses immediately alongside the river, causing their occupants to flee in fear of their lives. Reaching the dam he saw a massive gap in the wall with the water pouring through. The air was filled with a continuous roaring thunder. Four of his colleagues had been working the night shift, and he feared for their safety. Later, as dawn broke, lights could be seen on the roof of Hemfurth I power station and in the morning three men who had climbed up to escape the rising waters were brought down to safety. The body of the fourth was only discovered the following August, having apparently been swept from the basement where he had taken shelter and buried in the silt and gravel which filled the turbine outlet.

In the Hemfurth II power station at the southern end of the dam, the engineer Karl Albrecht had been taken by surprise by the detonation of Shannon's 'Upkeep'. He did not register Maudslay's detonation on the parapet but was standing on the steps at the entrance to the power house when the shockwave of Knight's bomb was transmitted violently through the structure. He sought shelter inside the building, which by now was in total darkness. Water and debris crashing through the roof brought him to his senses and he raced up the steps to the crest of the dam. There, breathless from exertion and fear, he watched as the breach grew wider. On the north side of the breach, another official, August Rubsam had been knocked off his feet by the detonation. With all telephone links severed, he was powerless to warn the authorities in Hannoversch-Münden of the impending disaster.

The breach in the Eder was smaller than that created in the Möhne, measuring 230 feet wide and 70 feet deep, with water pouring through the gap at an estimated 1.9 million cubic feet per second (marginally less than the Möhne's initial discharge) into the narrow valley below, producing a 20- to 25-foot flood wave which thundered as far as 19 miles downstream. By the time its force diminished in the wider lower Eder floodplains, and had run into the rivers Fulda and Weser, some 14,000 gallons per acre had flowed, causing widespread destruction and claiming the lives of some 68 people. Within 36 hours an estimated 74 per cent of the reservoir had emptied. It would take another 12 hours until the flow finally stopped: longer than the Möhne, since the lake was 1.4 times the size and the breach marginally smaller.

A mile downstream from the dam, the occupants of Hemfurth, reassured by that evening's civil defence meeting, had taken to their basements and shelters on hearing the air-raid warning. Now they were being summoned from them with great urgency and told to flee to higher ground – the dam had been hit. The water was first seen coming across the playing field alongside the river, north-east of the village – a thirty-foot-high wave, shining brilliant white in the reflected moonlight.

Meanwhile, Bürgermeister Ochse of Hemfurth called a relative who lived in Affoldern, two miles further down the valley to warn him: 'The Eder dam's been breached. The water's coming. Warn the village and pass the word on.' Meanwhile the Bürgermeister's son and a friend cycled around Hemfurth, warning the inhabitants. In the lower parts of the settlement eight houses and six commercial properties were completely wrecked.

At Bad Wildungen the postmaster received a phone call from Affoldern reporting that the dam had been hit and that the water was coming, then the line went dead. The postmaster relayed the message to the local police and those in Fritzlar, further down the valley. After initial disbelief they too passed the message on, alerting those in the path of the approaching flood. Above them, the crews of the orbiting Lancasters marvelled at the force that had been unleashed as they followed the water for a short distance down the valley. Harry O'Brien and Len Sumpter both recalled seeing a car inundated as it tried to escape the water, its lights going from white to green and then suddenly going out.

A tidal wave 36 feet high swept down on Mehlen, five miles below the Eder. A mile further on, at Bergheim, both the road and rail bridges succumbed to the deluge, the latter collapsing as the initial wave struck, forcing the tracks into the air amidst a shower of sparks, as whole sections of the bridge simply crumbled.

The Eder Valley was much wider than that of the Möhne. The flood wave flattened out rapidly since the water had sufficient space to spread, and its velocity decreased. The affected area increased and substantial amounts of topsoil were stripped from fields for the first ten miles. In other places the ground was left covered with scree and silt.

Chapter 9
Mobile Reserve and Return

0153 AJ-J As success was being achieved at the Eder, Maltby completed his journey across enemy territory. Gee was still jammed, and navigation was by dead reckoning as he crossed the neck of the Helder peninsula north of Alkmaar, heading for the North Sea. Maltby appears to have omitted an intermediate leg from Meppel, opting to take a route direct across the Zuider Zee. As they crossed the coast north of Callantsoog the last of the defences fired a few bursts of flak and a searchlight possibly near Den Helder, or on the southern tip of Texel, swept the sky, but without causing any serious problems.

The aircraft of the mobile reserve were encountering moderate opposition over the Netherlands. They had passed Roosendaal and were now picking their way between the night-fighter airfields of Gilze Rijen and Eindhoven. Dutch witnesses recall that there was activity around these airfields throughout the night, which would relate both to the 'Chastise' aircraft and also Mosquito intruders. At Molenschot, west of Gilze Rijen, some of the four batteries of 88-mm and 75-mm heavy flak and two batteries of 37-mm medium flak defending the airfield opened fire on the first of these, Ottley's, as he threaded his way through, some of the shells falling on neighbouring Dutch homes. This aircraft was then engaged by searchlights and further guns in the Nerhoven area on the south-eastern perimeter of the airfield, but it appeared to escape unscathed. Local witnesses report this engagement as occurring at 0130, but this timing appears to be too early and may be a mis-recording of 0150.

Recounting events of this night post-war, Freddie Tees recalled: 'We took off from Scampton at midnight, a clear night, a full moon, and we thought it would be an easy trip as we crossed the North Sea. We were halfway across Holland before we ran into any trouble. We hit our first light flak concentration and got through it without a scratch.'

0157 Four minutes later P/O Burpee was passing Breda but was four miles north of the planned route and heading directly for Gilze Rijen. It is also possible that Burpee was aware of a possible navigation error and may have climbed shortly before reaching this point in an attempt to pinpoint his position. There were a number of witnesses to the next few minutes, although their testimony is inconsistent and in part contradictory.

0200 Ken Brown was flying as third in the reserve wave, and was approximately a minute behind Burpee. His crew reported seeing an aircraft about 10 miles ahead of them explode in mid-air and crash in flames. Brown's description of events was summarised on the official Loss Card for ED865: 'Exploded in mid-air near Tilburg, outbound. Cause not known.'

According to Brown: 'Burpee was just off our port wing ahead of us when he was shot down.' Stefan Oancia, Brown's bomb aimer reported: 'The Lancaster ahead of us flew over a German airfield, was hit by ground fire, fuel tanks exploding and the ball of flame rising slowly – stopping, then dropping terminated by a huge ball of flame, as it hit the ground and the bomb exploded.' Behind Brown, Doug Webb, front gunner in Townsend's O-Orange, saw 'a bloody great ball of fire' ahead and to port.

The official report recorded:

> Aircraft 'S' is thought to have exploded in mid-air [sic] in the Tilburg area at 01.53 [sic] hours. The observing aircraft 'F' was in longitude 0506 at 0153 and 3 miles south-east of the town so that 'S' was observed at longitude 0453E and about 8½ miles WSW of Tilburg. There is no report to indicate that this aircraft was following the same track as 'F' but if the crashed aircraft was on track it was about 3 minutes behind 'F'.

The eyewitness accounts are all clear that the doomed aircraft was ahead of both AJ-F and AJ-O, although Brown's position given in the report quoted above would put him east of Gilze Rijen, and Burpee would be behind him. It is more likely that Brown was at a position near 04°40′E, placing Gilze 10 miles ahead and Brown about 3 miles south-west of Tilburg.

While there is no doubt that the aircraft in question was Burpee's, there are conflicting accounts as to the cause of its loss. In 1974 a Luftwaffe eyewitness, Herbert Scholl, in 1943 a Ju 88 wireless operator with E/NJG 2 (an operational training unit attached to NJG 2), gave an account stating that the four-engine aircraft (which he identified as a Halifax) came in from the west and was caught directly in the beam of a tower-mounted searchlight located between an aircraft repair hangar and the flak command post. The aircraft was so low that the searchlight beam was horizontal, shining directly at the approaching bomber. The aircraft dropped even lower, striking trees on the western edge of the airfield and cutting a path through them before crashing on an empty motor transport shed about 100 yards from the command post where it burst into flame. A few seconds later there was a tremendous explosion as the aircraft's 'Upkeep' detonated, shattering the windows and doors of buildings on the base and blowing members of E/NJG 2 who were standing some 800 yards away, off their feet. A huge column of smoke rose a thousand feet into the air and the wreckage burned fiercely for a considerable time, accompanied by the smaller detonations of exploding ammunition.

Examination of the wreckage the next morning revealed that the aircraft had been totally destroyed, save for the rear turret and tail unit which had broken off at the aft fuselage joint. Inside the turret, the lifeless gunner showed no visible signs of injury; it was noted that he was wearing a pair of ordinary walking shoes with worn soles, and thin uniform trousers. All seven crew were originally interred in Zuylen temporary cemetery, Breda-Prinsenhage, before re-burial in October 1946 in Bergen-op-Zoom War Cemetery.

This German account is of note in that it maintains that although the searchlight illuminated the aircraft there was no fire from the anti-aircraft defences. It presumed that the aircraft was brought down on account of the pilot being dazzled by the beam. This contradicts the other reports which clearly refer to the aircraft being hit by anti-aircraft fire and catching fire in the air, and makes no mention of the aircraft allegedly switching on its navigation lights in an apparent attempt to deceive the defences into believing that it was a friendly machine.

The flak command post adjacent to the crash site, which filtered information from radar stations along the Dutch coast, was heavily damaged, and out of action for several months as were other buildings, the cost of repair being cited as 1½ million guilders.

The burning wreckage of AJ-S was later also witnessed by one of the No. 456 Squadron Intruder Mosquitos. F/O Oxlade and his navigator F/O Shanks took off from an advanced base at Castle Camps at 0125, crossing the Dutch coast at 3,000 feet over Westhoofd Ouddorp, to patrol airfields in the southern Netherlands. They observed the occulting beacon positioned north-east of Gilze Rijen and also noted a fire burning on the ground to the north-west of the airfield – almost certainly the remains of Burpee and his crew. Circling the vicinity of the airfield at 2,500 feet Oxlade's Mosquito was engaged by heavy flak and machine-gun fire from the very alert defences.

The reason for Burpee taking a route that led him directly over Gilze-Rijen will never be known, but the official record noted that after 3°E the wind direction changed to between 30 and 60 degrees while increasing in speed to 14 mph. It is possible that he had adjusted his heading to allow for a wind that may not have been as northerly as earlier detected, thus overestimating his southerly drift, with the result that his track was taking him north of the planned route, and right over the airfield defences.

0154 Hutchison transmitted 'DINGHY' to No. 5 Group Headquarters, confirming the successful breaching of the Eder dam.

0155 Group rebroadcast 'DINGHY' on full power to all aircraft. Hutchison replied confirming: 'CORRECT'.

0157 Each aircraft of Gibson's wave had released its 'Upkeep' and now the sole objective of each of the captains who had witnessed the Eder's destruction was to return safely to Scampton. Nevertheless, there was still a great deal of excited exchange over the intercom as Gibson called up: 'Good show, boys. Let's all go home and get pie.'

0157 AJ-Z was approaching the Möhne reservoir on the first leg of its return flight. Some seven minutes after Maudslay's attack, and his last, faint contact with the other aircraft, his wireless operator Alden Cottam sent confirmation of their attack to Wally Dunn at No. 5 Group Headquarters: 'GONER 28B'. This was three minutes after Gibson's wireless operator had sent 'DINGHY' confirming that the Eder dam had been breached, but neither this anomaly nor the later signal received confirming Shannon's release seem to have been questioned by Group Headquarters. They were already too pre-occupied with allocating targets to the third-wave aircraft. Additionally, they were ignorant of the fact that as far as the other attacking aircraft were concerned Maudslay and his crew had already perished.

AJ-P At about the same time Martin had reached the North Sea coast and continued north-west on a heading taking him to the next waypoint 30 miles out.

0200 AJ-N Three minutes later, as if to further confirm the previous 'DINGHY', came 'GONER 710B' from Les Knight's wireless operator, Bob Kellow – Mine exploded in contact; large breach in Eder dam. It seems plausible that the chronological dislocation of reports may be attributed to the fact that crews were preoccupied with the activity over the target and the concentration and teamwork required to execute an attack. Once a crew had made their attack their focus became the issue of setting course for home. Reporting the result of their attack was not necessarily seen as critical to the success of the operation, and they also may not have appreciated the importance of this information in helping Cochrane assemble a picture of the operation's progress so as to allocate the resources of the reserve wave effectively.

0204 The air-raid warning centre at Kassel was still receiving reports of a four-engine aircraft over the Eder lake, although it seems likely that all the attacking aircraft were now heading back to the Möhne. A minute later there was a report of a light over the dam, which again remains unexplained.

0205 approx. Shortly after two o'clock the SS recruit regiment stationed in Arolsen was alerted by means of the phone line set up by Bürgermeister Ochse of Hemfurth. They then tried to contact the 3rd Battalion, 603rd Infantry, at Hemfurth, but already the lines were down.

0205 approx. AJ-P Martin was now nearly 30 miles over the North Sea from Callantsoog on the Dutch coast. At this point he should have altered course towards Skegness. For an unknown reason he appears to have kept on, heading north-west for another 70 miles before turning towards the English coast.

0206 AJ-J Maltby was some 45 miles from the Dutch coast when Sgt Nicholson managed to obtain a faint signal from Gee, sufficient to fix their position. Satisfied, he also replaced the cartridge in the Very pistol with the new colours of the day.

AJ-T McCarthy reached Vlieland and continued heading for his next turning point over the North Sea. In contrast to the force's inbound journey across the island the defences seemed caught unawares and they crossed it without incident. Since he was flying the reciprocal of his inbound track, rather than his briefed exit route, the crew had no details of convoy positions in the area at that time. At one point at 100 feet over the North Sea, McCarthy spotted a line of ships ahead. Not knowing whether they were friend of foe, and well aware of the Navy's propensity to fire at any approaching aircraft, McCarthy kept low and threaded his way past them seemingly unobserved and unchallenged.

0208 AJ-N reached the Möhne dam. Knight and his crew were fascinated to see how the decreasing water level had changed the shape of the lake. Although shaken, the dam's defences were still alert and one gun, presumably that on the parapet roadway, opened fire on the approaching Lancaster. Knight swiftly evaded. Using the dam to confirm their position, F/O Hobday re-set the API and they set course for Ahlen, flying at 100 feet and with an indicated airspeed of 220 mph, although a slight northerly wind meant that they made marginally slower progress over the ground.

0210 Gibson, Young and Shannon would also have reached the Möhne at about this time. For a distance of three miles below the dam the river had swollen to 'several times its normal size' while upstream, behind the remains of the dam, the reservoir level was noticeably lower and pleasure boats moored to the shore were already stranded on exposed mudbanks.

0210 approx. Eder Valley The flood warning initiated by Bürgermeister Ochse at Hemfurth had been transmitted down the line to Anraff, on the western flood plain of the Eder River, some 7 miles below the dam. The warning saved many lives; people had a little time to protect themselves and perhaps a few basic possessions before the water hit the village. During the next hours many of the occupants of neighbouring Bad Wildungen, safe on ground 450 feet higher, came to see the awesome spectacle of the flooded valley. They immediately realised the severity of the situation and began to assist, driving cattle out of barns, helping the aged and infirm from their homes and supporting the inhabitants in salvaging what they could. The residents of Anraff were proud to recall that despite the devastation there was not a single report of any looting. Amongst those assisting was Jan Gumila, a Ukrainian forced labourer who, with little concern for his own well-being, helped the rescuers. He later remarked that the villagers had always treated him well. Later firefighters helped recover the bodies of seven flood victims which were taken to the local church to be prepared for identification and collection.

After the confirmation of 'DINGHY' at Grantham there must have been discussion at No. 5 Group Headquarters while Cochrane collated the available facts and sought to build a mental picture of the current state of his force and remaining aircraft.

He would have known that, of the Sorpe wave, Rice and Munro had returned early without reaching their target.

The fate of Byers and Barlow was unknown, but by now it is likely that either Munro or Rice would have reported seeing an aircraft, most likely one of their wave, being shot down over the Waddenzee. Owing to his wireless problem, McCarthy's successful but inconclusive attack on the Sorpe had not been reported. No further attempt was made to contact any of this wave and at this point the impression must have been formed that it was unlikely that any attack had been made on the Sorpe.

Cochrane's first concern was to obtain confirmation as to whether any of Gibson's nine aircraft were still carrying 'Upkeep'. If so, they should be directed to the Sorpe.

0210 No. 5 Group HQ Dunn asked Gibson: 'How many aircraft of the first wave are available for "C" [the Sorpe dam]?' A minute later Gibson responded: 'None'. The Operation Order had detailed that the reserve would be under the direct control of Cochrane from HQ No. 5 Group. He now had to decide how best to allocate them.

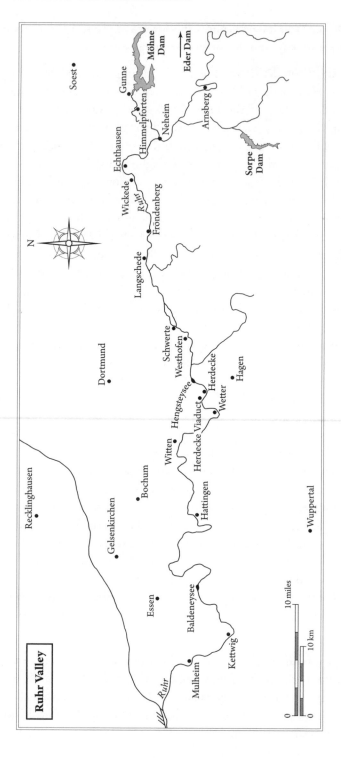

0212 Ruhr Valley Thirty miles downstream from the Möhne, Schwerte had experienced an air-raid alert all night. After imprecise rumours of flooding, the local railway air-raid warden was warned by officials from the stations at Neheim and Wickede of an unprecedented tidal wave sweeping down the river. A warning was issued to the inhabitants of the lower part of the town to seek higher ground and try to rescue livestock. Again, this was misunderstood as a general flood risk. They were used to occasional seasonal flooding, but this was entirely different. When the water arrived at 5.30 it did so with unprecedented speed, estimated at 15–20 mph, rising rapidly and trapping occupants in their upstairs bedrooms. It took four hours for the levels to recede sufficiently for many to be rescued.

0212 Kassel. The air-raid warning centre received a report that the Eder dam had been hit.

0213 AJ-T Don MacLean, McCarthy's navigator, obtained a fix placing them 15 miles west-northwest of Vlieland.

0214 AJ-N Knight reached Ahlen. He then headed for the lakes at Dülmen despite the flak there, rather than reverting to the original route south of Haltern.

0214 AJ-J Based on dead reckoning from his Gee fix, Nicholson estimated their position as 53°00′N 03°00′E and gave Maltby a minor course correction to take them to Scampton. Six minutes later, 100 miles from the Lincolnshire coast, speed was reduced to 185 mph and the Lancaster climbed to 500 feet before descending again, inexplicably, 'to test spotlights'.

0217 AJ-T McCarthy was now 38 miles north-west of Vlieland when Mac-Lean gave him his final course, due east, for Scampton. With 190 miles to go and a groundspeed of 220 mph, they would be home within the hour.

0217 approx. AJ-C and the reserve wave would almost certainly have taken a more southerly track to avoid the flak warned of at Dülmen. In an uncorroborated post-war account Freddie Tees stated that approximately seven minutes before their eventual demise: 'Over the German border we hit our second lot of flak, and although our guns in the aircraft made an effective toll of the enemy guns, they scored a direct hit on our starboard outer engine. We suffered no casualties and P/O Ottley succeeded in keeping us in the air.'

Although Tees's 'seven minutes' can only be an approximation, had the aircraft been following a more southerly route this would place the aircraft in the vicinity of Haltern and close to the northern defences of the Ruhr.

0218   The air-raid warning centre at Kassel received a report 'Enemy aircraft from the Eder lake area on return flight to the north-west.'

0219   Back at Grantham, after a five-minute consultation with Satterly, who had been tracking the progress of the remaining aircraft by dead reckoning, Cochrane had formulated his plan to deploy them and passed his instructions to Dunn. Dunn then broadcast 'DINGHY' to each of the aircraft in turn, confirming again that the Eder had been breached and to stand by for instructions.

0220 approx. AJ-Y   At a position which he later estimated to be 'five minutes before Dülmen' Anderson ran into searchlights which forced him off course. His exact route following notification of Gibson's flak warning is unknown, but this calculation of his position would appear to place him in the vicinity of Raesfeld, only two or three miles from Marbeck where Astell had collided with the pylon.

There was a searchlight on the outskirts of Raesfeld and there were other searchlights in the Marbeck area. These were activated after Astell's crash, which brought the defences of the area, including those in Borken to the north and Marl twelve miles to the south, to a state of heightened alert as testified by witness Anni Reining, who worked as a maid for the Thesing family, living adjacent to Astell's crash site: 'The flak batteries defending Marl didn't start firing until the bomber [Astell] had already crashed. The searchlights at Marbeck also shone straight up into the sky after this. The enemy aircraft were flying so low that the searchlights couldn't have lit them up anyway.'

0221 AJ-O   George Chalmers, Townsend's wireless operator, acknowledged No. 5 Group's call and a minute later Dunn transmitted the single codeword: GILBERT – attack the last resort target.

0222 approx.   Townsend ran into a defensive position as he attempted to cross a canal. Startled by the suddenness and intensity of the fire, he turned back on a reciprocal for about thirty seconds while the crew had a quick discussion as to the best way through. Realising that they were over a forest, he took a decision that was possibly to save their lives. '[The flak] was so intense that we turned off course, circled over a forest area, then flew down very low through the fire breaks in the tall pines. I suppose the flak lasted for about five minutes, but the critical period was probably little more than a minute.'

As they sank below the level of the trees members of the crew recalled seeing the angry lines of tracer lowering and then scything through the treetops as the German gunners depressed their barrels in an attempt to keep the Lancaster in their sights. According to Lance Howard, the navigator, Townsend 'threw that heavily laden Lancaster around like a Tiger Moth and we flew out of it'. Just as remarkable was that after all these gyrations O-Orange left the area almost exactly on track for their next turning point.

Previous accounts of 'Chastise' suggest that this encounter took place earlier in the flight. Circumstantial evidence may indicate that it was in the area of Haltern. There are large, wooded areas north and south of Haltern, the Haltern Borkenberg and the Schwartzwald respectively. The approach to the latter from the Rhine follows the originally planned Rees–Ahsen–Ahlen route and crosses the Wesel–Datteln canal immediately west of the Schwartzwald.

0222 AJ-N At about the same time, Knight skirted the lakes at Dülmen on his homeward run, turning onto a course of 300 degrees for the 49-mile leg to Zutphen.

0224 No. 5 Group HQ Dunn broadcast 'DINGHY' to Harry Hewstone, in Ken Brown's crew.

0225 AJ-F Hewstone acknowledged Dunn's broadcast.

0225 AJ-O Not having received any reply from Chalmers of 'GILBERT' broadcast at 0221, Dunn re-broadcast 'GILBERT' to O-Orange, who this time acknowledged a minute later.

In theory, Townsend should have been approximately three minutes behind Ottley, and Chalmers's four-minute delay in responding to No. 5 Group's original 'GILBERT' perhaps provides confirmation of their encounter with the defences – the crew being otherwise pre-occupied, entering the flak zone at 0222 and leaving it at 0226.

It is also conceivable that it was this concentration that threw off Anderson's navigation (see 0220) and that his assessment of 'five minutes from Dülmen' was in error – although his reference to searchlights would appear to refer to a different incident.

(Some accounts attribute this flak encounter as being earlier in the flight – just after the re-broadcast at 0145 of the warning of flak at Dülmen. This may be due either to confusion with flak in the Gilze-Rijen area at that time, or with the receipt of 'GILBERT' at 0221 and the flak in the Haltern area.)

0228 No. 5 Group Dunn called Anderson in AJ-Y, broadcasting 'DINGHY'.

At this stage of the flight Anderson should have been a minute behind Townsend which would place him roughly in the defended area that had given the latter so much trouble. If he was taking a slightly different route as a result of the flak warning, and had been forced off course fifteen miles from

Dülmen, it can only be assumed that he was now probably in the area east of Haltern.

0228 AJ-C Dunn then called Ottley.

0229 AJ-Y Anderson confirmed receipt of 'DINGHY'. He would attack the Sorpe. At this point it appears that he was still heading for Ahlen and still confident that he would be able to find the Möhne lake even though navigation may have become more difficult. He was now probably more than one minute behind Townsend.

0230 approx. Möhne dam Police Reservist Hannermann reported that 'Several aircraft' appeared at the Möhne and attacked the flak positions which responded. Farmer Nettlebeck's barn was set alight by this 'second' group of aircraft, but the blaze was soon extinguished. Another report, written four months later by Dr Pruss, the Superintendent of the Ruhr Valley Dams Association, also recorded that at about this time 'scout planes' flew over the Möhne dam and engaged the dam's defences with machine guns and set fire to a barn in Gunne with incendiaries. Although the timing is imprecise, these reports may well relate either to aircraft returning from the Eder, or those outbound aircraft using the Möhne as a waypoint on their route to their individual targets.

The barn may have been ignited by the 100 per cent tracer rounds fired by the Lancaster's Brownings, or by the additional 4 lb incendiary bombs carried by each of the aircraft. Further credence that it may have been the latter is provided by Gibson's account in *Enemy Coast Ahead* where he states that on the return flight Trevor-Roper called over the intercom: 'I am almost out of ammo, but I have got one or two incendiaries back here. Would you mind if Spam tells me when a village is coming up, so that I can drop one out. It might pay for Hoppy, Henry and Bill.'

0230 AJ-N Hobby Hobday obtained a fix 2 miles north-west of Aalten, using this confirmation to re-set the API which had wandered over the last leg. This may have been a further manifestation of the problem he had experienced with this instrument on the outward route when approaching the Scheldt estuary. With his position established, he set course for Elburg, on the coast of the Zuider Zee, 11 miles north-east of Harderwijk.

0230 No. 5 Group contacted Ottley in AJ-C, which was acknowledged.

0230 No 5 Group instructed Ottley 'GILBERT'. He was to attack the Lister dam.

0231 A minute after sending Ottley his 'GILBERT' instruction to attack the Lister, No. 5 Group re-broadcast to him, amending his target to the Sorpe.

0232 No. 5 Group tried to send 'DINGHY' to AJ-S, Burpee. It was repeated a minute later and went unacknowledged since Burpee and his crew were already dead.

Two documents suggest that Anderson was first allocated the Diemel as his last resort target and subsequently diverted to the Sorpe. If so, the messages sent at this time suggest that No. 5 Group originally intended two aircraft (Brown and Burpee) to attack the Sorpe, and that one aircraft each was to attack the Ennepe (Townsend) and Lister (Ottley). If Anderson was originally to attack the Diemel this would have meant that at least one aircraft would have attacked each of the six dams detailed in the Operation Order. It appears that subsequent reconsideration then switched Anderson and Ottley to the Sorpe as evidenced by the radio messages. Given that No. 5 Group had yet to receive confirmation of McCarthy's attack and that Wallis had stated that it might require five 'Upkeep' to breach the Sorpe it seems surprising that Townsend was not also switched to the Sorpe.

The reserve wave, now comprising Ottley, Brown and Townsend, supposedly spaced at roughly two-minute intervals but with Anderson probably trailing further back, were approaching the end of their transit north of the Ruhr and on their approach to the turning point at Ahlen.

0232 AJ-C Ottley and his crew had survived their recent encounter with the defences but, according to Tees's testimony, had an engine knocked out. However, on emerging from the defended area, unlike Townsend, they appear to have been able to regain the required course to Ahlen. It is possible that evasive action resulted in a displacement of their track and that they emerged from the area south of route and continued their progress parallel to, but about a mile and a half to starboard of their planned track. Alternatively, damage to the aircraft may have resulted in a gradual deviation to starboard. Whatever the reason, the result was to bring them closer to the defences of Hamm.

As they skirted Hovel on the city's northern outskirts, Freddie Tees heard the wireless operator confirm over the intercom that the Eder had been breached. Ottley's subsequent 'We go to ...' was abruptly interrupted by a tremendous noise. The aircraft was caught by searchlights and Tees suddenly felt the thump as a burst of flak, mainly from the port side, found its mark. Sparks and smoke streamed past his turret from the port inner engine, the smoke intensifying and making it difficult to see the ground. He attempted to rotate his turret but realised that hydraulic power had been lost. Ottley's voice again sounded in his headphones 'I'm sorry boys, I think we've had it.'

The aircraft was obviously doomed but, unlike Burcher, Tees had no chance to rotate the turret by hand in order to reach his chute.

These events were witnessed by the crews of AJ-F and AJ-O. Ken Brown saw an aircraft on the starboard bow, which he estimated was flying at 500 feet, come under concentrated fire: 'He immediately blew up. His tanks went first, and then his bomb . . . the whole valley was just one orange ball.' Oancia, Brown's bomb aimer, saw an aircraft ahead of them being hit and explode.

Brown recalled the event in more detail during an after-dinner talk at the Bomber Command Museum of Canada at Nanton in July 1993:

> As we came along to Hamm they were really waiting for us. We and the other two waves had passed that way. So, they poured it (flak) down. As a matter of fact, they were firing down at us. They were on a little bit of a lip as we went through the valley. Ottley was on my starboard side at about one o'clock and they hit him. He immediately blew up. His tanks went first and then his store.
>
> When that happened the whole valley was just one orange ball. I didn't have too much of an alternative: I don't think there was any bravery connected with it. There was a road off the port side. Everything was trees and this road, I couldn't see because of the fire from his aircraft. So I dove and went along the road. Then much to my consternation that damn road led right into a castle, and I'll never forget that castle door. We had to dip, and the left wing went between two turrets as we went through the castle.

The timing and location suggest that the castle in question was the Schloss Westerwinkel, Ascheberg.

Farther back, Townsend saw a massive flash to starboard and his navigator recalled seeing an aircraft flying at over a hundred feet coned by searchlights and hit by intense flak. The fuel tanks caught fire, after which it climbed slightly before exploding in the sky.

Ottley's demise was also allegedly witnessed from a distance by Gibson returning via Ahlen, having taken a final look at the emptying Möhne lake. If so, this suggests that Gibson may have lingered a little longer at the Eder and over the Möhne before setting course for Ahlen. Gibson incorrectly interprets the loss as being Burpee: 'They had got him somewhere between Hamm and the target,' but the official report by No. 5 Group identified correctly that Ottley had crashed 'at Hamm, seven miles off track', implying incorrectly that he was already on the Ahlen–Möhne leg when he was shot down.

Ottley's loss is attributed to one of Malte Schrader's rail-mounted units at Bochum-Hovel which reported aircraft approaching from the west. With no known Luftwaffe activity in the area the gunners were given authority to open fire. A short while afterwards the battery reported that they had hit one of the bombers and a glow was seen in the direction of Mann-Heesen, marking Ottley's funeral pyre. Later that day Schrader would receive orders to deploy some of his battery to defend the Sorpe dam, lest a second attack be mounted the following night.

0233 No. 5 Group repeated 'DINGHY' to AJ-S, which of course went unacknowledged.

0235 AJ-C came down on the edge of a wood 1½ miles north of Kotterberg, a village on the northern outskirts of Hamm. As the aircraft hit the ground the tail section and turret with Tees still in it were blown clear of the subsequent inferno and detonation of the 'Upkeep'.

At the time the official report on 'Chastise' was written in June the identity of this aircraft was still unclear and the presumption was made that this may have been one of the early aircraft detailed to attack the Sorpe, namely Byers or Barlow. If so, then the timing would suggest that the aircraft may have been on its homeward track having made an attack on the Sorpe which had not yet been notified to Grantham:

> An aircraft was seen shot down at Hamm at 02.35 hours. Hamm is 7 miles off the track between position 5148 – 0713 and Ahlen and 7 miles off the track between Ahlen and target X. The defences of Hamm are likely to be less than 7 miles from the tracks so that the aircraft turning more than 2¼ minutes too early at Ahlen on the way to the target would probably fly across the Hamm defences. As the leg from 5148 – 0713 to Ahlen was only 8 minutes long, an error of 2¼ minutes seems to be too large to be credible. If the aircraft shot down was one of the first or second Wave returning from Target X, it would indicate that the course was set from some point west of Target X or that the aircraft set course direct from Z to Ahlen and cut the corner at X. It is thought that 'K' or 'E' attacked Z so the crash reported probably refers to one of these aircraft.

The assumption may also have been influenced by the difficulties reported by Townsend and Brown at debriefing, of identifying the Möhne after it had been breached on account of the new 'lake' created by the released water.

Another paragraph in the same report concedes that the casualty may have been Ottley, while also adding Young to the possibilities:

Another aircraft was shot down near HAMM at 02.35 hours and was observed to hit the ground with a large explosion by F/617 which was proceeding towards its target at 150 feet. This aircraft might have been C/617 of the third Wave or might have been A/617 of the first Wave or K/617 or E/617 of the second Wave.

Freddie Tees regained consciousness on the ground. Bruised and burnt he extracted himself from his turret and started to make his way from the crash site. As he came out of the trees, he encountered a schoolboy making his way to look at the crash site. Injured and in a state of shock, the airman surrendered and was soon handed over to the police and taken to hospital before being transferred to a prisoner-of-war camp. The remainder of the crew were all killed, including Strange who had swopped turrets with Tees. They were originally buried in the South Military Cemetery, Hamm, and re-interred in Reichswald Forest War Cemetery in December 1947. Tees died in 1982 and in accordance with his wishes, his ashes were scattered on the graves of his comrades. Reunited in death.

0235 AJ-P   At about the same time as Ottley and his crew died, Martin was about 100 miles from the Lincolnshire coast and turned onto a course of 276 degrees, making good a track parallel to, but 20 miles to the north of the briefed approach to the English coast.

0236 AJ-Z   Maudslay had successfully completed his route back to the Möhne and the turning point at Ahlen taking him north of the Ruhr and was heading west at the end of the long leg towards the Rhine. This area had presented some of the strongest opposition to the outbound crews and batteries would now be wakeful, anticipating the returning aircraft. At the turning point at Rees his planned return route turned north to cross into the Netherlands and pass by Harderwijk on the southern shore of the Zuider Zee.

Crews had been briefed to make the return flight at a speed of 220 mph. It would appear that Maudslay was either flying more slowly, at about 180–185 mph, or had taken a slightly longer route around the north of the Ruhr. Whether he was on track and turned correctly, but then strayed slightly off course, or whether he was already north of track cannot be confirmed, but five minutes later he was heading directly towards Emmerich, 20 miles north-northwest of Rees and only a mile or so from the Dutch–German border.

The town's functions as a Rhine port and oil refinery centre, combined with its location on the approaches to the industrial Ruhr made it sufficiently important be defended by several light *'Heimat'* flak batteries. Units in the area had been brought to readiness earlier by the squadron's outbound Lancasters and were now alert for the enemy aircraft as they returned to base.

0235   Marburg area, 28 miles south-west of the Eder dam: Kassel received a report of 'one enemy aircraft circling in the Marburg/Lahn area'. Suggestions that this may have been Maudslay – lost and disorientated – can be discounted since at this time AJ-Z is known to have been approaching the Rhine.

0236 AJ-Z   An aircraft was heard approaching Emmerich at low level from the south-east. Visibility was good and the sky marginally lighter in that direction. The sound of engines increased and the gun crews identified the dark shape of a four-engined bomber. It was flying low and would come within the range of the 20-mm batteries to the south and east of the town.

The battery in Der Ward was the first to open fire, soon to be joined by other 20-mm sites along the Nierenbergerstrasse and near the river port. The plane turned away to the right in an attempt to evade the stream of shells curving towards it. As it did so the rear gunner returned fire, directing a continuous stream of tracer at the battery near the harbour area. By now about a dozen guns were firing. With sights at maximum depression, their fire cut through the tops of nearby poplar trees. At first the aircraft seemed to avoid the flak but then suddenly there was a flash as either an engine or fuel tank was hit, followed by a burst of flame. The aircraft continued for a short distance, heading in the direction of Klein Netterden, to the east of the town. Witnesses could see the fire was spreading rapidly and the aircraft lost height until it hit the ground in a ball of flame.

The aircraft had come down in a flat field close to Osterholt, to the east of the Industria Brickworks alongside the Osterholtweg, a short distance before the Dutch border, between Kleine Netterden and 's Heerenberg. Later that morning German officials came out to inspect the smouldering wreckage. The machine was identified as being a British Lancaster bomber. Searching through the debris the authorities recovered the remains of the crew, all of whom had been killed instantly as the aircraft hit the ground. Their bodies were originally laid to rest in the Nord Friedhof, Düsseldorf, and subsequently re-interred in Reichswald Forest War Cemetery.

0236   The air-raid warning post at Waldeck reported to the local centre at Bad Wildungen that Affoldern was now under water and that buildings were collapsing and being swept away.

0240 AJ-T   McCarthy was just over half-way across the North Sea, following almost exactly the reciprocal of his inbound route. Flying at 100 feet above the waves and making 190 mph they were now 84 miles from the English coast.

0241 AJ-N   Knight was still picking his way out over the Netherlands and was 16 miles east of Harderwijk, after passing between Deventer and Raalte, slightly starboard of track, some ten miles from Elburg which was identified on the port beam and reached three minutes later.

After witnessing the loss of Ottley, Townsend had identified Ahlen and made a starboard turn onto the leg taking him south-east to the Möhne lake.

0243 approx.   AJ-F and AJ-O arrived in the area of the Möhne. The latter crew had difficulty in identifying the dam itself.

Sgt Charles Franklin, Townsend's bomb aimer, reported seeing a large, elongated lake stretching away westwards towards Neheim, prompting a response by navigator Lance Howard that this could not be so; there was no such lake on his charts. As they approached Townsend took the Lancaster closer and they could see the roofs of buildings with clusters of people clinging on to escape the swirling water. It was then that they saw the breached dam, 'a great stream of water rushing out of the breach and rolling down the valley beyond the wall'. Satisfied that his reputation as a navigator was intact, Howard marvelled at the awesome but terrible sight.

At debriefing the crew reported: 'Had a look at Möhne dam on way in and could not find it for some time. Found sheet of water about seven miles long and extending to four miles wide up the valleys with dam in middle. Roofs of houses could be seen sticking up above the water which was flowing very fast.'

By this time the escaping water had travelled down the Möhne valley, through Neheim, past Wickede and by 2.30 a tidal wave estimated at 12–20 feet high had reached Fröndenberg, bringing with it uprooted trees, rocks, mud and the remains of buildings, and as many as 160 human victims from further up the valley.

There had been advance warning. The roar of the water could be heard coming from the direction of Wickede. Hitler Youth were despatched to warn the inhabitants and fire sirens sounded the alarm. As elsewhere there was no specific alarm for a flood situation, and it was difficult to persuade people to leave their shelters. When word eventually got through as to what was happening, it was believed only to be a flood, and no one anticipated a tidal wave with strong currents. A number of people went down to the Ruhr to see the spectacle and were simply swept away.

As elsewhere the damage was extensive. Both the road and double-track girder rail bridge were swept away. Eleven houses were destroyed, numerous properties flooded, and 34 inhabitants died. A nearby slave-labour camp was inundated with the cost of 30 workers and 4 guards. A further 160 unidentified dead, presumably carried down from upstream locations, would also be buried in the town cemetery.

0244 AJ-N Knight was flying on Return Route 3, which had also been allocated to Maudslay and Young. He identified Elburg on the coast of the IJsselmeer, 12 miles south-west of AJ-J's exit point just over an hour previously and turned port onto a westerly course taking him across 30 miles of water to cross the eastern coast of the Den Helder peninsula near Edam, and thence to the North Sea coast between Castricum and Egmond.

0247 AJ-T Confirming his fix obtained seven minutes earlier Don MacLean obtained a second position, placing them 70 miles east of the Lincolnshire coast.

0250 No. 5 Group Dunn re-broadcast 'DINGHY' to all aircraft of the mobile reserve.

0253 AJ-J Maltby crossed the Lincolnshire coast at Wainfleet, familiar to No. 5 Group crews as a bombing range, and used by the squadron crews in their early low-level bombing practices.

0254 approx. AJ-L Shannon climbed to 800 feet before putting the nose down to cross the coast near Castricum aan Zee at nearly 300 mph. For an unknown reason, which can most likely be attributed to the elation felt by some of the crew members returning from this operation, Brian Goodale, David Shannon's wireless operator, re-transmitted the code 'GONER 79B' to No. 5 Group Headquarters confirming their successful drop at the Eder.

0256 AJ-T McCarthy's navigator F/Sgt MacLean continued to obtain his fixes, which now placed them 37 miles from the Lincolnshire coast, making a straight run for Scampton.

0257 AJ-N Knight was approaching the North Sea near Castricum aan Zee. The selection of this stretch of coast as a crossing point seems surprising since it is only 5½ miles from the port and industrial centre of IJmuiden which was strongly defended by a mixture of Navy and Luftwaffe batteries comprising both light and heavy weapons. Navigation was aided, however, by the Noord-hollandskanaal and the readily identifiable landmark of a body of water, the Alkmaardemeer/Uitgeestemeer. Directly ahead were two radar masts at Castricum – their final exit pinpoint – beyond them the sea.

Unlike the others it seems possible that rather than climbing prior to building up speed for crossing the coast, Knight opted to keep as low as possible. As they approached the beach Knight kept the aircraft right 'on the deck', pulling up only to clear a high dune ridge that rose across their path. From his turret, rear gunner Harry O'Brien noted with horror as the Lancaster sank back down and a large concrete block, believed to be a 60-foot-high *Flakgruppenkommandostand* (Flak command and observation post), part of the coastal defences, flashed past a mere few feet below his turret. The obstruction had been lurking in the dead ground immediately behind the ridge, unseen by Knight. It had been a close call, but they had caught the defences by surprise and passed over without a shot being fired.

0258 AJ-A At almost the same moment, Melvin Young was following route 3. He appears to have had an uneventful return across enemy territory. From Harderwijk he had made a pinpoint on the island of Marken, and after crossing the Den Helder peninsula seems to have passed south of the lake and was approaching the coast nearer to Wijk aan Zee, increasing height slightly, ready to dive and gain speed, making his exposure to the defences as brief as possible.

Young was some six miles south of the tracks taken by AJ-N and AJ-G at this point, and thus closer to the northern defences of IJmuiden; there is also the possibility that these had been alerted by the passage of Knight's or another aircraft, although again the evidence is contradictory as to the order in which Knight and Young crossed the coast. Young's tendency to fly a little higher than the others may have compounded the risk. It is reported that after crossing the east coast of the peninsula he pulled up, rather than keeping low. This was in accordance with briefed tactics, more so if he was uncertain of his position, but by doing so he sealed his fate.

Accounts vary, some stating that a mixture of four 88-mm and six 37-mm guns opened fire, others that only one 88-mm fired at the Lancaster which then attempted to turn north away from the defences, parallel to the coast, For a moment it looked as though the aircraft had escaped unscathed but it was then struck by a shot fired by one of 81st Marine Battalion's 88-mm guns. The tail of the Lancaster was hit and it descended into the sea, coming down on a sandbank some 100 yards offshore. Although some reports suggest that Young had attempted to ditch the aircraft the impact was heavy. Photographs show that while the centre section and wings remained relatively intact the fuselage of the Lancaster broke up on impact sufficient for the bodies of its crew members to be carried out to sea, being taken by the current and washed ashore further north, between Wijk-aan-Zee and Bergen-aan-Zee, a week or so later. All now rest in Bergen General Cemetery (Bergen-aan-Zee).

0259 AJ-N Knight's navigator recorded 'Crossing coast, reduce airspeed' and recorded a groundspeed of 176 mph. This relatively low speed suggests that they were now past the coast and over the sea, reinforcing the hypothesis that they had passed through the defences marginally ahead of Young and possibly alerting them to the following Lancaster.

While the Lancaster crews were coasting out over the southern Netherlands, between 0237 and 0326 Wellington minelayers were 'gardening' the 'NECTARINES' area off Vlieland. The island's defences were quiet despite their activity earlier in the night.

0300 AJ-T McCarthy was now only about 60 miles or 20 minutes' flying time from Scampton when No. 5 Group Headquarters received the signal 'GONER 79C' – mine exploded in contact with the Sorpe dam and optimistically predicting 'a small breach'.

This was the first confirmation that those at Grantham had received of an attack on the Sorpe. Knowing that Rice and Munro had returned early, and with no response from Byers, Barlow, Burpee and Ottley, this left only Brown and Anderson from the reserve wave detailed to attack this target. Nothing had been heard from Townsend since acknowledging 'GILBERT' at 0226, but it must have been assumed that he would now be in the vicinity of the Ennepe and that it was too late to switch his attack to the Sorpe.

0300 Anraff, Eder Valley Karl Burk's SS regiment proceeded towards the Eder lake. Until that moment he was under the impression that the dam was being attacked by a British Commando troop. As he saw the extent of the catastrophe, he declared the area a disaster zone and set up camp in the railway station at Buhlen. He divided the area into two parts: the upper part Hemfurth–Affoldern–Mehlen–Bergheim–Giflitz–Anraff with Captain Bernhard in charge; and the lower part, Wellen–Wega–Mandern–Ungedanken–Geismar under Lieutenant Michaelis. Both would be overseen by Major Back, commander of 29th Armoured Pioneers Recruit Battalion from Hannoversch-Münden. A further emergency operations and first-aid centre was established in an Affoldern barn. Priority was given to the re-establishment of telephone communications and shortly after ten o'clock the next morning they were able to issue commands to the villages and settlements concerned.

From all over the region a swarm of officials and quasi-officials from various government bodies, institutes, self-important Nazi functionaries or self-appointed spokesmen started a kind of 'inspection tourism' (*Inspektionstourismus*). Colonel Burk would have none of this behaviour and quite ruthlessly put a stop to it.

Lieutenant Wilhelm Michaelis, one of the local commanders, recalls:

At around 1045 a.m. a member of the rescue task force reached Anraff. We immediately had to report the damage to his staff. In our place virtually everything was still intact, there were no immediate casualties to care for, and we were immediately told: 'Take care of yourself as you can, we'll help you later.' Then, around 5.00 that afternoon, the tidal wave slowly subsided, and the situation eased. All those affected were found shelter in the village. It was a case of help and help alike.

The following day help arrived in the form of fire brigades from central Germany. The assistance given then built bonds that survived a great many years later.

Seven miles further down the valley lay Fritzlar airfield, being used by Junkers for test and development work on the new Ju 352 transport. There was sufficient warning to prevent loss of life, and the broad width of the valley meant that the airfield was only flooded to a depth of 4–6 feet. Development of the aircraft was disrupted for a few weeks.

0305 AJ-P Martin completed his crossing of the North Sea. He appears to have steered a course which brought him to North Coates, some 20 miles north of his intended landfall, thus requiring a turn south-west to bring him to Scampton.

0306 A minute later, Maltby arrived over Scampton. After circling the airfield for five minutes he touched down at 0311, the first of those who had carried out an attack to return.

0308 AJ-T McCarthy crossed the Lincolnshire coast at Mablethorpe at 100 feet. With 34 miles left to run he adjusted his course two degrees to port to bring him over Scampton.

0310 AJ-Y With his rear turret unserviceable and forced off track by search-lights at about 0220, approximately 'five minutes short of Dülmen', Cyril Anderson had been struggling to regain track. It is not known how far he had progressed beyond the Haltern/Dülmen area, although his acknowledgement of 'GILBERT' at 0228 confirms that at that stage he was continuing his mission. Now, forty minutes later, he too should have reached the Möhne dam and have been setting course for the Sorpe dam.

However, he was still uncertain of his position. With ground mist beginning to obscure landmarks, and with the increasing likelihood of not being able to find his target, make an attack and clear the Dutch coast before daybreak, he decided to abort the operation. His briefed return route was as that followed by Martin, Maltby and Shannon, via Nordhorn and across the Helder peninsula, but as in the earlier case of McCarthy, he chose to return by the reciprocal of his inbound route, in this case heading back to Rees and then to Beek and out of Holland via the Scheldt estuary.

0311 AJ-J Maltby landed at Scampton and taxied to dispersal. The crew disembarked to find a large number of personnel waiting to greet them, including Harry Humphries:

> I went to Flights and met Dave Maltby. I said, 'Hello Dave. How did it go?' and he said 'Marvellous, absolutely marvellous. Never seen anything like it. Water, water, everywhere. Wonderful, wonderful.'

There was a great sense of euphoria, tempered by the knowledge that some of them, almost certainly including Hopgood and Astell, would not be returning.

Martin arrived overhead in the Scampton circuit as transport arrived to take Maltby and his crew back to the briefing room where the Intelligence staff were waiting together with others to debrief them and offer hot drinks and cigarettes – their first proper refreshment since the pre-flight meal nine hours earlier. While Maltby and his crew were taking in the scale of what they had achieved, Ken Brown and Bill Townsend were approaching the Möhne, their next identification point and datum for setting course to their respective targets.

0314 AJ-F The transit from the Möhne to the Sorpe had been only four minutes, and although Brown arrived in the area at about 0247 he found it impossible to locate the Sorpe dam precisely. His bomb aimer, Stefan Oancia recalled: 'All low-lying areas were covered with a fog or mist leaving only the tops of the hills exposed and thus making a determination of the exact ground location impossible.' It took some time and searching until the crew were convinced that they had located the right area, but after circling the area it seems that the turbulence of their passing helped the visibility improve and they were finally able positively to identify the dam. Further investigation revealed the same issues that had beset McCarthy – the descent past the church spire, the brief run along the dam before having to pull up to clear the steeply rising ground on the eastern shore.

Brown too found the approach extremely challenging:

> I tried to position myself from the spire. I didn't do too well. I got behind the dam on the first run. When I found myself at ground level, behind the dam, I had to climb up roughly eighteen hundred

feet. It didn't do my nerves any good at all. Because I was on top of the trees, I had to do a flat turn. I couldn't move the wing down to get around. I had to stand on the rudder to get around and then we were down in the valley again.

On the third attempt, after climbing the hill on the far side they descended again only to find themselves in the mist-filled valley of the adjacent River Rohr. It was easy to become disorientated and lose the position of the lake and dam. Brown then resorted to a tactic that he had used while trying to land in poor conditions during training. As noted earlier, each aircraft carried six incendiary bombs to be used as required as navigation markers. Brown located the dam again, using the church as a starting point and then flew a circular orbit, encompassing the attack run, during which the incendiaries were released down the flare chute at timed equal intervals by Harry Hewstone, the wireless operator. On completion of the circuit a glowing necklace on the ground provided a datum indicating the position of the dam.

By now the area over the dam had cleared, although the approach and exit routes were still mist-shrouded. Making the attack required three further attempts. Brown described the technique finally adopted:

We came in over the church spire. I had to cut the power back almost to a stall, then shove the stick forward and come screaming down the side of the hill with the power right off. When we hit the level where I thought it was 60 feet, I shoved on the power and ran along the sloping side of the dam, an extremely short run I might add, to the point of release. There was no time for lights before we had to climb like mad to clear this hill.

Oancia was finally able to release the 'Upkeep', unspun, at 0314. The weapon 'dropped about 10 feet away from the dam about two-thirds of way across'. Its detonation created a 'semi-circular swelling of water against the dam, followed by a spout of water 1,000 feet high' (an observation which was repeated on McCarthy's questionnaire, suggesting that the wording was that of an Intelligence officer). The blast at a shallower depth caused a percussion ring which was seen to rise rapidly, dissipating the mist. After the water and spray had subsided, Brown made a low pass over the dam to observe the results.

The direction of Brown's final attack run has become a matter of some debate. According to German witnesses, Brown made his attack at 90 degrees to the wall. Josef Kesting, the engineer who had witnessed McCarthy's attack, was in the power station at the time and 'didn't see the plane until it was flying over the dam with its lights on'. His testimony maintains that Brown did two circuits of the reservoir, dropping his bomb on the second run. Its detonation blew out the windows of the power station and stones and debris rained down in the area of the compensating basin.

Kesting's account is unclear as to whether he actually witnessed the second attack, and also omits Brown's several attempts to perfect his line of attack. It seems likely that he was inside the building at the time that Brown dropped his 'Upkeep', and thus did not see the bombing run. He then emerged to see AJ-F making the subsequent reconnaissance run at right angles over the dam to assess the damage and may have assumed that this represented the direction of the actual bombing run.

A second witness, night watchman Josef Brinkschulte, also saw and made a distinction between the two attacks, claiming that the second was made at right angles to the wall, again by an aircraft showing lights. His claim is more difficult to refute.

Officially Brown released his 'Upkeep' at a groundspeed of 180 mph from 60 feet on a heading of 130°. This indicates a run along the dam, rather than at right angles to the wall, and as such was in accordance with the prescribed method for the release of 'Upkeep'.

Brown's debriefing questionnaire records that visibility was 500 yards but that he said he could see 'everything' and that the moon was 'on the starboard beam'. The moon at the Sorpe at 0314 on 16 May 1943 was at an angle of 14 degrees above the horizon and on a heading of 245° (i.e. in the south-east) which equates with it being on the Lancaster's starboard beam when making an attack along the dam from Langscheid on a heading of 130°. The reference in the questionnaire to the 'Upkeep' falling about two-thirds the way across again suggests a run along and parallel to the dam, rather than one towards it.

If Brown did make an attack at right angles to the wall the assessment of range would have been more critical and extremely difficult to achieve. Also, the ring of incendiaries enabling an orbit of the target used for a parallel approach would have been unnecessary. At the Canadian Bomber Command Museum in 1993 Brown gave no indication of making a run at right angles to the dam:

> Our tactics were to run parallel with the dam and drop our bomb
> in the middle . . . it was a near perfect drop. We were pleased with it
> and as far as the explosion was concerned, the waterspout went up
> to about a thousand feet and so did we. I think we ended up about
> eight hundred.

Regardless of the method of attack, Brown's was also inconclusive. He assessed that the crest had crumbled for a distance of 300 feet, but the dam still appeared intact with no obvious signs of leakage.

0318 AJ-T Back at Scampton McCarthy was about to join the circuit in preparation for landing following Martin who was a few minutes ahead of him.

0319 AJ-P Martin landed and taxied to dispersal, the second to return. As he shut down an excited group gathered beneath the starboard wing to view the damage received over the Möhne dam. For the crew it was their first full appreciation of how close it had been. Martin's rear gunner Tammy Simpson:

> Things were a bit sombre when we got back. The first thing we learned when we got out of the aircraft was that there was a great hole in the [starboard] outer wing where the aircraft had been hit by ground flak. The outer tank was completely denuded of petrol at the time, so it saved our bacon.

Martin took a more laconic perspective, remarking to Mutt Summers: 'Hello Mutt. Look what some bastard's done to Popsie.'

0323 approx. AJ-F After completing his assessment of the Sorpe, Brown arrived back at the Möhne. Approaching the reservoir from the south-west his navigator Dudley Heal had the same disconcerting experience as Howard earlier, of seeing a lake which was not on his charts and an absence of landmarks. Flying upstream they reconnoitred the rapidly emptying dam: Brown noticed that 'the water level had gone down considerably and there was a fast-flowing river below the dam'. The crew's debriefing report recorded their observations:

> Flight Engineer saw two large breaches close together between the two targets. Each breach was about a quarter width of the space between the two towers. Water was pouring through both gaps, shooting well out before falling in two powerful jets. The valley seemed to be well covered with water. Report confirmed by air bomber [sic]. Front gunner reports a third breach beyond tower on NE end of dam. Breach about half the size of the other two. Water pouring through.

While the apparent appearance of two breaches between the towers might be explained by the effect of disturbed water at the edges of the breach, the reference to a further small breach remains a mystery, akin to the similar claim made by Shannon after his attack at the Eder.

One incident the crew omitted to mention in their debriefing report was that while Brown was taking stock of the scene at the Möhne, one of the dam's gun crews, probably that which had fired on Knight as he passed the dam nearly an hour and a half earlier, opened fire on them. The resolute defenders were silenced by rear gunner, Grant McDonald. Brown recalled:

> As we came over the Möhne, they were throwing 20-mm at us . . . so we came real low, below the towers, straight on at them. We opened up at about five hundred yards and carried in over the tower and the rear gunner depressed his guns and we raked the thing as we went through. Well, there was no firing coming from that tower when we left.

0323 AJ-T   At Scampton McCarthy was cleared to land having successfully completed his return flight by flying the reciprocal of his outward journey to overcome the problems with the compass deviation card. As the aircraft touched down the starboard wing dropped, but McCarthy reacted swiftly, applying aileron to hold the wing up until the speed dropped and the ride became exceptionally bumpy, even for Scampton's grass field. Looking out to starboard the deflated mainwheel could be seen twisting erratically around the rim and the significance of the jolt felt while attacking the train at 0057 became apparent. A single shot had entered the undercarriage bay and burst the tyre. As the speed decayed the aircraft began to ground loop but the undercarriage held, and a relieved crew climbed out.

0326 AJ-F   As with McCarthy, the next stage of Brown's return flight, the 21 miles from the Möhne to the turning point 1 mile east-northeast of Ahlen, was not without incident. Increasingly concerned about the possibility of night fighters – a view shared with McDonald – he kept the Lancaster at rooftop level, hugging the ground, as Feneron urged maximum power from the Merlins. As they approached east of Hamm the defences opened up. Already on high alert since Brown's outward flight and doubtless encouraged by their victory over Ottley, they began laying two low-level box barrages on track and ahead of the Lancaster. It was an intense time, but the Lancaster came through without damage.

0330 AJ-N   Knight had maintained 100 feet for the crossing of the North Sea. Now, 85 miles from the coast, he began to climb to 4,000 feet. Five minutes later he was 23 miles east of Sea Paling on the Norfolk coast, approximately 118 miles from Scampton.

0337 AJ-O Following the loss of Ottley north of Hamm, Townsend had trailed Brown by several minutes to the Möhne. Using this as his departure datum he headed for his allotted target, the Ennepe dam, thirty-five miles to the south-west. He too had great difficulty identifying the reservoir amongst the many mist-filled valleys. Identification was further hampered by inaccurate information about the target. The target maps showed an island in the middle of the lake 320 yards ahead of the dam rather than the correct narrow spit of land.

Eventually Townsend found a reservoir of the correct configuration which he identified as the Ennepe. Further concerns emerged when George Chalmers started 'Upkeep' spinning. Though supposedly balanced, at 500 rpm, a tremendous noise and vibration was transmitted through the entire airframe, to the crew's great consternation.

Three runs were made in an effort to release the problematic 'Upkeep', without success. Each time Charles Franklin the bomb aimer called 'dummy run' and Townsend had to pull up and to the left to go round for another attempt. Although the run-in was across the lake, its narrowness and proximity to the rising shoreline meant that it was extremely difficult to achieve the vital combination of line and height. During these runs Howard noted 'a large manor house' on the starboard side.

A fourth run was made at 0337, and the 'Upkeep' was released on a heading of 355 degrees at 220 mph. The bomb made two bounces and sank as AJ-O cleared the dam. About 30 seconds later the weapon detonated with the familiar thousand-foot plume of spray. As it subsided Howard saw that the dam was still intact.

He recalled: 'We were well inside enemy territory. The moon was starting to set and we could see signs of dawn breaking. A lone daylight flight over hostile territory faced us.' Sunrise was now only an hour and a half or so away. Townsend set course back to the Möhne, anxious to make the Dutch coast before daybreak.

As with Brown's attack on the Sorpe, ambiguity surrounds Townsend's attack. The squadron Operations Record Book reports: 'Ennepe Dam. 1 Mine, 60 ft. 0337. Mist on the reservoir caused this aircraft to make three runs at the target. Mine dropped accurately on third attempt and seen to explode.'

To add to the mystery, the War Diary of the German Naval Staff (Operations) reported that the Bever dam, an earthen dam some 7 miles southsouthwest of the Ennepe, was attacked without result on this night. One bomb was dropped, falling in the middle of the reservoir, but causing no damage. This claim is reinforced by an account by Paul Keiser, a soldier home on leave, of a bomb being dropped into the Bever reservoir at about 0300 hrs on 17 May.

Hearing the sound of engines, he went out and witnessed an aircraft making three runs over the Bever dam at a height estimated as 50 metres. On the third run it dropped a bomb into the lake some 800 yards from the dam. This exploded about 250 metres from the site of an earlier masonry dam, used at that time as a bridge across the lake, which had been replaced downstream by the earth dam to enlarge the reservoir in 1938. In addition, on the northern end of the old dam was a large house – Haus Uhlenhorst, which might equate with Howard's 'manor house'.

Much of this account accords with the details of Townsend's attack – but there are significant problems in reconciling the two. An attack on the Bever dam would have required a run on a heading of some 225° not 355°. Keiser also stated that the aircraft was clearly seen to be a twin-engine machine with RAF markings, not showing any lights, which after attacking, circled and then flew off in the direction of Cologne. He also recalled that the explosion was relatively small – causing a waterspout about 60 feet high, rather than the thousand feet created by 'Upkeep'.

The seismograph at Göttingen recorded a detonation at 0337, so there can be no doubt that Townsend's 'Upkeep' was released at that time. Three of Townsend's crew reported that during the attack the moon was on the starboard beam, as it would have been for the Ennepe. Townsend stated that the attacks were made 'running into [the] moon in half-light reflected on mist and water'. For the Bever dam the moon would have been on the starboard bow, thus approximating to Townsend's recollection.

The Bever had no towers, although buildings at each end might have been misidentified as such and being 479 yards apart rather than the 110 yards of the small towers on the Ennepe, these would have given a false release point of over 800 yards. With this the 'Upkeep' would have submerged halfway to the target and detonated in the manner recorded on the debriefing form: 'A circle, afterwards meeting dam' as the outward-spreading ripples from the distant detonation eventually reached the wall.

Paul Kreis's testimony describing a twin-engine aircraft has been ascribed to an attack by one of the No. 105 Squadron Mosquitos sent to Düsseldorf – and the smaller explosion would also equate with a single bomb from this type of aircraft. No reference is made to any such diversion in the No. 105 Squadron Operations Record Book which states that their Mosquitos operated at above 20,000 feet and all returned to base by 0123. It would seem a remarkable coincidence if one of these Mosquitos had unilaterally diverted to and attacked the Bever dam on the night that another aircraft was attacking a neighbouring dam – the more so given that security for 'Chastise' and its targets was so stringent.

To add to the confusion, the post operation de-briefing pro-forma refers to Townsend's attack being made against the Schwelme dam. This name, with various spellings, appears in subsequent reports. It has been suggested that this name, taken from a town within 10 miles of both the Ennepe and Bever dams, was used to resolve the uncertainty about the target – the 1940 listing of Operational Targets records the dam on the River Ennepe as the Schwelm (*sic*) while the Bever dam, on the River Bever, is not listed.

Further perpetuating the ambiguous dam, on 29 June, Sir Arthur Harris instructed that the Service Records of those who lost their lives on Operation 'Chastise' should be endorsed: 'On the night of the 16th/17th of May 1943 this airman [or officer] took part in the extremely hazardous and highly successful raid on the Möhne, Eder, Sorpe and Schwelme Dams, from which operation he failed to return.'

0343 AJ-O was back in the area of the Möhne dam, again finding it difficult to identify. Howard noted: 'We turned for the Möhne – found it, and stared amazed at the drop in the water level on the banks of the lake – and still the water gushed in a white sheet down the valley.'

0355 AJ-N Over the sea off Brancaster and nearing the Lincolnshire coast, Knight switched on his navigation lights.

0400 The water arrived at Fröndenberg at 0345 and at this time the flood was reaching its peak, 27 feet above normal levels, and spread across the valley for nearly two miles to Menden-Bosperde. Gas supplies were cut, as were the phone lines with Menden across the valley. The force of the water was so great that it brought down the pylons of the 25,000-volt power line, illuminating the landscape with a brilliant flash that lasted several seconds like a false dawn. The local hydroelectric plant weir was washed away, and the concrete road bridge collapsed into the torrent. Half an hour later, as the peak of the flood began to subside, the double-track railway bridge a few hundred metres downstream collapsed under the pressure of the road bridge debris.

Across the valley, at Halingen on the south bank of the Ruhr, opposite the village of Langschede, they were used to the river flooding. Tonight, as before, people went out to fetch the livestock in from the fields as the waters rose up to their bellies. One of them, 60-year-old Bernhard Kuster, a farmer and innkeeper, assisted by his 9-year-old son, was bringing in livestock from the fields. They were used to the river flooding, but not like this; the water was flowing swiftly, first up to the horses' bellies and still rising quickly, now a tidal wave several metres high. The force of the water swept him off his feet and against the trunk of a beech tree near his cowshed. With difficulty and in fear of his life he managed to lodge himself in the branches above the increasing spate while he watched the world he knew disappear. His livestock and the root crops and potatoes he cultivated were all under water. It had all happened so quickly. Within minutes his life had been irrevocably changed. His wife, daughter, son and sister all drowned in the rising waters, their bodies being recovered in Schwerte, eight miles downstream. His home was destroyed, and with it his belongings, his memories, his life. All that remained were the geese, which returned the following day, and a dog.

Over the following days the bodies of many Neheim residents and foreign workers were recovered in Hattingen, carried fifteen miles by the waters. In the church a plaque commemorates locals who perished, amongst them a married couple, an entire family, and a well-respected and much-loved elder. Officials placed strict censorship on obituary notices to conceal the extent of the catastrophe, permitting only the phrase: 'According to God's unfathomable will found death by a tragic fate on May 17.'

As AJ-N was approaching the English coast Les Knight reduced ground speed to 185 mph. Harry Hobday fixed their position 10 miles due east of Cromer and 5 miles north-east of Mundesley before switching on the navigation lights.

0406 AJ-L landed at Scampton. Shannon had not spared the throttles for most of the journey, following the same return route taken by Maltby earlier, and in all probability also taking the shorter route across the Zuider Zee and Den Helder peninsula to arrive a quarter of an hour ahead of Knight.

0408 AJ-N crossed the coast at Skegness, arriving over Scampton at 0412.

0411 AJ-O George Chalmers finally transmitted news of their attack back to Grantham: 'GONER 58E' – 'Upkeep' released against the Ennepe; exploded 50 yards from the dam with no effect. Now heading north-west towards Zutphen, Sgt Powell was coaxing maximum power from the Merlins trying to put as much distance between them and the beginning of a disconcerting glow in the eastern sky. As they tore low across the countryside at speeds in excess of 240 mph, they were hard pressed to look out for approaching obstacles and power lines, many requiring a last-minute hurdle to clear them.

0415 AJ-Y Cyril Anderson passed Roosendaal and was approaching the Scheldt estuary.

0415 AJ-G Three minutes after Knight, Gibson landed at Scampton.

0419 The all-clear sounded in Kassel at 0419. After four hours of taking shelter, the inhabitants of the city began to emerge, thankful that they had not been the target for Bomber Command that night. It would be another six hours until the unleashed waters of the Eder reservoir reached the city.

The maximum discharge through the breach is computed to have been 8,500 cubic metres per second, a similar magnitude to the flow from the Möhne dam. It would take 36 hours to empty the reservoir of 1.64 million cubic metres out of a total of the 2.15 million cubic metres which were in storage at the time of the attack.

0420 AJ-N Knight landed at Scampton. Including the two early returns of Munro and Rice, seven aircraft had now come back. LAC Keith Stretch, a member of AJ-N's groundcrew, was waiting. Knight came over and said, 'I hope I haven't treated your engines too badly, they behaved beautifully but we did have to call upon emergency power for a while.' Otherwise, the Lancaster had performed impeccably.

After the aircraft were bedded down, the groundcrews reported to the flight office and were told to return at 0800.

0420 AJ-Y With the enemy coast 20 miles behind them, William Bickle, Anderson's wireless operator switched on the IFF. Reaching the intermediate waypoint 30 miles off the Scheldt estuary, Bickle changed frequency on his TR 1154 transmitter to call No. 5 Group, a minute later sending a message in the standard bomber code: 'Returning to Base. Unsuccessful.'

As the last aircraft picked its way across the Dutch countryside, Gibson and his crew were being debriefed. F/O Bellamy, who had photographed the crew as they boarded their aircraft eight hours earlier, was again on hand to capture the crew seated around a table as they related their experience to S/Ldr Townson, Scampton's Intelligence Officer. Harris and Cochrane, whose only information had been the staccato Morse messages, stood, watched and listened, now keen to hear first-hand from the leader of the attack.

The harsh light of Bellamy's flash bulb captured the faces of the crew (except Pulford, who was out of shot), reflecting different reactions – an animated Spafford, expressing nervous relief at their return. Next to him, on the end of the table, Terry Taerum his gaze focused across the room, his thoughts elsewhere. Across the table, Deering was seated next to Gibson whose furrowed brow and sunken eyes were testimony to the physical and mental effort of the night, not to mention seeing two, possibly three, of his squadron's crews meet their end in a sudden burst of flame. Bob Hutchison was to Gibson's left, with Trevor-Roper, a large mug of rum-laced tea near his elbow, thankful that he had survived to see his 29th birthday in two days' time.

Across the table, the paraphernalia of debriefing – a sheet from the Eder dam target folder – a view of the target from above Waldeck Castle, a pre-war German photograph of the dam used for briefing the crews as to the line of attack. Also visible is a grey and purple shaded target map, the white serpentine reservoir showing starkly against the darker terrain. The Intelligence officer leafs through his notes, possibly reviewing the pro-forma questionnaire specially produced for this operation.

The record of this debrief is succinct: Gibson reported that visibility was excellent during the bombing run: 'Saw the whole thing', picking up the target 'from 3–4 miles' with his 'Upkeep' making three bounces before detonating with an 'enormous column of water'. According to the crew 'There are two holes in the dam', though subsequent photographs clearly show only one breach, and in his account in *Enemy Coast Ahead*, written a year later, Gibson only refers to one 'great breach 100 yards across'. Gibson was complementary about the use of VHF radio to control the operation – summing it up in a single word: 'Perfect'. His gunners, likewise, praised the decision to use 100 per cent daylight tracer in their guns: 'Very satisfactory effect against gun positions. No dazzle, perfect for this job,' a view not shared by all gunners on the raid, some of whom found the constant stream of brightly burning rounds too bright, diminishing their night vision. Regarding the attack on the Eder, the notes are brief – 'A large hole was definitely knocked in it and a great deal of water was seen flowing out.'

Other observations were recorded: route planning and navigational details, the location of flak along the route. Gibson had witnessed the demise of F/Lt John Hopgood at the Möhne. The crew had also seen Maudslay's mine detonate on the parapet of the Eder dam and near Hamm they had witnessed another aircraft go down in flames. Concern was doubtless raised about the fate of Young of whom nothing had been seen or heard since leaving the Eder.

0434 Civil twilight minus 30 The time by which the Operation Order specified that no aircraft should be beyond 3°E. On this basis, AJ-Y had made this point with about ten minutes to spare.

At about the same, time Brown in AJ-F was picking his way out of Holland. Crossing the IJsselmeer his greatest concern was night fighters, so he kept as low as possible – going down to 50 feet or less, recalling that he had been advised: 'If you are low, never pull up.' It was still dark, but the eastern sky was brightening, the light making it extremely difficult to distinguish between the shallow water and mud of the IJsselmeer and the horizon. As they approached the Helder peninsula some 8 miles south of Den Helder they ran into a searchlight battery which lit up, throwing beams across their path, through which they would have to pass. As they entered the glare the cockpit was bathed in light. Dazzled outside the cockpit, Brown concentrated on his instruments and pushed the nose down. 'We were right on the deck and I felt I could reach out and touch the water.'

Next to him Basil Feneron crouched as low as he could as about a dozen light flak guns opened up, tracer shells whipping over the canopy as the gunners lowered their sights. Then the shells were striking home, passing through the Perspex and raking the top of the fuselage. As the guns got closer Allatson in the front turret realised that he was firing up at the defences, who in turn were firing down on the Lancaster. Allatson's return fire caused the searchlights to waver momentarily – enabling Brown to see a land wall ahead. Pulling back on the column, the Lancaster hurdled the obstacle, the gunners scattering as the aircraft passed seemingly feet overhead at maximum speed. Then they were over the sea – Brown prudently keeping the aircraft at wave-top height. Grant McDonald fired back at the remaining flak which followed their progress until they were out of range and able to assess the damage.

AJ-F was badly scarred, though fortunately nothing vital was hit and the crew were uninjured. As Brown later recalled: 'Those Jerry gunners did a first-class job on us. They must have thought the roundel on the side was a target because they blew it completely off. We were badly damaged, and it was a miracle nobody was wounded.'

0445 approx.   Townsend, in AJ-O, the last of the 'Chastise' aircraft, was still in the Zutphen area – at about 6°E – and with dawn set to break within the next half-hour Lance Howard decided that it would be better if they revised their route to pass over the Zuider Zee rather than cross the Helder peninsula. Accordingly, instead of heading west at Elburg for Bergen aan Zee, they continued north-west towards Oudemirdum, near Stavoren, intending to exit to the North Sea between the islands of Vlieland and Texel.

0510 approx.   AJ-O was crossing the Zuider Zee and preparing to slip between Vlieland and Texel. Approaching these islands' defences, with the rising sun behind them they came under fire from a battery on Texel. Fired at maximum depression, shells bounced off the water around them, some appearing to ricochet over the aircraft as it hugged the sea. Deciding to abort this exit route, they turned to starboard and then tried again, this time passing north through the channel separating Vlieland and Terschelling.

Some ten minutes later at Bergen aan Zee airfield, Sgt Kraft of IV./NJG 1 was scrambled and ordered to the 'Zander' zone at Zandvort at the neck of the Helder peninsula in the hope of intercepting Townsend. This time he flew for 41 minutes but again, orbiting until 0600 and 60 miles south of the Lancaster's exit point, he saw nothing.

It appears that Townsend's briefed route was return route No. 2, Zutphen–Oudemirdum, then west across the Helder Peninsula, to cross the coast near Callantsoog, while Cochrane's post-raid report records that he turned west at Elburg and followed Gibson's route to cross the coast near Castricum aan Zee. Neither of these is correct: further examples of conflicting documentation connected with 'Chastise'.

Sgt Kraft's radio operator, Handke, later learned that Townsend had flown out 'north-west over Texel/Vlieland at low level'. With a tinge of regret, he observed: 'The fact that this last aircraft was at low level and had changed its course from west to north-west probably saved it from being shot down.'

0515 approx. As Townsend was threading his way through the last defences, dawn had broken in Schwerte. Fifteen-year-old Herbert Nockelmann lived with his parents, grandmother, two younger brothers and older sister on the outskirts of the historic old town, directly adjacent to the Ruhr meadows.

There had already been two air-raid alerts. For the first the family had taken shelter in the cellar of a nearby school, but after the all-clear at two o'clock most of them had gone back to bed, but Herbert's parents were worried. His father had heard engines and explosions to the east – from the direction of the Möhne dam. His fears were confirmed later that night when a policeman knocked at the door. The dam had been bombed, but there was no cause for alarm, any flooding would be minimal. But then, at 5 a.m, 'a wave of water, a metre high, rolled over the entire width of the valley'. The water rose slowly but unceasingly, advancing over the riverside meadows up to the houses of the old town. 'The water in the cellar was up to the ceiling. Soon it had reached my navel on the ground floor and the oak beams in the hallway and the flagstones were already rising.'

He helped his mother gather bedding and groceries and with his siblings went up to his grandmother's flat upstairs. He watched the water rise until it was just above the windows of the ground floor, where it halted.

0525 AJ-Y Dawn was breaking at Scampton as Anderson approached the circuit. Two minutes later Bickle switched the TR 1154 off and made sure his trailing aerial was wound in as Anderson switched to the TR 9 to call up Scampton control for permission to land.

0530 AJ-Y landed at Scampton, the second aircraft to return with its 'Upkeep' aboard.

One pilot who had made an attack and returned from the operation remarked cynically that Anderson had been 'in a hurry to get to bed', but others felt that they too might have returned home if they had met the problems encountered by Anderson.

Gibson would not be as sympathetic. Anderson and his crew were almost immediately posted back to No. 49 Squadron.

0533 AJ-F Brown brought the badly damaged AJ-F in for a rather shaky landing.

0540 approx. AJ-O Contrary to instructions to climb over the North Sea, Townsend kept low over the water. Part way across a faulty oil gauge caused his port outer to be shut down, marginally reducing their speed. Oil leaking from the front turret also hindered his forward vision.

0600 The water level in Fröndenberg was beginning to drop noticeably, but even by noon the water was too deep and the current too strong to facilitate the rescue of those now trapped for over six hours; 36 inhabitants of Fröndenberg and its surrounding villages had perished, including the switchboard operator in the local water and electricity works who remained at her post until it was too late to escape. It was doubly tragic that her efforts to raise the alarm caused many to seek shelter in cellars, unaware of the real nature of the danger. Many were saved only by courageous neighbours running from house to house urging them to get out and find higher ground, or even their roofs or attics.

0615 AJ-O With clear forward vision only available out of the direct vision panel Townsend executed a bouncy landing in broad daylight, downwind into the sun, and taxied to dispersal. It was now three-quarters of an hour since the previous return and most of the station personnel were up preparing for the forthcoming day.

0620 AJ-O Shutting down at dispersal, Townsend and his crew made their way down the fuselage to find a reception committee gathered round the foot of the ladder to the entrance door. As they climbed down the group began to question them as to the night's fortunes. Irritated by the unwarranted intrusion, Townsend responded brusquely to an enquiry by a gold braided senior officer, telling him to wait until they had been debriefed, not realising that he was speaking to his Commander-in-Chief. All that mattered at that moment was that they were safely home.

The enormity of the previous night began to sink in. Across the airfield, eight empty dispersals and 56 empty places in the messes bore testament to the cost of Operation 'Chastise'. For the aircrew it was a fact of life. Each man handled it in his own way. But for Wallis, his focus had been on developing his idea, convincing others of its validity and then perfecting the weapon. 'Chastise' had been the final test, the proof of the theory. With perhaps the exception of Gibson, the aircrew had been a necessary, but anonymous element of that final test. He now recalled their faces at the final briefing only a dozen or so hours earlier, and for the first time appreciated the tragedy of the human cost.

As Mick Martin later recounted: 'Well as the morning wore on there was a state of tears and laughter, in the way that one was jubilant about the success of the raid and naturally desperately sorry about the losses. But this was war.'

Chapter 10
Effect

While the crews were debriefed at Scampton and relaxed after the tensions of the last twelve hours, a day of torment was dawning in the Ruhr valley as its inhabitants took stock of overnight events, some learning for the first time of the disaster.

17 May, 0700 At Schwerte, 31 miles from the Möhne, Norbert Kaufhold had remained in bed through the earlier air-raid alerts, but was now woken abruptly by a neighbour hammering on his door in a terribly distressed state: 'At first we didn't understand what had happened. Then we began to realise how terrible the night had been. The Möhne dam had been hit by bombs. The whole Ruhr valley is flooded. Mühlenstraße and Hellpoth are a torrent!'

Climbing to the top of his house he looked out to see for himself. The two streets had been warned at around 3 o'clock. Nobody anticipated the scale of the danger. It was not until 5.30 a.m that the flood arrived, with such rapidity that most could only save themselves. At 7.30, Norbert heard that a woman was stranded up a tree in Ruhrstrasse. He found her high in the branches, wearing only her nightgown and shouting for help. It took another half hour for her to be rescued. The water would reach its peak at about 8.30, and by 10 o'clock the level began to fall, leaving a thick layer of mud, littered with animal carcasses. The stench would hang over the streets and gardens for months.

The water struck the neighbouring town of Westhofen at about 5.55, inundating the waterworks and the hydroelectric power station, with a tremendous roar. Civil defence workers and firefighters who had warned the occupants of low-lying Garenfeld across the river were driven back across the bridge and watched from high ground as the bridge lights turned opaque – 'like stained glass' – before going out, as the waters rose, cutting off the officials who had to be rescued later that day by boat. As with many in locations this distance downstream from the Möhne, farmers had sufficient warning to move many of their livestock to higher ground. Now as they surveyed the scene, bodies of dead cattle from less fortunate herds floated westwards, past the adjacent steelworks.

0715 Ruhr Valley At Herdecke, eyewitness Erich Schmidt recounted:

> At 7 o'clock in the morning, the Ruhr Valley lay quietly in front of me. Fifteen minutes later I could not believe my eyes. I saw a grey mass breaking through the fog and rolling down the valley, it was an eerie sight, I called to my family, and walked towards the bend in the River Ruhr, assuming that the weirs [at the southern end of the Hengsteysee and the bend of the river at the confluence with the Volme] had broken, but within minutes the access path was already flooded by the rising waters. By standing on the cemetery wall, I could see people desperately wading through the freezing cold water to bring their belongings to safety. Many witnesses report that the main tidal wave, by now 15 feet high, was preceded by a smaller wave about 5 feet high as the river water was forced ahead of the torrent. Uprooted trees, furniture, house parts, even horse-drawn carriages, drifted past in the swirling current.

The 132-MW output pump-storage plant, one of the most important power stations of the Rhine-Westphalia Electric Power Company, was under 6 feet of water and out of action for 14 days.

The enormous environmental damage, caused by sewage, sludge, animal carcasses, fuels, heavy metals and industrial pollution, was not mentioned in an otherwise detailed contemporary damage report; yet these pollutants are now revealed in core samples taken from the riverside areas of Hagen, on the south side of the Ruhr across from Herdecke.

0730 Ruhr Valley Some 6½ hours after it had been breached 1,500–2,000 cubic meters (329,000–444,000 gallons) of water were still flowing from the Möhne dam each second. At the Hengsteysee, four miles upstream from Herdecke and 32 miles downstream from the dam, the wave of water was travelling at a speed of 7 miles per hour. Here the turbine houses of the two power stations on the Hengsteysee, which were listed as important Ruhr targets in Bomber Command's original 'Ruhr Plan' of 1937, would be flooded.

1000 Kassel, 40 miles from the Eder and on the River Fulda, had already been warned. Inhabitants of areas of potential risk had sufficient time to prepare for the rising river level, clearing cellars and lower floors, moving possessions and themselves to upper levels. The water arrived at 10 a.m. and continued rising until 3 p.m, by which time over 1,300 houses and 1,200 apartments had been affected.

1030 Ruhr Valley The Möhne's waters reached Witten, 47 miles from the dam, flowing at 3,000 cubic metres/sec and reaching a depth of 23 feet, 4 feet above its previous record in 1890. The road bridge soon became impassable, so the railway viaduct became the only crossing option. Bommern on the south side of the river escaped lightly, but the island near the river lock was hit hard. Almost all the timber-framed buildings were washed away, the sewage treatment plant and sluice gates destroyed. In the lee of a half-demolished house 15 inhabitants climbed up into a large tree, waiting until the waters subsided. The Wengler & Kalthoff steel forgings plant was under water and the river was up to the sheet steel rolling mill. Part of the town's steelworks were underwater, along with workers' hutted accommodation.

1200 The flow from the Möhne reservoir finally abated. It was after mid-day when the floods began to reach the Essen suburbs of Steele, Wirden and Im Ruhrtal after a period of false security, since the river level had seemed to remain normal. Part of the reason for the temporary stay of execution was the emergency emptying of the Hengstey and Harkort lakes as soon as the breaching was reported. The sluices were then closed again, creating two storage basins to accommodate some of the torrent and slow the rate of flooding downstream, but they could not hold it indefinitely. At about 2 p.m. the water in Steele rose so rapidly that those at ground level had to flee for their lives, with no chance of saving possessions.

Five miles downstream, the Baldeneysee, which had been drained in 1941 to deny Allied aircrew a distinctive landmark, also provided a relief reservoir to capture 7 million cubic metres of flood water. When at last the flood water, now estimated at 17 million cubic metres, reached the Rhine, the river rose a few metres.

1330 By now the water levels were receding, but even those areas that thought they had seen the worst of the flooding could find that worse was to come. At 1.30 p.m. on 17 May, a pier and two arches of the 12-arch, 103-foot-high Herdecke viaduct – which carried the main double-track link between Dortmund and Hagen over the Ruhr – collapsed just as a passenger train was about to cross, leaving the tracks suspended across the gap.

By evening, as the waters subsided, the full scale of the devastation was revealed. Although the British planners had been cautious in their estimate of the damage caused by local flooding, they were correct in predicting that it 'would cause a disaster of the first magnitude, even in the lower reaches of the

Ruhr'. Over 250 million cubic metres of water were released from the Möhne and Eder dams within the space of 12 hours. Water from the Möhne flooded an area of some 32 square miles for nearly 100 miles to the Ruhr's confluence with the Rhine at Mulheim, while that from the Eder affected some 27 square miles around the Weser downstream from Kassel.

According to eyewitness reports, the speed of arrival of the water, its volume and effects were considerably varied. In the Möhne Valley and at Neheim reports refer largely to the huge tidal wave. While some residents were able to flee to higher ground, many were quickly forced to take to the upper floors of buildings. In other areas, where the valley was less constricted, casualties were first aware of lapping water before the flood arrived on a broad front, travelling and rising more slowly. The debris carried by the water influenced the course and intensity of the flooding. Trees, boulders and other detritus often created temporary barriers between buildings which slowed the flow or even diverted it for a time. Eventually such barriers might fail as the water pressure built up behind them causing periodic local surges, the debris from the barriers intensifying the erosive effect as the water broke through.

It does not require great imagination to contemplate the horror and fear experienced that May night.

Figures for the total number of deaths as a result of 'Chastise' vary, but the generally accepted total is around 1,300. In 1943 high civilian casualties were seen as an acceptable part of the bomber offensive. Indeed, those of 'Chastise' would be far eclipsed by the attack on Hamburg on 27/28 July, which created a firestorm killing an estimated 40,000 and injuring a similar number.

Likewise, the figure of 47 drowned by the waters of the Eder dam, pales in the light of the subsequent attack on Kassel of 23–24 October 1943 when at least 5,500 were killed. Today such civilian casualties, collateral damage to use current parlance, would be utterly abhorrent, but in 1943 it was deemed acceptable as a price that had to be paid. Much store has been placed on the fact that at least 593 of the Möhne deaths were foreign workers housed in a camp at Neheim 7 miles down the Möhne Valley. These deaths have become a contentious issue for 'Chastise' – with suggestions that if the workers' presence was known beforehand then the raid should have been cancelled. There is no evidence that this was so, and if it were, it then also raises questions of the morality of forced labour and human shields. Foreign workers were employed in great numbers in the Ruhr – especially in the extractive industries. The attack of 4/5 May 1943 on Dortmund killed 200 prisoners of war and 75 other foreigners.

The debate is not unique to 'Chastise'. The offensive use of water through the destruction of enemy hydraulic installations to cause major damage to agriculture, water supplies, and other infrastructure has been employed in armed conflict throughout history. In 596 BC, Nebuchadnezzar breached the aqueduct that supplied the city of Tyre to end a long siege. Likewise, in the second century BC, the Achaeans obstructed the spring that supplied the Greek city of Phana. In 1938, Chiang Kai-shek's Chinese Nationalist armies attempted to block a Japanese military advance by breaching the Yellow River's dikes, resulting in nine years of flooding and the death of over 800,000 people. Operations against dams and dykes were considered amongst the most successful strikes carried out during the Korean War by the US Air Force, notably the attack on the Hwacheon dam. After a failed attempt by heavy bombers, an attack on 1 May 1951 used 2,000-pound torpedoes to destroy the sluice gates. In the Vietnam War many dykes were damaged or destroyed by systematic bombing, and North Vietnam reported a death toll of 2–3 million inhabitants due to drowning or starvation because of these attacks. In more recent conflicts terrorist groups have continued to exploit dams and reservoirs as a potential weapon of war despite international legislation and condemnation.

Today Operation 'Chastise' would be prohibited by Article 56 of the amendment to the Geneva Convention agreed in 1977. This outlawed attacks on works or installations such as dams 'if such attack may cause the release of dangerous forces and consequent severe losses among the civilian population'. However, hindsight is an exact science and historians need to exercise caution when applying present-day mores to judge events of the past.

Looking more closely at how 'Chastise's' results matched the expectations of the planners, 'Chastise's' prime objective was to undermine the Ruhr's industrial production by creating a shortage of water and other sources of power.

The Möhne dam had been built to maintain the level of the River Ruhr during the dry summer months. By controlling the flow of water, over 300 pumping stations and waterworks in the Ruhr Valley could supply the towns of the Rhine-Westphalia region. The Möhne dam was the backbone of a system serving 4½ million people. Its destruction immediately halved the available reservoir capacity.

Three waterworks in Neheim were destroyed, temporary respite being obtained by the laying of overground pipes from neighbouring Husten which was unaffected. Hamm's water supply was shut down and Hagen lost 60 per cent of its supply. Of 25 other waterworks affected along the Ruhr, that at Fröndenberg was out of action for 17 days. Echthausen, the largest and most modern plant of its kind in the area, commissioned in 1942, remained inoperative until August. Steam-powered waterworks were more quickly brought back into operation: that at Steele after only a day, others serving the northern Westphalian coalfields after a week.

Dortmund lost 80 per cent of its water supply for about two days. The reactivation of a duplicate system of obsolete steam pumps enabled 80 per cent supply to be flowing again within 8 days. Nevertheless, horse-drawn drays distributed kegs of fresh water drawn from the wells of the city's two main breweries for about 6 weeks to maintain an adequate supply of potable water.

The more significant damage was to waterworks with electric pumps, which reduced industrial capacity, as Speer later admitted. These pumps had to be removed, dried, and cleaned. In many cases key parts had been ruined. To speed the process, pumps had to be commandeered from other less vital parts of German infrastructure, which then in turn suffered – robbing Peter to pay Paul. If loss of industrial output in the Ruhr had been mitigated, it was at the expense of other production elsewhere in Germany.

Overall, the Ruhr's water use fell 75 per cent from 1 million cubic metres on 15 May to 260,000 two days later, but after six weeks returned to normal levels. Favourable precipitation in the summer and autumn of 1943 helped alleviate the supply situation. Nevertheless, there was a shortage of water for firefighting during the final two months of the Battle of the Ruhr. On 23/24 May when 826 aircraft attacked Dortmund in the heaviest raid of the Battle, 2,000 buildings were destroyed, many through fire, although some reports claim that water shortage was not a contributory factor.

An even greater workload was required for the cleaning and maintenance of settlement beds and the introduction of new filter sand layers, many of which were sited on the flood plains of the River Ruhr, such as that at Warmen. This work took several months to complete. Nevertheless, after a short time almost normal volume was reached again, this being mainly due to an unexpected benefit of 'Chastise'. Due to years of pollution of the water, the bed and banks of the Ruhr had become muddy and impermeable. The flood waters cleaned these and were supplemented by the groundwater, though experience would show that they re-silted in a relatively short time.

Equally serious was the destruction of sewage works, allowing untreated wastewater into the Ruhr further polluting the river and adding to the risk of disease. These either had to be rebuilt or else temporary, makeshift waterworks had to be created to supply the cities concerned.

With regard to domestic supplies, Oliver Lawrence of MEW had concluded in a report of 2 April 1943 that it was: 'Not possible to state that a critical shortage of water supplies in the Ruhr would be a certain and inevitable result of the destruction of the Möhne dam.'

A large part of the district's industrial and domestic water came from underground water-bearing strata of sand and gravel supplemented by water pumped from collieries and used for industrial purposes. Excessive extraction had led to a depletion of these strata – leading to the construction of a number of storage dams in the headwaters of tributaries, and of filter beds further down the valley fed by the river, to keep the underground strata filled with water. In addition, water could be drawn from the Rhine. Thus, the Möhne was only part of a very complex system, and not the direct supply of water to end users. Lawrence thought that the system would still be able to meet industrial and domestic requirements with only a slight risk that the underground beds would suffer temporary depletion.

Water-supply problems would be exacerbated by damage to mains and pipework from conventional attacks. Boiling water to make it potable would be difficult owing to lack of gas – so wood fires would have to be used.

A contemporary report from the diary of Heinrich Wefnands of Spreng-kommando (Bomb Disposal Team) Kalkum, which had dealt with Barlow's unexploded 'Upkeep': 'Almost the whole Ruhr area is without water. Infinite car teams bring in drinking water. Women, children, and old people are every-where with vessels to receive water … Whole villages human and animal, swam in the Ruhr.'

A Reichs-Bahn (German railways) report for Schwerte Station also noted that the water production facilities in the Ruhr area had become unusable, and that almost the entire area had no tap water for about a week. A temporary solution was supplying the population with drinking water through existing wells. Even after recovery and restoration of the water supply from the mains, the water had to be boiled before use since it was heavily infected with bacteria. Due to the failure of the waterworks and the resulting lack of water, several companies in the area of Hamm, Dortmund, Hagen, Witten, Bochum and Essen had to cease their work for some time.

Wallis had predicted a 'substantial loss of electricity supplies', not because of the destruction of the Möhne's hydroelectric plant – negligible – but because of the shortage of water for the cooling towers of coal-powered generating stations. Lawrence, however, had also predicted that the Ruhr River authority would be able to provide sufficient water for the thermal power stations and the effect on electricity supply would be of 'secondary economic importance'. The dams generated only limited hydroelectric power. Interruption of electricity supplies for blast furnaces and coke ovens would probably be slight.

Dortmund's steam-powered turbines closed down for 2 days, and the large pump-storage facility at Herdecke (Koepchen) 40 miles from the Möhne, one of the most important power stations with a capacity of 132 MW, was out of action at first because the generator room was flooded to 2 metres, but was restored after a fortnight. Further damage was inflicted on the numerous hydroelectric plants along the Ruhr. Some 80 miles from the Möhne, at Mulheim, the 4.5 MW Kahlenberg power station was destroyed.

The consequences to the electricity supply were not long-term. Throughout 1943 approximately 733 MW of generation capacity was permanently lost. Overall, some 372 MW of local generating capacity was lost as a result of 'Chastise', but this was alleviated by an efficient grid system fed by surplus capacity from elsewhere topped up by hydro-power stations in the Alps.

Local distribution suffered because substations were flooded or silted up, but most damage was to overhead and underground electric cables. This was repaired within two weeks. Nevertheless, the disruption was sufficient to necessitate a further electricity load-management system to supplement the existing electricity and gas load distributors. Many users had to be taken off the grid temporarily to balance the district load, leading to additional disruption to production.

The water requirements of the Ruhr coalfields were met by seeking alternative sources. Water was drawn from the River Lippe; more was pumped back from the Rhine to the lower reaches of the Ruhr. Further reserves were obtained from the Sorpe reservoir. Nevertheless, Ruhr coal production fell by nearly 300,000 tons in May as a direct consequence of 'Chastise'. Further losses due to other bomb damage to pits and workers' homes reduced it to its lowest since the outbreak of war. This in turn compromised Germany's promise to supply 1 million tons of coal a month to Italy – which had been used to justify the employment of migrant Italian workers in the Ruhr mines.

Attacks prior to 1943 had had little effect on coking plants, but after 'Chastise' those in Dortmund experienced a 9 per cent production loss for two months. Consumption of electricity and gas was reduced by almost a third by the imposition of an emergency load-management system and full production was not restored until January 1944.

By-products of the coking process also suffered: light oil, tar, ammonia and sulphur – used for aviation fuel, synthetic fuel, rubber, and explosives. A 1945 report by Bomber Command's Operational Research Section states that post-'Chastise' coal mining, coke and synthetic oil production in the Dortmund area fell, stopping completely for at least a week due to water shortage.

German steel production had doubled during 1942 and increased overall a further 20% the following year. Nevertheless during 1943 the Ruhr's production declined by 8 per cent, with 200,000 tons lost in the first quarter of 1943 and an additional 300,000 tons in May and June of that year, much undoubtedly due to 'Chastise'. The armaments industry faced a shortfall of

400,000 tons. To maintain production the Germans drew on existing stocks of steel ingots. This in turn created a long-term cost as these stocks were never replenished and production of military equipment and ammunition fell markedly.

Many of the steel plants had their own gas and electricity generation systems as well as being connected to the grid, but they were solely reliant on outside suppliers for their water. This was an issue following 'Chastise'. Hoesch steel in Schwerte lost 24 per cent of its output between May and August 1943. During this period water was cut off for three weeks, halting the company power station and practically stopping production. Steel produced in this area was often used to make chains (including anchor chains) but during the second quarter of 1943 deliveries fell by 45 per cent for several weeks. Due to the combination of water shortage and bomb damage, production was only 10–15 per cent of normal in June and did not regain normal levels for six months.

The steel works at Hagen-Kabel and Harkort-Eicken in Wetter were both working at full pressure and suffered heavy damage when the Möhne floods arrived. At Hagen, 30 miles downstream, the smelting ovens and rolling mills had also been working and were heavily damaged. In Essen, the Krupp works was unaffected, being able to maintain its water supply from the northern Ruhr area of the Rhine and Lippe rivers.

The combined effects of 'Chastise' and air attacks on Dortmund caused engineering output to drop by 30 per cent. Werk Dortmund was already suffering from shortage of electricity and gas caused by an earlier raid in May, and problems were compounded by water shortage from 'Chastise'; the combined effect brought the whole plant to a standstill for five weeks. Production was down 21 per cent during the period May–August, before rapidly recovering to full output. The manufacture of components for 'Würzburg' and 'Mannheim' radars ceased temporarily due to lack of power in May 1943 and production of 17 Panther tanks was lost. Great concern was voiced about the lost production of self-propelled guns, required to replace losses in North Africa and the Eastern Front.

Commonly cited figures record eleven factories destroyed. Amongst them were several in Neheim, which was a centre for electrical assemblies and light metal fabrication. There, the Kaiser lamp factory – employing 600–700 workers, many of them women from Eastern Europe – was totally destroyed, as was the Hillebrand lighting firm. Broecklemann, employing 220 workers and with a rolling mill producing aluminium sheets for the aviation industry, was destroyed. Reconstruction did not commence until 1945 and full production was not attained until 1950. In Fröndenberg two major factories ceased production for nearly three weeks. A further 41 factories are recorded as severely damaged, 40 more moderately damaged and 33 suffering minor damage. Numerous smaller factories came to a standstill due to flooding and lack of water and power, though their size and the nature of their production is unspecified, preventing any accurate assessment of output loss. Nevertheless, the impact of 'Chastise' was sufficient for Josef Goebbels, Hitler's Propaganda Minister, to write in his diary: 'The attacks of British heavy bombers on the dams were very successful. Damage to production was more than normal.'

Aside from the physical damage to factories, infrastructure was heavily disrupted. All bridges up to 30 miles downstream of the Möhne were destroyed and communications across the River Ruhr severely disrupted for several weeks until emergency structures could be built. These were then often timber-piled and single-lane with weight restrictions, limiting the transport of goods and materials.

The collapse of the Herdecke viaduct severed the rail line between Hagen and Dortmund. The line between the Ruhr and Kassel – one of the main supply lines for the Eastern Front – was out of use for several weeks. At Wickede, the destruction of two bridges carrying twin tracks across the Ruhr and Obergraben watercourses cut another main supply line for materiel destined for the Eastern Front. By 7 June the track was back in operation, but only as a single line, carrying but a fraction of its former capacity. Five miles downstream the twin-track girder rail bridge over the Ruhr between Fröndenberg and Menden was swept 50 yards downstream. The pier foundations were too badly damaged to be repaired and a new single-track replacement on timber piles was constructed. Until this was complete, locals had to be ferried across the river in rubber dinghies, but freight was impossible. Even 60 miles from the Möhne the water retained sufficient force to sweep heavy freight locomotives and their wagons from the tracks. Throughout the network, ballast was washed from beneath tracks which were buckled or thrown out of alignment; embankments, stations and signalling apparatus were washed away and locomotives and rolling stock, both in short supply, wrecked.

Over 20 miles of roads were badly damaged – from potholes to complete destruction; others suffered to a lesser degree. On the Rhine, barge traffic was dislocated and both the Duisburg and Ruhrort ports were closed for several days. Travel from Cologne to the Netherlands was delayed for up to six days. Such disruption also hindered the deployment of mechanical equipment for rescue and repair, necessitating the use of more manual labour, much of it imported, placing further strain on food and accommodation resources.

A less recognised, and to an extent unexpected, effect of 'Chastise' was that on agriculture and food production. The valley of the Ruhr along the river and its tributaries was a major source of food for the industrial work force. In rural areas deposits of sand, gravel and scree a metre deep covered over 10,000 acres of once fertile farmland rendering it unusable for up to two years. There was also a great deal of debris – including trees, rubble and household effects. Sewage and industrial pollution caused enormous environmental damage. In many cases the topsoil was degraded. In Arnsberg nearly 1,000 acres of arable land and 250 acres of park, horticultural or woodland were flooded; 20 per cent of the wheat and barley crop was destroyed; and of the rest, a harvest yield of only 30 per cent was expected. Overall damage to cultivated agricultural land was estimated at 50 million Reichsmarks.

Some 6,800 head of livestock perished and only a month after the raid meat rations for 'normal customers', excepting workers in industrial areas in Germany threatened by air attack, were reduced for the second time in two months, by 100 grams per week, forestalling a planned increase for the winter months of 50 g. Instead, the general population was offered an extra 300 grams of bread and 15 grams of fat, plus extra cheese and pasta. This had a serious psychological effect.

The British Ministry of Economic Warfare did not consider the Eder dam a major economic objective. Its chief purpose was flood prevention; its destruction would inundate large tracts of agricultural land in the Eder, Fulda and Weser valleys but it was unlikely that any densely populated areas would be affected, other than low-lying districts of the city of Kassel. The effects would be distinct from those of the Möhne and/or Sorpe. Official records indicate that only 47 lives were lost in the Eder floods, although other sources claim as many as 68 victims, whilst in seven villages between the Eder dam and Kassel 213 houses, stables and barns and 101 places of work were either destroyed or damaged. Affoldern was particularly affected, with 75 buildings destroyed and 12 inhabitants drowned, along with 19 others in the surrounding district; 200 cattle and 250 pigs were lost, along with 40 horses.

In the Eder Valley the topsoil was eroded from 123 acres of arable land and another 40 acres were ruined by silt and gravel. Some 1,200 horses, cattle and pigs along with countless smaller animals, goats, hens, chickens and so on were lost. Root crops suffered the greatest damage. The year's harvest was ruined in many places and great effort was expended to salvage wheat from flooded barns. An additional loss at the Eder was the fish stock in the reservoir which had recently been replenished.

As predicted, the breaching of the Eder resulted in the destruction of the four power stations situated below it, reducing the capacity of the Prussian electricity supply system.

As in the Ruhr great damage was done to communications: 15 bridges were destroyed, including virtually all between the Eder and Kassel, amongst them that between Grifte and Wolfershausen, 30 miles from the Eder dam, carrying the twin main line between Kassel and Frankfurt-Main. Nearly all were replaced or repaired by 17 July.

Compared to the Ruhr Valley the effects within the city of Kassel were limited. With a population of some 220,000 this was the only significant manufacturing centre affected by the Eder floods. By 10 a.m. when the water arrived most people had taken their belongings out of threatened property. The flood reached its peak by 3 p.m. – 4.2 metres above normal, inundating an area 4 miles long and up to a mile wide, affecting 2,500 homes, mainly in the low lying Unterneustadt and Bettenhausen districts. By 7 p.m. that evening the water was beginning to subside.

Regarding utilities, although two of the city's six pumping stations were flooded, its water supply was maintained from natural springs and river resources. Within 24 hours supplies were back to 83 per cent of normal. Since the city had its own power station and was linked to the Prussian grid system the effect on electricity supply was minimal and largely one of distribution. Flooding of the gasworks resulted in 3–4 days' loss of service – the first time it had been affected by air attack.

As MEW predicted, the effects on industry were minimal. The airfield at Fritzlar, 13 miles downstream from the Eder dam, used by Junkers for development work and test flying, was flooded for a day. Some works in the Bettenhausen district suffered minor disruption: the Salzman company, which produced heavy-duty fabric for tents, groundsheets and inner tubes, was partly flooded, but production resumed after two days. Machinefabrik Dianawerk, producers of shells and components for the Henschel company, was without power for several days. Major industries – the three Henschel locomotive and tank production works, the Fieseler aircraft plant and Junkers aero engine works – all escaped significant material damage. The most serious problem for industry appears to have been the difficulty of workers getting transport from their homes to their place of work, partly on account of a loss of electric power for the tram system for a short period.

It took about 10 days to make roads passable, build temporary bridges, salvage foodstuffs, pump out cellars, clear mud, and repair buildings, many of which had been partly submerged. All told Kassel got off lightly, but it was a brief respite. Five months later, on 22 October, the city would be subjected to an attack in which 569 aircraft dropped 2,000 tons of bombs, damaging 63 per cent of the city's living accommodation, killing 5,500 people and making 120,000 homeless. This major attack resulted in the city losing 50 per cent of its water supply for 4 weeks, 75 per cent of its electricity for a week, and all its gas supply for 12 days – making the results of 'Chastise' seem a minor inconvenience.

Although water from the Eder reservoir helped maintain navigability of the lower Weser and supplied the Mittelland Canal, MEW considered it unlikely that the dam's destruction would lead to a critical situation and that effects on navigation would be of short duration. Nevertheless, flooding necessitated the use of boats in settlements up to 88 miles downstream of Kassel. The sluices of several small lakes were silted up and suffered structural damage. Serious damage was caused to the banks of the Fulda and Weser which had to be rebuilt and dredged to restore navigable channels. With a shortage of water, priority was given to maintaining the level of the Mittelland Canal, but without water from the Eder the level of the Weser fell, and its barges could only be partly loaded. Since the river carried little industrial traffic the economic impact was not considered significant.

The extent of the physical damage belies any supposition that 'Chastise' was primarily a propaganda attack. Nevertheless, the Ministry of Economic Warfare's predictions had recognised that a vast population would witness the destruction and suffer its consequences. There would inevitably be a tremendous morale effect.

At first, the German press attempted to play down the scale of the disaster, reporting:

> Weak British air forces entered the Reich territory last night and dropped a small number of explosive bombs in some places, damaging two dams, the ensuing floods causing heavy civilian casualties. Eight of the attacking aircraft were shot down, nine other enemy aircraft were destroyed over the occupied enemy western areas, including one by the army.

The damaged dams were not named, and foreign reporters were prohibited access to the affected area. Filming and photography were strictly controlled. In Neheim and other localities the press were only allowed to print four obituaries in any single issue. The wording was carefully controlled to conceal the extent of the casualties.

Aside from the physical deprivation which would sap morale, MEW construed the population would also become susceptible to rumour and false alarm. The German authorities quickly began to pick up rumours circulating of up to 30,000 deaths. On 19 May the German News Agency issued a rebuttal of these; the death toll was lower than anticipated, amounting to 370 Germans and 341 POWs.

On 20 May, panic broke out amongst residents of Neheim who had congregated in the town cemetery for the funeral of 53 of the victims when a false alarm suggested that the Sorpe dam had broken as a result of the damage sustained. Inevitably the population was susceptible to rumours regarding a likely shortage of drinking water, risk of disease and inability of the fire services to deal with incendiary attacks.

The same day, in London, the OSS Morale Operations Branch, responsible for 'Black Propaganda', suggested seeding a rumour in the Ruhr that the water reserves for two years had been lost and that the drinking water supply had become hopelessly contaminated, resulting in an epidemic of typhoid and intestinal diseases. Within a week, radio broadcasts purporting to come from 'Der Chef' – a patriotic German officer – but in reality originating in Buckinghamshire, were transmitted criticising the authorities for their failure to evacuate affected areas and refusal to provide additional soap to prevent the spread of infection and disease. Another rumour suggested that the Möhne dam defences had been earlier reduced in order to provide guns to protect the property of a high-ranking Nazi official.

Conversely, the reconnaissance photographs of the breached Möhne dam and flooded tracts of the Ruhr provided strikingly graphic images that were used by the Ministry of Information and Allied press to maximise the propaganda value of the operation. Headlines ranged from the *Daily Telegraph*'s 'RAF blow up three key dams in Germany' and *The Times* 'Ruhr Dams Breached. Daring Low Level Attack by Lancasters, Walls Blasted Out with 1,500-pound Mines', to the *Daily Express* with a style that pre-dated its switch to tabloid format 34 years later: 'Floods Roar Down Ruhr Valley' and the *Daily Mirror*: 'Germany Receives the Floodblitz'. Not only did they inspire their readers, but graphically demonstrated yet again the skill, determination, accuracy, and effectiveness of Bomber Command.

The British press also subscribed to the rumour mill predicted by the Ministry of Economic Warfare. 'Ruhr railways at a standstill after Dams Raid. Dortmund said to be threatened by complete inundation. 120,000 homeless in Upper Ruhr. Rioting at Duisburg and Mulheim: Many cities flooded. 4,000 reported drowned,' ran the headline in the *Lincolnshire Echo* of 18 May. The following day they continued, 'Packed refugee trains leave the Ruhr. Flood tide spreading after inundating 54 towns and villages. 50,000 homeless families: Nazis Show alarm for Southern Germany.'

Ministry of Information Home Intelligence Reports monitored public reaction. News of the operation travelled quickly and was a prime topic of discussion: It was seen as a 'brilliant and daring achievement' arousing feelings varying from 'jubilation' to 'grim approval', although 'some later tempered their views with a tinge of horror' at the likely civilian casualties (reported in inflated terms by the press). Equally, there were some who were apprehensive as to 'what the Germans can do here in return', though 'well informed people do not believe that any of the dams in this country could be hit with comparable effect'.

Leaflets showing photographs of the breached Möhne dam were quickly produced and dropped as part of the on-going campaign to maintain the spirit of those in occupied territories. Winston Churchill was in America at the time of 'Chastise', seeking to dissuade the Americans from switching their focus from Europe to the Pacific. During a crucial speech to Congress on 19 May, he referred to the operation as demonstrable proof of the effect that bombing was having on Germany. 'You have just read of the destruction of the great dams which feed the canals and provide power in the enemy's munition works. This was a gallant operation . . . it will play a very far-reaching part.' Likewise, it was hoped that Stalin would see it as evidence of the Western Allies' support. Such was the impact of the operation that both allies requested information on the weapon used and the nature of the attack. Whilst details were passed to the Americans, who would conduct trials with 'Highball', diplomatic subterfuge was conducted to restrict Soviet access to details of Wallis's weapon.

Initial reaction in Germany was very much one of 'shock and awe'. From the late nineteenth century Germans had prided themselves on using their engineering skill to overcome nature, building dams and canals and improving the Rhine – it was part of the national psyche. Now British engineering skill had been used as a weapon to turn nature against them.

Hitler was furious at the inadequacy of the defensive measures, blaming the Luftwaffe for failing to prevent the attack. It reinforced his prejudices about the inability of air power to provide an effective defence against bombing, and possibly contributed to his insistence that the Me 262 jet be developed as a fighter-bomber. Goebbels was convinced that the British must have had inside information to mount such a precise attack. He sought to exploit a story in the Swedish Press that the raid had been at the instigation of a German Jewish refugee. However, such propaganda was dismissed by many Germans, who called for the punishment of those guilty of neglecting the dams' defence.

The authorities tried to play down the size of the attacking force, but with rumours of up to 30,000 casualties the extent of the damage could not be concealed from those in affected areas. It was clearly apparent that the RAF was able to penetrate a small force deep into the heart of the Reich at night, locate a small, defended target hitherto seen as invulnerable, and by destroying it cause disproportionate levels of damage.

After visiting the dams Speer told Goebbels that the damage was not as serious as thought and he hoped to have the armaments industry running at half production by the end of May. Identifying shortage of water as the greatest problem, he sought to restore supply to the Ruhr industry 'within a few weeks', focussing on the restoration of the pumping stations. Within 24 hours Speer recorded with pride that he had '7,000 workers' on their way to commence initial clear-up, without mentioning that most were foreign labourers. A further 20,000 would follow. Over 1,800 troops were also employed. This added to the logistics problems – all had to be transported, accommodated, fed and watered in an area already overburdened.

In Neheim 3,000 members of various parts of the Wehrmacht, fire brigades, the Organisation Todt (OT) and the Reich Labour Service (RAD) arrived to pump out cellars, remove mud, clear debris, dry furniture and provide field kitchens. Looting was punishable by death. Food was available without ration coupons, and emergency rations – real coffee, spirits and confectionery – were provided for three days to boost morale. But beyond this much of the recovery was dependent on self-help. In the Melsungen area, south of Kassel, all inhabitants aged between fourteen and sixty, who had not been affected by the disaster and who were not engaged in agriculture or other official labour, were formed into emergency working parties, each of twenty people. These were despatched to assist with rescue and clearance. Priority was given to the rescue of people and the salvaging of surviving livestock from fields and byres, and wheat from flooded granaries, then recovery of corpses.

Aside from the immediate rescue and re-establishment of basic services, attention turned to the reconstruction of the dams. To prevent winter flooding and for the Ruhr to have sufficient water for 1944 it was essential that they were sealed and at least capable of constraining water again before the start of the autumn rains. Everything was given utmost priority.

This urgency further stretched demand for manpower. Skilled workers were required from all over Germany. Only fifty stonemasons were available, so others were brought from the Austrian Tyrol, Italy and Belgium. Most of the labourers came from France, others were Italians who had been working in Berlin; 100 Dutchmen worked as carpenters to construct massive wooden scaffolding. The rapid introduction of such numbers of foreign labourers sparked fears of sabotage and rigorous quality control checks had to be made to ensure that work met required standards.

It is a common claim that the use of Organisation Todt workers delayed construction of the Atlantic Wall, thereby assisting the D-Day landings. The diversion of equipment such as cement mixers and materials was doubtless detrimental to the coastal defences. The greater issue was not so much that these were taken from the Atlantic Wall, rather that this was the first time that OT workers had been used in Germany. It set a precedent, and from now on increasing numbers of these workers would be used to provide resources within Germany, rather than in occupied countries. By the end of 1943, more than 10,000 OT workers had already been deployed in the Ruhr. In his post-war interrogation Speer maintained that he appointed a special OT group which then pulled skilled workers from France, without his approval. The inept transfer caused a crisis of trust amongst French workers and a mass exodus from OT, described as a catastrophe by Speer at Nuremberg in 1946. Many of the workers brought to rebuild the dams remained in Germany to repair and restore industry and communications and did not go back to their original work. Rommel later inflated the number of workers diverted from his defences to 20,000, blaming this for the lack of progress on the Atlantic Wall – but this may have been an attempt to justify his failure to defeat the Overlord landings.

Materials were also a problem: Organisation Todt wanted to expedite work by using concrete to fill the breach, but the Ruhr Reservoir Authority insisted that the dam should be re-built in exactly the original manner. Local quarries that had provided stone when the dam was built were unable to meet demand. Thousands of tons of stone had to come from quarries over a large area – causing transport problems. Some 2,000 tons of structural steel, in short supply, was also required – adding to the 6,000 tons needed to repair damaged industrial plant. Trains transporting materials for the reconstruction were given priority over other traffic.

At lunchtime on 17 May Speer pessimistically predicted that it would take at least a year to repair the Möhne. Subsequently both he and Goebbels recognised after their initial reaction, that, though extremely serious, the effects were not as catastrophic as they first appeared. As the latter wrote in his diary:

> At first very dramatic reports are given by the affected districts; but the effects of the attacks turn out to be less than devastating during the day . . . The Americans and the British, of course, make the flooding of a large part of the surrounding area of the dams the greatest sensation you can ever think of. Thankfully, the death toll is not as high as we initially feared.

Reconstruction commenced on 9 July and continued by day and night, seven days a week. It was not merely a case of making good the gap blasted by 'Upkeep'. About 12,500 cubic metres of wall had gone but cracks had penetrated the remaining structure, necessitating the removal of a further

6,800 cubic metres – a total of 19,500 needed replacing. The force of the torrent had created an 8-metre depression in the footings and the foundations of the dam had been eroded so new foundations had to be secured into the rock. The valve machinery controlling the release of water and hence the level of the Ruhr, also had to be replaced.

The work was entrusted to Butzer of Dortmund, employing 1,600 men, initially in round the clock shifts, stopping only for occasional air-raid alerts. By 14 September 2,500 men were on the site. Such was the energy directed to the reconstruction of the Möhne that the breach was sealed on 24 September – after only 79 days– but the repair was basic and sufficient only for water containment. Even by April 1945 the reservoir was only at two-thirds capacity. The repairs were far from complete, and concrete was still being injected into the dam to reinforce it as late as 1953, ten years after 'Chastise'.

Repair of the Eder dam was contracted to the Frankfurt firm of Philipp Holzmann who had built it. Although the breach was smaller than that at the Möhne, the task was more complicated owing to the drainage outlets in the wall. In the event they were not replaced, enabling the repair to be seen easily today. The dam was sealed at the same time as the Möhne, but reconstruction was not completed until June 1944. In their haste to make the wall watertight, cement had been injected under pressure to seal it. An unforeseen result was that essential drainage channels were blocked and had to be re-drilled – a technically demanding and extremely time-consuming operation. Even after the war further injections were required and it was not until 1947–8 that the dam was allowed to fill to capacity. Later, in the 1990s, further remedial work was found to be necessary – directly attributable to the effects of 'Chastise'.

Repairs were also prioritised at the Sorpe, now the major source of water for the Ruhr. Although the dam had been hit by two 'Upkeeps', damage was limited to the clay sealing and the concrete core itself was undamaged. Concern that a follow-up attack might be mounted against the damaged areas added to the urgency of repairs which were completed within a month.

The above is only a broad overview, and it is very easy to underestimate the massive scale of the issues facing those affected, more so when placed in the context of ever-increasing damage from area attacks and shortages of manpower and materials. It is estimated that the total reconstruction cost of the effects of 'Chastise' was the equivalent of at least £5.9 billion at today's prices.

A vexing question remains in respect of why no attempt was made to bomb and disrupt the reconstruction work, which was clearly observed by subsequent photographic reconnaissance flights and monitored by the interpreters. Speer identified this potential threat: 'a few bombs on the repair sites would have produced cave-ins and a few incendiaries would have set fire to the wooden scaffolding'. For this reason, duplicate sections of scaffolding were kept nearby, and key machinery was dispersed to reduce the risk of complete destruction in the event of an air raid.

There is no definitive answer: MEW estimated that the dams would not be repaired before the winter set in. This would result in further flooding, and the economic impact of 'Chastise' would thus be extended. This opinion appears not to have changed despite regular reconnaissance of the repair work. Over-optimistic assessments of the damage may also have been a contributory factor. Indeed, one interpretation report even suggested inaccurately that the Möhne dam might have moved off its foundations, increasing confidence in the severity of the damage, yet the progress being made on reconstruction was visible in clear sight.

Increased defences including light flak and barrage balloons precluded any further low-level operation. Any attempt to disrupt the repair work would have to be carried out from high level. This brought its own issues with regards to accuracy – particularly if considering the use of incendiary bombs to ignite the scaffolding. These were impossible to aim with precision and any attempt would therefore have to be as an area attack. This would require large numbers of aircraft and bombs, partly to ensure sufficient strikes on vital points, and a force of adequate strength to saturate the defences. In such a case it is easy to imagine that Harris's response would be that it was better to employ a force of such size over a major area objective. There, he would have argued, almost every bomb might strike a useful target, rather than the potential wastage which would accrue from the area bombing of a precision target.

Equally, as would be seen a few months later with the end of the Battle of the Ruhr and switch to other priorities, there was a tendency for Harris and the planners to underestimate the Germans' resourcefulness and capacity for recovery from what appeared to be devastating attacks. However, hindsight is an exact science, and it is easy to be critical of decisions made at a time when the efficient allocation of scarce resources was paramount.

The Germans quickly assessed the potential threat now facing them. On 17 May, within hours of the attack, the OKW estimated that about 25 further dams were vulnerable to attacks of a similar type. Speer demanded the provision of flak for other important dams 'by that evening'. He had no means of knowing that following the losses of 'Chastise' the RAF no longer had the specialist force required to mount another attack. Only 23 Lancasters had been converted to carry 'Upkeep' – and 8 of those were no more and 4 were badly damaged.

The efforts now being engaged to defend German dams were enormous and ongoing. The Möhne dam was given quadruple light flak and 88-mm guns, searchlights, and mobile weapons. In addition, the reservoir was surrounded by 300 smoke pots, and 55 balloons, with 1,500 men employed to man these. In February 1944, rafts intended to act as 'bomb deflectors' were constructed using 40 tonnes of metal and timber. Yet more metal was required for anti-torpedo nets and high steel masts erected on each shore to carry a curtain of steel cables carrying contact mines. More steel netting was strung on the air side of the dam to deflect bombs. The two towers that had served as sighting marks were removed. In May and June 1944, fearful of an anniversary attack, the Möhne defences were reinforced temporarily by additional heavy flak, withdrawn from Hagen. Similar defences were provided for the Eder and to a lesser extent other major dams – including others on the squadron's target list – the Sorpe, Diemel, Ennepe, and Lister.

The Germans additionally expended further resources developing new means of defence including the so-called *'Aktion Blumentopf'* (Action Flower-pot) – 24 mines moored in three rows in the reservoir, remotely detonated to throw up plumes of water in the path of low-flying attackers to bring them down or at least deter their run. Such devices were far from reliable, as demonstrated when a number were detonated prematurely by static electricity generated during a thunderstorm. For two years the protection of dams would engage an entire division's worth of military assets, much of this diverted from the Eastern Front. By the end of the war the demand for men and resources elsewhere prevailed and these units were redeployed, leaving instead wooden dummy guns, still waiting in vain for attacks which never materialised.

In this respect, 'Chastise' was also a double-edged sword. Within days of 'Chastise', the Air Ministry and Ministry of Home Security, fearful of a retaliatory attack by the Luftwaffe, instigated a survey of strategically valuable British reservoirs, potentially vulnerable to similar attacks. Over the next year defences were positioned for some 18 British dams. These included Derwent and Howden, and the Blackwater Reservoir supplying hydroelectric power for the aluminium smelter at Kinlochleven. Although no attacks transpired, such fears were not fanciful speculation. Sheffield's Derwent Reservoir and Craig Goch dam in the Elan Valley, supplying Birmingham's water, featured amongst the Luftwaffe target folders, and attacks by long-range aircraft such as the He 177 or Fw 200 Condor approaching from the west after flying round Ireland were at one stage under consideration.

Chapter 11

Assessment

Historians have long debated the results and effectiveness of Operation 'Chastise'. Was it the outstanding success championed by the media of the time, and echoed by Paul Brickhill's book *The Dam Busters* and the subsequent film of the same name, or was it merely an expensive sideshow that did little to affect the course of the war? There is no easy or definitive answer.

For many reasons, not least its unique weapon and the tactics devised for its delivery, Operation 'Chastise' has been perceived as being a stand-alone strike, part of, yet apart from, the main area offensive. Another unique factor of 'Chastise' is that although it was a precision strike it achieved area effect.

Although the results achieved by the operation are in themselves significant, it should be remembered that this was also an integral part of the Battle of the Ruhr. Its effects need to be viewed in conjunction with the achievements of the main force of Bomber Command.

Any attempts to assess the results of 'Chastise' are complicated by a myriad of complexities:

- The vast scale of the geographical area affected.
- The effect on all facets of life, personal, social, domestic, and industrial, both physical and emotional.
- Disruption across continuous areas, both urban and rural, rather than isolated pockets.
- The operation was but one element of the Battle of the Ruhr – its results were not only immediate, largely cumulative, and need to be seen in context with other effects of the Bomber Offensive.
- The sheer geographical scale and physical diversity makes comprehensive assessment impossible.
- Data relates largely to individual areas – making historical quantification difficult.

The key results anticipated from the destruction of the dams had been:

- Cause considerable local flooding.
- Disrupt industrial production by creating a shortage of water and other power sources, notably electricity.
- Disrupt transport and infrastructure.
- Have a considerable psychological impact on the population.

The effect would be different for each of the primary targets owing to their purpose and differences in their hinterland. It was also clear that the greatest industrial impact would result from the simultaneous breaching of both the Möhne and the Sorpe dams, which together held the majority of the water catchment for the Ruhr Valley.

If the objective of 'Chastise' is seen purely as being the permanent dislocation and even the stoppage of the Ruhr's armament production, and through this, a serious reduction of Germany's ability to wage war, then the operation cannot be considered a success. For such a result to be attained the Air Ministry and Ministry of Economic Warfare recognised that both the Möhne and Sorpe dams would have to be destroyed.

That the latter was not achieved was due largely to 'Upkeep's' unsuitability for use against an earth dam such as the Sorpe. Yet the planners recognised this weakness and allocated a separate force of five aircraft solely to this target, on Wallis's belief that cumulative hits might crack the watertight core, leading to erosion and subsequent failure. It was ill-fortune, rather than any failing on the part of the crews detailed for this as their primary target, that resulted in this solution not being put to the test.

The situation was further compounded by 'the fog of war' which prevented Cochrane from gaining an accurate picture which might have resulted in him diverting more aircraft to this target. In the event, only two aircraft attacked the Sorpe, which though cratered, withstood both mines. The Germans were forced to lower the reservoir level (although not 'empty it' as some accounts have claimed) both as a precaution and to effect repairs. Nevertheless, as Speer later admitted, post-war: 'The British came close to a success which would have been greater than anything they had achieved hitherto with a commitment of a thousand bombers.'

Significant economic effect was achieved. Although the planners had been cautious in their estimation of the damage caused by local flooding, they were correct in predicting that it 'would cause a disaster of the first magnitude, even in the lower reaches of the Ruhr'. Otherwise, the planners' expectations for 'Chastise' were undoubtedly met regarding the loss of utilities, reduction of available water supply and general dislocation of infrastructure.

Referring to the overall cost and effects of the Battle of the Ruhr, German historian Horst Boog notes that some 18,500 Bomber Command sorties, costing some 873 aircraft (4.7 per cent) and 6,000 aircrew, resulted in the loss of only four to six weeks of industrial output. The Battle ended in July 1943 and industry in the Rhineland and Ruhr had largely recovered by the end of that September. Against this, the results of 'Chastise', achieved by only 19 aircraft, compare well. It has been calculated that the partial dislocation of means of production caused by Operation 'Chastise' was at a 40th of the cost, in aircrew and aircraft terms, of an equivalent conventional bombing campaign, and with 20 times the destructive effect.

Although other operations during the Battle of the Ruhr incurred losses of between 4 and 5 per cent, these were for forces of 400–500 aircraft, so in 'real' numbers of aircraft lost these attacks were a far greater cost. In terms of bomb tonnage, the damage done by 8 'Upkeeps' (approximately 30 tons) compares well against main-force loads in the region of 860 tons of HE and 500 tons of incendiaries for a typical attack against a Ruhr city by, say, 500 aircraft. It may, of course, be argued that this effect should be offset against the time and resources allocated to the development of 'Upkeep', modification of aircraft and the training of the crews. At a time when Bomber Command was on average losing 15–20 aircraft a night in area attacks the results achieved at the cost of only 8 aircraft (despite being an unsustainable loss rate of 42 per cent) suggest a very positive return.

Despite the importance of the dams, the planners also failed to appreciate the energy and resources that the Germans would employ to effect their repair within a relatively short period, thus ensuring that there would be sufficient water reserves for 1944. Likewise, the water-pumping stations were very speedily restored. Against this must be offset the vast quantities of men, materials and resources that had to be diverted from other tasks which accordingly suffered, so effect was still achieved, albeit in different locations.

But beyond the immediate material damage, the effects of 'Chastise' were more diverse and far-reaching and take on a whole new dimension well beyond the planner's initial intent. These include the costs, effort, and opportunity costs of reconstructing the dams and defending them and other similar potential targets, against further attack, the additional psychological and propaganda opportunities, plus the political considerations. Add these further elements to the destruction and disruption caused by main-force attacks on the Ruhr and the whole begins to become greater than the sum of the parts.

Despite Harris's objection to elite units, having been ordered by Portal to form No. 617 Squadron he was not slow to grasp the benefits of such a unit.

Following 'Chastise' he maintained the squadron as a specialist bomber unit to carry out precision attacks against difficult targets requiring specialist training or using new or unique weapons. To paraphrase his original comment when being told of 'Upkeep' it might be said that he saw No. 617 Squadron as being the equivalent of 'giving them [the protagonists of precision bombing] a Lancaster, while we get on with winning the war'.

By utilising the skills of experienced crews who might otherwise have been rested in an instructing role, he now had a resource which at minimal cost enabled him to address precision targets requested by the War Cabinet and Director of Bomber Operations without diluting his main force or disrupting his offensive against area targets. In this respect, having been forced to undertake 'Chastise' (and form No. 617 Squadron) under duress, Harris saw an opportunity to turn this to his advantage. For the remainder of the war he was a firm supporter of the aircrew and cheerleader for the achievements of No. 617 Squadron. Post-war he would continue to champion them, referring to them affectionately as his 'old lags'. Yet, despite capitalising on the immediate success of 'Chastise' and using it to promote the achievements of his Command and garner political support, he paradoxically wrote to Portal in January 1945: 'It achieved nothing compared with the effort and the loss. The material damage was negligible compared with one small area attack.'

However, 'Chastise' and No. 617 Squadron spawned a far greater legacy.

The use of VHF during 'Chastise' to control aircraft in the vicinity of the target demonstrated the benefits of close tactical control at the sharp end enabling an experienced force leader to co-ordinate and direct an attack. This permitted a high degree of flexibility to adapt to local conditions which might have changed since the original briefing. The concept was quickly seized upon, creating the role of Master Bomber to direct the main force, used for the first time during the attack against Peenemünde on the night of 17/18 August 1943.

Likewise, No. 617 Squadron went on to develop precision target-marking techniques, first to mark their own special targets and subsequently to place accurate markers for main force attacks. Cochrane then adopted the technique for use by No. 5 Group and later created his own independent Marker Force to improve the effectiveness of main force area attacks – acknowledged by official historian Noble Frankland as a significant change in the prospects for Bomber Command during the run-up to D-Day when the accuracy of attacks against French targets was of significant concern.

For Wallis, the success of 'Upkeep' and 'Chastise' earned him his spurs as a weapon designer. Harris's scepticism was largely overcome and within months Wallis was given the go-ahead to develop his 12,000-pound Tallboy deep-penetration bomb, used with devastating effect by 617 Squadron from the summer of 1944 against V-weapons sites, U- and E-boat pens and the battleship *Tirpitz*.

Tallboy was used by No. 9 Squadron in a further attack against the Sorpe dam in October 1944. Reconnaissance photographs revealed three direct hits on the roadway on top of the dam, one of them on the crest at its mid-point. Three more had cratered the earth bank on the air side. However, the dam still held. This appeared to contradict Wallis's belief that more 'Upkeeps' might have done the job. Yet on a visit to see for himself in April 1945 he discovered that the concrete core was indeed broken and cracked, necessitating a lowering of the water level. Subsequent seepage, attributed to the Tallboy attack, caused internal erosion and settlement that took six years to repair. Wallis's forecast was thus vindicated, although over a much longer timescale than his prediction of 1943.

Tallboy was followed by the 22,000-pound Grand Slam used to destroy key railway viaducts in March 1945 which, along with main force attacks to drain the Dortmund–Ems and Mittelland Canals, effectively isolated the Ruhr, starving it of raw materials and the means to transport finished goods. (This achievement was in effect the delayed execution of a proposal put forward immediately after 'Chastise' for No. 617 Squadron to deliver a *coup de grâce* to the Ruhr by severing its major water and rail links using 'Upkeep' dropped overland with a forward spin, against embanked sections of canal and viaduct piers, an operation which, had it been executed, the planners suggested might be even more significant than 'Chastise'.)

Viewed in this broader context, although unsuccessful in its primary objective of halting industrial production in the Ruhr, the Dams Raid caused severe economic and material disruption. In addition, it delivered a substantial range of military and political effects, along with a marked effect on morale, not only in Germany, but also across occupied territories and among the Allied nations. Strategically and tactically, in the longer term it gave rise to developments which increased the efficacy and accuracy of Bomber Command, and the weapons at its disposal. It demonstrated not only the skill, courage, and dedication of Bomber Command's aircrew, but also its ability to strike at targets with a degree of precision hitherto considered unattainable by night. There can be no doubt that, far from being a sideshow, Operation 'Chastise' made a significant and valuable contribution to both the Battle of the Ruhr and the longer-term fortunes of Bomber Command.

Acknowledgements

This work owes much to the support and encouragement provided by many individuals and organisations who over the years have offered the benefit of their experience and knowledge. Each in their own way has contributed to the body of knowledge recording this epic operation. Even if not connected directly with this work, I owe each a great debt of gratitude.

I am particularly grateful to the following individuals who, at various times, helped either confirm facts, provide additional detail, read draft sections of text, or act as a sounding board for analysis: Werner Buhner, Steve Darlow, Charles Foster, James Holland, Dom Howard, Richard Morris, Clive Richards, Paul Stoddart, John Sweetman, Arthur Thorning and Jan van Dahlen.

I would also like to thank the following individuals and institutions for facilitating access to archives and other material: Sebastian Cox and Alan Thomas of Air Historical Branch, Nina Hadaway, Peter Devitt and Andrew Dennis of the RAF Museum, and its former Head of Archives, Peter Elliott. Also, former Commanders of No. 617 Squadron and the Chairman and Members, past and present, of No. 617 Squadron Association.

Last, but not least, my sincere thanks to my publisher, Michael Leventhal, who suggested that I undertake this work, and editor, Donald Sommerville, for his constructive advice and guidance.

Index